If you have ever felt like you've be[...] in your questions, this book will feel like the breath of fresh air you need. Page after page you will find encouragement as if a good friend is sitting next to you saying, "me too." Russ has been one of my dearest friends for many years, the kind of friend that is always in your corner. In his writing as well, he has a way through humor and transparency to be the friend sitting in *your* corner, reminding you that you are not alone. *Hope for the Wilderness* is the life raft we all need in our painful seasons.

**MATTHEW HERNANDEZ**
*Young Adults Pastor (Gateway Church, SLK)*
*Dallas, Texas*

*Hope For The Wilderness* by my dear friend, Pastor Russ, pushes you to trust in Jesus in every situation, whether it's a joyful season or a dark one. His writing is convicting, but warm, honest, transparent, filled with hope and wrapped in truth. It's a book that every new believer can digest, and every mature believer can be challenged by!

**JOEL LEGGETT**
*Lead Pastor (Cor Church)*
*Atlanta, Georgia*

This is book is for everyone navigating a wilderness experience in their life. Insightful, inspiring and filled with unique biblical observations for those who need hope. John Russell Moore is one of my favorite authors!

**LEE CLAYPOOLE**
*Lead Pastor (Union Road Church of God)*
*Gastonia, North Carolina*

Russ Moore demonstrates great humor and knowledge in his debut book for anyone who's had a wilderness experience, which applies to all! He is well-versed, and his use of quotes from multiple genres and church leaders is astounding. He writes plainly, doesn't sugarcoat the hard topics, and his transparency will give all who read *Hope for the Wilderness* courage to do the same.

**KRISTIN TERRETTE**
*Author and Women's Ministry Leader*
*Woodstock, Georgia*

We must all acknowledge that pain is part of the human condition. It is inevitable and can't be avoided. However, there is a parallel truth: life's most painful lessons can become life's greatest teachers if we choose to learn. Russ did. You can too. This book is a story of transforming pain into power and purpose.

**ED FUNDERBURK**
*Executive Director (Ed Funderburk Ministries, Church Consultant)*
*Former Executive Pastor (Gateway Church, DFT)*
*Dallas, Texas*

Regardless of your season in life, you'll find yourself in the pages of this book. I strongly recommend *Hope for the Wilderness* to those serious about finding purpose in your pain. Russ offers honest dialogue and practical insight in finding hope in your most difficult seasons.

**CLINT CLAYPOOLE**
*Lead Pastor (Cary Church)*
*Raleigh, North Carolina*

# HOPE

*for the*

# WILDERNESS

# HOPE
## *for the*
# WILDERNESS

Through all the *Pain* to all the *Promise*

RUSS MOORE

gatekeeper press™
Columbus, Ohio

HOPE for the WILDERNESS: Through all the Pain to all the Promise

Published by Gatekeeper Press
2167 Stringtown Rd, Suite 109
Columbus, OH 43123-2989
www.GatekeeperPress.com

Design by Tucker Johnson
Foreword by Tim Moore
Photography by Christi Whitt

ISBN (hardcover): 9781662916083
ISBN (paperback): 9781662916090
ISBN (eBook): 9781662916021

# CONTENTS

# FOREWORD

It's been said we will meet more than 10,000 people in our lives. Most are forgettable. But every once in a while, you meet someone that has something special. You know what I mean? That special quality that immediately melds your heart to theirs.

That's Russ.

If you are fortunate enough to meet him, you two will probably end up being life-long friends. I know he and I will be. And thankfully, you have a chance to meet him on these pages.

Several years ago, I had the privilege to not only meet Russ but hire him. Yes, we have the same last name, but I promise—nepotism was not in play.

Russ currently serves as our Executive Pastor of Ministries at *X Church*. His leadership and spirit have lifted our church from a wilderness season to a place thriving with health and unity. I am forever grateful for the way he helps me carry the weight of ministry.

I've had a front-row seat to watch him live out the principles on these pages. The words he puts to paper aren't just contrived theories, they are chapters from his life inked for your benefit. Russ writes with the transparency of a double-pane window freshly *Windexed*. He invites you to relive his painful journey through the wilderness while speaking hope to yours.

Don't be surprised if you find yourself laughing with him and at him throughout this book. I've never met anyone with more embarrassing, self-deprecating stories. Ever! And if while reading any part of this book you think to yourself, "is he making this up?"– I assure you he is not. No, this is Russ. All of him. His brilliant writing, affinity for quotes, love of adjectives, grasp of Scripture, and moments that make you want to face-palm.

In surprising irony, you will find clear direction for finding your way *out* of a wilderness. Ironic because Russ has the worst sense of direction of anyone I've ever known. Even after living in Columbus for six months, he still needed to use his *Maps* app to get to and from work.

So. Hop in the passenger seat and buckle up. Your *Uber* driver is waiting to navigate you over the sand-covered, cactus-laden dunes of your life and to the oasis of a better future.

The promised land is waiting.

*Tim Moore*
*Lead Pastor, X Church*
*March 2021*

# INTRODUCTION

*"The most difficult time in your life may be the border to your promised land."–Christine Caine*

*My* life might be over.

It's a thought I couldn't shake in the late summer of 2016.

Over the past few months, I had entered a season of depression, circumstantial storms, heartbreak, and self-inflicted wreckage.

Over the past few months, I had entered a *wilderness*.

My soul was withering, so I flew out to Dallas, Texas to give it shade among friends. By day three, I found myself slowly pacing in front of the shallow end of my buddy's neighborhood pool, recounting the events of the last month, pouring out my heart. Inside I was wondering how I was going to make it through all this intact.

My buddy, Logan, just smiled through the whole thing. When I was done with all my confessing and carrying on, he told me how visible the grace of God was in every detail of my story. How God was going to redeem every moment.

I sat back down on my towel, gathering my things. We were about to head into the city for dinner when he looked at me and said matter-of-factly–

"You will write out of this season. And it will help a lot of people."

He might as well have said, "Hey, one day you're going to churn butter from a unicorn."

Write?

I was just hoping to *survive.*

However, his prophetic words bubbled up only three months later as I began to heal. As I began to process what God was already teaching me. Doing in me. How he was mending me. Preparing me.

Through tears, I began to pen words and concepts that carried me like a life-raft to safety. Principles from God's Word. Nuggets of truth that kept me fed during the famine.

I'm believing for all that meat to be nourishment for your soul.

Truth is, I'm nowhere near where I want to be or need to be, and I'm certainly no expert. Nor have I seen the worst desert out there (many of you have been through far worse). Nor do I think I've seen my last desert.

But as I share observations from my journey, and more importantly, observations from the *original* wilderness journey from Scripture, I believe with all my heart God's Spirit is going to shoot waves of life, wisdom, refreshment and energy into your hope-weary bones.

If you're holding this book, I can only imagine what you're feeling. What you've been through. I can only imagine the loss.

We're all familiar with what it's like to feel crippled by fear, disabled by anxiety, crushed by disappointment, and stuck in a dry and discouraging place.

And I, for one, definitely know what it's like to get *lost*.

In fact, since Pastor Tim so kindly let you know how bad I am with directions, I'll share a doozie. Just don't tell anyone.

One Thursday, I drove from my house in Atlanta, Georgia to my hometown of Greenville, South Carolina to meet my parents and some friends for dinner. This was the 2016 season, so every minute of the drive felt like an eternity, me completely lost in my head. Call it an excuse if you want. All I know is I can still taste the battery acid of panic when I saw the "Welcome to Greenville, *Alabama*" sign instead of the "Welcome to Greenville, *South Carolina*" sign.

Yep. I had driven three hours in the *wrong* direction.

Face-palming already?

To add insult to injury, I started racing home in the *right* direction in such fury that I was pulled over ten minutes into the return trip and given a fantastically expensive speeding ticket.

Yeah....

Now. Maybe you haven't punched in the wrong address on the GPS. But maybe you *did* point your proverbial life in the direction of Cozumel, Mexico and yet somehow found yourself in what feels like Toronto, Canada. And you have no idea how you got there, how to get back, how long you're camped out for, or where to go from here.

Even worse, maybe you hit a pothole or two along the way so big the tires are blown, and the engine is shot. Now you're stranded, hands on hips, just staring at the damage of your life while the sun beats mercilessly down on your back.

I just want you to know, God has not left us alone on this road trip.

He's given us a companion guide in the pages of His Word and a supernatural Guide in the Person of the Holy Spirit.

And He's going to get you and me back on our feet.

I'm not exaggerating or being dramatic to tell you that even as I type this, I weep. Tears fill my eyes as I think about you. As I wonder what kind of pain you might be facing. As I contemplate just how fiercely God loves you and the care He has for your soul.

Tears run down my cheeks as I plead with the Spirit to use this flawed, feeble book to bring much glory to God and much strength to your heart.

See, I know what it's like to wonder if you're going crazy. I know what it's like to feel your best days are behind you. I know what it's like to be in a season where you cry more than you'd ever admit to your closest friends.

I also know what it's like to hit bottom but then look up to see a God more faithful than you had ever quite imagined. A God ready to embrace you and father you and restore your soul. Ready to exchange beauty for ashes.

You know, deserts are rather unfriendly terrains. This was especially true in ancient times. In addition to all the natural elements of danger, the desert was the home of the fugitive. If someone was convicted of a crime, especially violent crime, to the desert they would flee. There, justice would hunt them down, even down to their lineage if need be.

However, there was an exception to this "law of blood revenge." One crucial exception to the hostility of the desert. That is the custom of "open hospitality" by a shepherd. The "golden piety of the wilderness," still practiced by many Bedouin cultures.

As well-known author Dallas Willard put it, "every wanderer in the desert, whatever his character or his past, was received into a shepherd's tent as a 'guest of God,' furnished with food and kept inviolate."

This is actually the context of Psalm 23, by the way, where the host prepares a table in the presence of the guest's enemies. It's a tent of safety and rest in the middle of swirling danger and difficulty.

This book is your tent.

My prayer is that under its shelter—in the pages—you find rest for your soul, balm for your wounds, lotion for your head, food for your strength, and *a map to get out.*

One quick, practical note on the tent. It's constructed into six major sections and is designed not just for *enjoyment* but *engagement.* At the end of each of the six sections, for example, is a page to journal your *Wilderness Writings* and a page to write out some *Desert Decisions.* There are also miscellaneous stops along the way to process and journal, and even to pray.

You can, of course, simply read this book at leisure and still be inspired and helped. But if I can twist your arm into keeping a pen and highlighter handy, well, here's to the twisting. For the hyper-diligent, you might even want to keep a Bible nearby. An exhaustive overview of the Israelite journey would be impossible in a book this size and supplementing an actual reading of the story from Exodus through Joshua alongside will only pile extra meat on the plate.

Either way, it's your tent to do with as you please.

I just want you to know you're not in this alone.

And deserts can't last forever.


Here's to the promised land,

*John Russell Moore*

*And now, God, do it again—*
*bring rains to our drought-stricken lives....*

Psalm 126:4 MSG

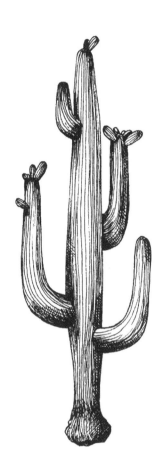

*the*

# JOURNEY

*from*

# EGYPT

## Chapter One

## NO WASTED TICKETS

*"I am the Lord your God, who brought you up out of Egypt."*
*—Psalm 81:10*

*"There are far, far better things ahead than*
*any we leave behind."—C.S. Lewis*

*"To step towards your destiny, you have to step away*
*from your security."—Craig Groeschel*

I remember falling in love.

Do you?

As for me, I'm not referring to Elizabeth at the middle school lock-in.

Only hours after meeting, she chased me through the night with a flashlight in some indoor version of "capture the flag." The moon gave me away by a classroom window and there she made the kill. So, we found chairs by the mystery shapes in the corner and sat down, me awkward and sweating. There in the dark, time stilled, and I felt the left shadow of her face turn dangerously close to mine.

"I like your voice," she whispered. "You have a happy voice."

My stomach melted and I mumbled something about the green in her eyes.

That whole next week I listened to *Say You Love Me* by Fleetwood Mac on repeat.

A week later her friend blocked me on the way to her locker to inform me, "Elizabeth doesn't want to go steady anymore."

The week after *that* I watched *The Wedding Singer* four times in theatres to sooth the ache in my shattered, sixth-grade heart.

Of course, I've had a few more loves since then but I'm not referring to those either.

No, I'm talking about the odd, mysterious love that happens in faith.

I'm talking about the mingling of souls between a human being and God.

It may sound awkward, especially if you're not religious or haven't experienced it, but I'm talking about falling in love with Jesus.

As a seventh grader, I had no idea my mother had been secretly twisting the arm of God in prayer for me to meet a new best friend. Someone who had an actual enthusiasm for spiritual realities.

Sure enough, I met Colt, now a brother for life, and passion began to explode in my heart for eternal things. And sure enough, I've never gotten over it.

I don't know your background. But for me, as a middle school kid, discovering Jesus was like falling over a cliff and landing on every forbidden treasure island I'd ever dreamed of as a boy. I was dizzy with wonder, and I had my whole life before me to explore the caves and examine the jewels.

Oh, I'll never forget that season, that honeymoon season, of falling in love with God. Like the shepherd boy David from Scripture, who I'm sure would sneak away with his harp to make melody out in the fields, I would sneak away for secret moments with Him. I dreamt of the Lord at night. He was on my mind as I laid down, and on my lips as I got up.

I became weirdly obsessive. I wore those stupid fish t-shirts and bought WWJD bracelets. I found a different church service to attend almost every night of the week. I devoured books and devotionals and Scripture. There was nothing too inconvenient. Nothing that could stand in the way of me experiencing God in a genuine way. Hear His voice. Sense His power. Be filled with His Spirit.

That first year was filled with joy. The miraculous. The hand of God that seemed to be over everything I touched.

I know everyone's story looks different, but if you're a Christian, surely you can recall the sweetness of those early days of walking with God.

If you're anything like me, though, somewhere along the way you bought into the idea the Christian life was like a straight line. You surrender your life to God and it's smooth sailing upward from there, point A of salvation to point B of heaven; smooth, diagonal and problem free.

However, just like finances, marriage or anything else in life, we get into trouble if we don't prepare ourselves for reality. And reality will teach us very quickly that walking with Jesus actually looks more like a rollercoaster, riddled with ups and downs, mountains and valleys, hills and ditches, and twists and turns.

It is not a straight line.

It is a zig zag.

It's a journey of the ugly and the beautiful. It's wading through the waters of frustration and reward. Tears and joy. Defeat and victory. Sin and repentance. Pain and healing.

Mountain peak moments, standing like Elijah on top of Carmel, fire having fallen fresh on all your obstacles, rivers of invincibility flowing through your veins. Contrasted against dark nights of the soul, where tears turn to blood, and you don't know if you'll make it to see the light of day.

In other words, life is full of *seasons*.

*"For everything there is a season,"* Solomon wrote.

And one of those seasons is *the wilderness*.

o o o

What is the wilderness?

According to Merriam-Webster, it is *"a wild or uncultivated state…an empty or pathless area or region."*

The wilderness is the wild. It is the undomesticated and the unpredictable. There's no marked path. No *OnX* mapping service. No cameras behind bushes after fording a shallow creek with Michael Scott. No, usually just dryness and desolation.

Depending on the location in the world, wilderness dangers vary. You could, of course, get lost forever. Dehydration or hypothermia could set in. This is assuming food can be found and bears, snakes, spiders and coyotes avoided.

Extremity of temperature. Exposure to the elements. Insect bites and infections. Lack of food and water. All combining to form a place of discomfort and pain.

It's no wonder we sometimes refer to the tough spots in life as a "wilderness" season. There are times in life that seem to have no path or purpose. There's a lot to fear. The hardship and pain can be difficult to bear. And occasionally we wonder if we will ever find our way out.

Wilderness seasons in life vary, too. They might be brief or long. Light or severe.

Your wilderness could be a dry stretch in your walk with God, where His voice seems distant and His Presence absent. Maybe you're reading this and feel like you've never even really known God in a meaningful way. Or you did at one time but now He's barely an acquaintance.

Maybe you've been fired from your job and are in a season of waiting, while navigating financial hardship.

Perhaps a relationship has fractured in your life. A romance fizzled, a marriage fell apart, or a friendship blew up. Maybe it's the long and lonely road of singleness, waiting for the right one to come, that soul mate for you to do life with. Or hoping for a child. Or waiting and believing for any promise from God you are starting to doubt will ever come to pass. Maybe you just feel far, far behind in where you'd hoped to be in life by now.

It could be a doctor's report has melted your heart in fear. Maybe a loved one just passed. Your kids are straying towards a destructive path. Or you feel like *you* are on a destructive path. A once-harmless habit has turned into an addiction with a vice grip around your life.

Maybe anxiety is beginning to encroach upon your daily life and spin things out of control. For someone reading this, a low-lying cloud of depression has been knocking on your door for a while, and now it seems to have come to stay.

Other times, we find ourselves in a wilderness based on the consequences of our own decisions. If we could take it all back, we would. But we can't. And now we're left in a land of regret to pick up the pieces.

Often, a truly difficult time in the desert is a combination of two or more of these scenarios, all coming together in a perfect sandstorm to complicate and frustrate our current season of life, and at times it seems almost impossible to navigate.

We know God is faithful. And we know seasons come to an end. But like David, we ache, *How long, Oh Lord?*

> *How long, Lord? Will you forget me forever?*
> *How long will you hide your face from me?*
> *How long must I wrestle with my thoughts*
> *and day after day have sorrow in my heart?*
> *How long will my enemy triumph over me?*
> *Look on me and answer, Lord my God.*
> *Give light to my eyes, or I will sleep in death…*
> (Psalm 13:1-3)

Now. One encouraging thing we do know about seasons right off the bat is *they don't last forever.*

Seasons change.

In my most troubled times as a teenager, when the problems of life threatened
to squeeze out all hope for the future, my youth pastor would look me in the eye and with fatherly authority remind me, *"Son, the way you feel now, you won't feel this way forever."*

If I could look past the paper into your eyes even now, I would speak that into *you* until you believe it:

"The way you feel now, you won't feel this way forever."

I know it's simple. But it is at least a starting place of hope to get underneath your feet.

Seasons end. Storms pass.

*But*—and this is a crucial *but*—this is the-reason-I-wrote-the-book *but*—

**How** *you walk through the wilderness is everything.*

The *way* you navigate this journey will determine whether or not your time in the wilderness was wasted. It will determine whether you make it to all the fertile ground of the Promised Land you're believing for from God. It can even determine *how long* you stay in the wilderness.

We can grumble our way through this time, learn nothing God wants to teach us, take nothing from it to prepare for our destiny, cause ourselves even more pain, and ultimately not enter God's best for our lives and future.

Or, we can grow closer than ever to Jesus, rise above our circumstances, learn and acquiesce what God wants to do in us, expedite our time in the wild, and then move forward in power and strength, ready to possess every Promised Land God has in store.

I know I was caught off guard the first time my treasure islands turned to desert sands. But the choice truly is up to us.

To choose the latter, however, we need a plan and some principles. We need a guide. We need a manifesto for the wilderness.

We need *hope*.

Fortunately, God has not left us in the dark.

In fact, *another* reason so many people parallel difficulty with the wilderness, apart from the obvious, is because we have a significant, historic example in God's own people in the Old Testament.

The sand winds of it all began to blow as early as the book of Genesis.

Skip past the first couple chapters of paradise and stars articulated into the cosmos by the tongue of God, all that gala-apple-biting tragedy, hold on for dear life through the careening scream of the human race falling off the rails, and the floods, towers, and scattered languages, and we eventually slam into the glass door of Genesis 12.

Here God speaks a covenant and a promise to a man named Abraham. This opens that glass door into the possibility of a new future for the human race. He promises Abraham a lineage, a land, and a worldwide blessing. Every syllable of Scripture from that point forward, all the way to the end of Revelation, and I believe through eternity, for that matter, is the unfolding of that promise.

At the last page of Genesis, over seventy of Abraham's descendants are living in the land of Goshen. Turn that page, and several hundred years later, and sure enough, the seventy has turned to millions, and these descendants are all enslaved in Egypt.

Joseph's long forgotten, and all the Pharaoh knows is these Hebrews have multiplied like rabbits and are a threat to be contained. Thus, as Exodus begins, God's own people are in chains.

Interesting, isn't it? I'm sure this is not how Abraham pictured the prophecy coming to pass. The more the promise is fulfilled, the harder it gets for God's people. Ever experience a blessing turn to a burden?

At this point, I'm sure hope was running thin through their veins. Day after day, brick after brick, sweat by sweat, they've resigned to live out the rest of their days merely surviving. God's very people grew accustomed to bondage.

But God had a plan.

When all was darkest, God introduced a deliverer.

Moses.

Pharaoh had issued an edict for all the Hebrew boys to be slaughtered, but a desperate mother sent her newborn down the Nile River in a reed basket.

In God's brilliant providence, this baby boy Moses would be found by the female slave of a princess and grow up in enemy territory, raised, trained and prepared in the very palaces of Egypt.

Later, as an adult, Moses experienced his breaking point over the mistreatment of his people. He observed a slave master beating a fellow Hebrew and he snapped, striking and killing the Egyptian once he thought the coast was clear.

By the next day, the news went viral, and Moses fled to the desert. Throughout the next forty, dry, mundane years, as Moses barely eked out a living, God secretly worked behind the scenes to prepare him for an epic task.

Suddenly, one day, in a holy moment, Moses encountered God at a fiery, burning bush. There he heard God's voice and received His call. The Lord brushed past Moses' insecurities with blunt questions and leveled his doubts with unflinching directives.

With Aaron as his mouthpiece and right-hand man, this unlikely hero, and one of our primary wilderness guides, was sent back to the most powerful man on the planet with one simple command from God Himself. Come on, say it with me:

*"Let my people go."*

Pharaoh didn't budge. Plagues and miracles followed.

Ironically, God Himself had hardened Pharoah's heart. Frustrating as it is, sometimes it's actually God making things harder, so when the promise comes, He alone will get the glory. He loves to stack the odds. Seems to be the essence of His very nature. Sometimes He likes to send the fire only once the wood gets wet.

Finally, the people were let go, but there was still one last Hail-Mary assault and chase by the Pharoah. In dramatic fashion, God parted the Red Sea for the children of Israel and made a way where there was no way. The Lord then dropped the watery walls back into place just as their enemies showed up, drowning them in a salty grave, never to rise again.

The people were free.

o o o

Free from Egypt's grip, the plan was to pass *through* the wilderness into a beautiful and bountiful land where homes were already built, waiting for them to possess.

The journey *to* the wilderness was three days. The journey *through* the wilderness was roughly eleven days "as the crow flies," though God factored in a two-year detour to prepare their hearts.

Tragically, however, an entire generation of over 1,000,000 people spent *forty years* in the wilderness and died, *never even seeing the Promised Land*.

They succumbed to the discouragement and sorrow of a difficult season.They sabotaged their own destiny through disobedience, sin, and a wrong spirit and attitude.

And so do millions of people today.

o o o

I'll never forget my twenty-ninth birthday. I was living in Lexington, Kentucky. I am an extrovert by nature but the older I get the more I cherish my alone time, and thus, I could not *wait* to treat myself to a full day in Cincinnati. I planned ahead and bought tickets to catch a daytime Reds game and then tickets to see my favorite band play that evening.

My glorious celebration was all going as planned until about thirty minutes after the game when I *still couldn't find where I parked my car*.

Now, to deflect, I could try to describe just how scattered, loose, vast and expansive the Cincinnati Reds parking was, but alas words would fail. I just know I looked *everywhere*.

After a solid hour of scouring every parking deck in sight, I walked over to *Yardhouse* to eat some sliders, and then walked around some more. Still nothing. I called a taxi, and we rode around for hours searching until I ran out of money. Again, nothing.

At ten o'clock that night, out of cash and having missed my concert, walking around in circles in Cincinnati, a grown man wanting to cry, I finally called the cops for help. A band of them startled me to death minutes later as they rolled up on large police scooters. I gave them the description of the car and within minutes one of the officers had pegged it. I'd parked it directly under a deck embankment, undetectable from the road. Again, trying to deflect.

"Thank you so much, Officer," I said. "I have literally been looking for hours. I can't believe I couldn't find my own car."

"Don't worry, happens all the time," he responded.

"Are you serious?" A bit of relief began to wash over me. "Thank goodness, because I really feel like an idiot."

"Oh, make no mistake," he quipped back, and—I'm not making this part up—"You definitely *should* feel like an idiot. I'm just letting you know it happens a lot with people from out of town."

I was on my way to my musical Promised Land that night for the concert. I had the guarantee on paper promising to get me in. But I circled the city and never entered.

*Everything that goes into a life of pleasing God has been miraculously given to us by getting to know, personally and intimately, the One who invited us to God. The best invitation we ever received! We were also given absolutely terrific promises to pass on to you—your **tickets** to participation in the life of God. (2 Peter 1:3-4 MSG, emphasis mine)*

The children of Israel had absolutely terrific promises. Tickets to their future. Yet just like I walked around in circles in Cincinnati that night, that first generation out of Egypt wandered around for forty years and died in the wilderness, the tickets still fresh in their pockets.

They never got to the concert. They never got to Canaan.

I wonder how many of us have been circling the same mountain for years. Still lingering in the same sin. Still wasting time failing the same tests. And the tickets have been in our pockets all along. The promises waiting to be activated. The wilderness ready to be walked through. The Promised Land waiting to be inherited and possessed.

Maybe you're wondering what relevance their journey has for you, considering your current modern scenario. Can their story really help us? According to Scripture, one of the sovereign purposes to their story even occurring was *exactly for the purpose to help us.* Reflecting back thousands of years to their epic journey, the Apostle Paul said this:

> *Nevertheless, God was not pleased with most of them; their bodies were scattered in the wilderness… These things* **happened to them as examples** *and were* **written down as warnings for us.**… (1 Corinthians 10:5,11)

You may be in a Starbucks right now, having never thought much about Moses or this peculiar people God delivered so many years ago. But according to Paul, the Holy Spirit had those words penned specifically for *you.* To encourage you. To warn you. To spur you on to enter into all God has for you.

To give us a plan and a hope for the wilderness.

o  o  o

I wish I could have been a bystander to that Red Sea riptide. Felt the breeze on my face and the goosebumps on my arms.

This is *Shawshank Redemption.*

Yet this movie has multiple endings.

See, sometimes it's tough to remember that even though *we* may know the ups and downs that would befall this people, *they* didn't.

All they know is God showed up. They've been rescued. They are about to dance and worship, and they're on their way to the Promised Land.

But there is a difficult path on the way to their destiny. With their WWJD bracelets secured and church merch donned, they anticipate a quick stroll to their dreams.

They have bought into straight line Christianity, but they are about to enter the zig zag.

As a former pastor used to remind me, life is divided into chapters. These Jews are about to enter some pages they're not ready for. They're approaching a chapter with an elongated detour. For some of them, this detour will lead to their descent instead of their destiny.

They've left Egypt.

But they're about to enter the Wilderness.

*The Lord is a warrior;*
*the Lord is His name.*
*Pharaoh's chariots and his army*
*he has hurled into the sea.*
*The best of Pharaoh's officers*
*are drowned in the Red Sea.*
*The deep waters have covered them;*
*they sank to the depths like a stone.*
*Your right hand, Lord,*
*was majestic in power.*
*Your right hand, Lord,*
*shattered the enemy.*
(Exodus 15:3-6)

## Chapter Two

# WELCOME TO THE WILDERNESS

*"We must take a three-day journey into the wilderness...."*
*—Moses (Exodus 8:27)*

*"God never loses any of our past for his future when we surrender ourselves to him. Every mistake, sin, and detour we take in the journey of life is taken by God and becomes his gift for a future of blessing."—Pete Scazzero*

*"Three days ago, we all died. We should all be able to start over."—Jack Shepherd, Lost*

There's no doubt about it. The children of Israel stepped straight from a miracle to a mess. A dry, discomforting mess.

The wilderness of the Sinai Peninsula to be specific, across from the Mediterranean Sea.

Of course, no two wildernesses are the same, not on earth and not in life.

The earth is covered by one-third desert, did you know that? We tellurians have places that haven't seen rain in over five thousand years, if ever.[1] Yet deserts vary.

You could visit the Atacama Desert in Chile, for example, to experience a typical sand-and-rock desolation by heat, or any number of melting deserts across the world.

And yet the driest deserts aren't the hottest ones, ironically; they're the coldest. On that note, we could point the compass straight south and travel down to the McMurdos Dry Valleys of Antarctica, practically a blue, icy Mars.

Or, to thaw, we could head a little north to Australia and explore the Great Barrier Reef. Though not a desert, it *is* considered by definition an *"aquatic* wilderness." That's a wilderness I wouldn't mind visiting.

The wildernesses in life vary too. We touched on it a little earlier, but let's dig a little deeper.

What has *your* wilderness looked like? Or the wilderness of those you love?

When I think back to people in my life who have traversed some endless dunes, who've survived some zigzags, my mind instantly lands on a few snapshots.

I think about the time I was shaving my roommate's head in Lexington, for example. Clipper in hand, I hit ignore on my best friend's phone call only to receive an immediate follow-up text of *"Please… it's an emergency."*

I could hear the tears choking in his voice on the other end. He had just found proof of his wife's infidelity.

Before I'd even checked with my boss or bank account or legs for approval, I found my foot on the gas pedal, my body and my Malibu hurtling through time and I-75 overnight to

Greenville. By the time I arrived, he had thrown up all the bodily fluids he could muster. So, we just sat there together in silence and I helped him stare at the wall until the sun came up. Then we went to Waffle House and cut our waffles up in chunks and moved them around our plates like chess pieces, scheming how to make the world right again.

That next year for him was a wilderness.

I think about Anthony from a church location I pastored. He and Holly had spent the last two years and their life's savings building their dream home for them and their kids.

I'll never forget the urgency in his voice when he called to say it was in flames. On a day colder than Antarctica—literally, a polar vortex—their dogs had knocked over kerosene lamps in the middle of the night. The day was so cold the firemen couldn't do anything about it. Water just kept freezing solid as crystal the moment it left the hose. A colleague with four-wheel picked me up, and we somehow navigated out there in time to stand with the family and watch the house burn down together, all the friendly ghosts of halls, pictures, memories and future hopes dying with the flames.

The next year for them, a wilderness.

I think of the time my youth pastor and his wife sat me down to let me know she had breast cancer. Wilderness.

I think of the funeral I conducted for a seven-year-old boy who had collapsed in the middle of a soccer game from a rare, undetected condition. Wilderness.

I think of students I pastored who were violated in the most intimate and irreversible ways by the very ones who should have protected them. Wilderness.

I think of a ministry friend in his late twenties who had to bury his wife right after he began pastoring a campus at the church. Wilderness.

I think of all the suicidal calls, attempts and threats I've received in the middle of the night. Wilderness.

Encouraged yet?

This is life, though, isn't it?

These seasons and moments come no matter what.

It's the promise Jesus made that none of us claim or have tattooed onto our lower arm:

*In this world, you will have trouble.* (John 16:33)

Maybe "trouble" is *exactly* how you would describe the state of your life right now.

If so, welcome.

Welcome to the wild.

Welcome to life in the zig zag.

o o o

The last chapter ended with Egyptian bodies floating like pool rafts in the Red

Sea, baptized completely into the past, God's people stepping dry and happy into a brand new future on the other side.

This moment, come to find out, was also an Old Testament foreshadowing of New Testament "baptism."

> *Or didn't you realize we packed up and left there for good? That is what happened in baptism. When we went under the water, we left the old country of sin behind; when we came up out of the water, we entered into the new country of grace—a new life in a new land!* (Romans 6:3 MSG)

And yet the Israelites quickly found themselves in a wilderness.

Notice the progression. God's people went straight from "baptism" to "wilderness."

Interestingly, the exact same thing happened to Jesus in the New Testament.

> ***As soon as Jesus was baptized***, *he went up out of the water. At that moment heaven was opened, and he saw the Spirit of God descending like a dove and alighting on him. And a voice from heaven said, "This is my Son, whom I love; with him I am well pleased."*
> ***Then Jesus was led by the Spirit into the wilderness*** *to be tempted by the devil.* (emphasis mine)

Baptism to wilderness.

Victory to testing.

Promise to hardship.

Ever experience that?

Ever taste the joy of a mountaintop experience and next thing you know you feel at the bottom of the ocean? Ever feel like God gave you a promise and then everything next seemed to counter every word God just spoke?

If so, you're not alone.

We could box-check the story of all our heroes in the Bible as well.

God gives young Joseph a dream. Then young Joseph spends the next fourteen years in pits, prisons and pain before it all cross-stitches together for what God planned.

God anoints young David to be king. Then young David spends the next fifteen years fighting giants, hiding for his life, avoiding King Saul's jealous sword, and encountering opposition at every turn before finally being crowned.

God speaks an unbelievable promise to old Abraham of an heir that brings about worldwide blessing and salvation. Then old Abe travels and travels, battles and battles, and throws in the proverbial towel before finally receiving the promise twenty-five years later at the age of one hundred.

Then there's Moses. Well, we're getting a front-row seat to his story through this book.

Maybe that's been you.

Maybe you've just walked out of a spiritual "baptism" of sorts, perhaps even a baptism of blessing or joy or financial provision, and then suddenly a wilderness breaks upon you that you never saw coming.

Or maybe you're in a wilderness of wait, the journey from the baptism of promise to the actual promised land dragging on painfully, depressingly longer than you had ever anticipated.

According to author and pastor John Mark Comer, the process of God's visions and dreams being fulfilled in our lives compared to when they're given and what we expect is always *"longer, different, harder, better."*

*Longer* is definitely true.

In fact, look at what happened immediately after the exodus...

> *When Pharaoh let the people go, God did not lead them on the road through the Philistine country, **though that was shorter**. For God said, 'If they face war, they might change their minds and return to Egypt.' So, God led the people around by the desert road toward the Red Sea. The Israelites went up out of Egypt ready for battle.* (Exodus 13:17-18 emphasis mine)

God intentionally took them the long way to their dreams.

He knew their strength wasn't ready for the battles ahead, that their character could not yet sustain the blessings yet to come.

This seems to be the wilderness-to-wildest-dreams way, huh?

If only they had known, though. If only they had trusted.

The Israelites eventually complained themselves into oblivion, thinking God was trying to *punish* them, never opening their hearts enough to understand God was trying to *prepare* them.

He was introducing *Crossfit for Canaan*, if you will.

And the gym hurt like hell.

So. If the Red Sea for God's people, the Jordan River for Jesus, and that moment at the altar, with that girl, in that promotion, or in that golden season for you were baptisms of life and joy, then the wilderness is our baptism of pain. It's a baptism of loss. A baptism of confusion. But also, it's a baptism of *purpose*.

It's important to remember the waters of that second baptism will eventually dry. If we'll just keep going, if we'll just not give up, if we'll just keep walking, crawling even, with God, we will look up one day with the sun of the promised land kissing our cheeks.

Until then, though, there are things God is looking for us to extract within the zigzags, some life to be drawn out of the waters of death.

o o o

I don't know what the zig zags of your life have looked like. I just know you've had them.

Just like Moses.

Just like me.

Alongside the Israelite journey, I'll interlace some of my own story. Though truth is, many of my wilderness seasons have been primarily internal.

Looking back on it now, the landscape's obvious. There seemed to be lurking in the personality of my dad's side of the family a subtle shadow of depression, nearly hidden, but always creeping in at the outcrops.

In fact, pangs of guilt still knife through my chest when I remember the season of watching my dad battle depression. I'd walk past him on my way out the door and he'd be sitting on the couch in silence. He'd even lost interest in sports. That's a *big* deal.

I loathe how self-absorbed I was in that season. I'm not sure what I could have said, but I remember an emptiness in his eyes that took a good year to refill.

And truth is, DNA is a powerful thing.

I've always been gregarious and outgoing, a life-of-the-party kind of guy in most settings. And yet disproportionately introspective in comparison to my fellow extroverts. Stuck in my head at times, melancholy periodically clawing at my door like an estranged cat.

I think most of us feel like a mixed bag of contradictions on the inside, if we're honest.

Now, the snapshot bio. I've had a very fortunate life. I grew up among the loblolly pines of Greenville, South Carolina, in middle-class suburban comfort with parents and family healthier and more wholesome than I ever knew to be thankful for. That capstone of stability provided a wide berth for all my insatiable passions, curiosities and pursuits.

Middle school and high school years were laced mostly with joy, quests for God, escapades with girls and friends, and a healthy dose of typical teenage angst. I grew in faith, while a few cracks in character let some demons begin to whisper their way into my story.

After my first semester in college, I spent a year of adventure in Buenos Aires, making memories, learning Spanish, and working on the ranch, riding horses bareback under the rustic Argentine sun like something out of a John Eldredge book.

Oh, please do cry for me Argentina.

Upon my return, I experienced what felt like nothing less than a supernatural summer of faith and ministry. It was golden, earnest, and book-of-Acts-like.

Yet an ache remained. All through my life and my many lores of romance, I found myself still longing, writing, and dreaming of Mrs. Moore.

A year after returning to the States I met a golden-skinned Asian girl. She looked like she'd been kissed by Hawaii and mystery. The day I walked into my first class, I said to myself, "that's the most beautiful girl in school." She sat right in front of me, and a week later, for God knows what reason, she asked for my number "so we could go over homework."

We dated for over a year and our souls got pretty attached. She was the envy of all my friends and the bronze of beach-sun would sing off her dark skin like a California song.

Still, I knew she wasn't the one.

All I know is the day I met the girl of my dreams, my heart came home.

I had liked a lot of girls and even loved a few.

But Hazel walked in and it was all over. Hazel walked in and I knew, this is the one I'll marry.

She came into the store where I worked and I began to help her, even though my brain began to short-circuit. Conversation with her made my soul dizzy. I said stupid things. Co-workers kept asking if I was okay, and why were my cheeks red, and why was I talking so *loudly*?

She bubbled over with a crackling energy and began trying on clothes as I donned the best professionalism I could muster. But those bright, almond-shaped eyes, rarefied with intensity, would turn towards mine, her fingers working casually through raven-black hair that drew waves down her shoulders, and I, well, I was undone.

Waxing poetic, I know, but it was far more than externals. It was the radiance of her personality, a soul as bright as the glowing rings of Jupiter. It was the depths of her passions. That she was a Spirit-filled follower of Jesus, a successful hair stylist, and a professional *Jeet Kune Do* instructor (are you kidding me?). That we liked all the same music and shows and clothes. All the things that matter and all the things that don't.

Suffice it to say, I was putty in her hands at first interaction.

She left the store and left an imprint on the inside of me.

I took a fifteen-minute break to call and tell my best friend I had just met my wife.

That when she smiled at me, the world tilted, and every forgotten dream came rushing to the top of my head like blood.

He said he could tell.

Lamely, I had asked for her number to invite her to a church event where I was going to be in a ping pong tournament (*what?!*), and we stayed up until 2 a.m. in my truck talking about life and feeling like we had known each other forever.

After two weeks, she ghosted me. It hurt, but oddly enough I was happy. Happy I could feel this way.

I spent the next year making wishes on stars and drawing her name with my finger into steamed glass in the shower, beckoning God to make the magic He'd spoken over my life come back.

He did.

Around a year later she sent me a text and asked me out for sushi. Over dragon rolls and stomach nerves, she apologized profusely for her behavior. Explained she had committed to a year of no dating and was petrified by how fast she'd begun to fall for me. She'd decided to over-compartmentalize. To retreat. But if I were to forgive her, if I were to trust her, she was ready, she was all in.

Two weeks later I took her to the mountains by *North Greenville University* to a spot called *Bald Rock*, a stony cliff hidden by trees that overlooks the city lights of Greenville. It was December so we took blankets and a thermos and a Macbook with Nicholas Cage's Christmas movie, *Family Man*. There under a pale, midnight moon we made it official.

We quickly dove headlong into what felt like a storybook romance, the sights, sounds and smells all still fresh in my mind: white chocolate peppermint mochas, *Angels and Airwaves* (best alternative pop-punk band of all time) pumping through the speakers, the herbal teas she would heat up for me before I'd sleep-drive back to my house, the intonation of her voice when she'd call in the morning.

I was fully alive, all of my senses on fire. I had found a smile, a smile I hadn't known since early youth, the kind you forget you have.

And I had caught a grand vision for my life. Me and her. Dreaming along cozy streets, arm in arm, conspiring how to change the world, but looking a little too long in each other's eyes to quite get to it yet. Of holding hands on benches and a thousand corny moments made for movies. Of chasing her frame up a grassy hill toward a tangerine sunset to laugh, to fall, to fight, to kiss deeper than angels would bear to look, to read, to play.

I remember there always being a knife fight in my stomach when she walked my way, her brown eyes sparkling with secrets and joy.

Everyone knew we were meant to be.

"You're Cory and Topanga from *Boy Meets World*," my buddy Josh would repeat.

Friends would refer to our times together as "the bubble." I imagine it was nauseating. Perhaps you've already thrown up on the pages yourself.

Together we planned our wedding and secretly I planned to buy a diamond.

I sold my truck and netted some cash. I got her ring size, discovered her favorite cut, called a jeweler a friend recommended, planned a down payment, plotted a ridiculously elaborate proposal, all the things.

Around the one-year mark, things weren't perfect. But that was any relationship, right? Her mom—her best friend—had turned a cold shoulder my way, later acknowledging jealousy of the place my voice had raised to in her daughter's life. I began to notice things that concerned me slightly. But still, this was the one.

I continued to plan my proposal.

And then I got back from a trip to Mexico, and she had changed her mind. Truth is, I heard it in her voice during my one long-distance call I had made from Vera Cruz there by the valley.

We plodded through a couple more weeks when I got back before she cut the plug. I can still recall the eternity of that Sunday afternoon. The next week, I flew out to Colorado with my family to Zombie-walk among the Rockies.

I remember a few days later her collecting her belongings from the back of my Jeep and smiling fakely while asking polite questions about my trip to Denver. Without an ounce of pride, I told her I didn't understand, that I thought we should talk about us, that we shouldn't give up. Her pebble-smooth façade broke quickly into frustration and she said she didn't have time for this, that she was hungry, that she really needed to leave.

The details are messy, and I never quite understood. But I remember how it felt, that much is true, along with the months to follow of trying to pull all the spurweed stickers out of my scabbing heart.

I just know within weeks she had changed her number, left our church, and bailed out on her closest friendships with anyone who knew me.

The devastation of soul I experienced would be hard to put into words.

I buried myself in work and church and concerts and even painted some horrible emo image on a canvas of God counting my tears in a jar, and don't tell anyone, but spent a good month drinking a quarter bottle of NyQuil each night just so I could sleep.

It sounds dramatic now, but to find your soulmate, then wake up one day with that future gone—it felt like waking up and the sun not being there. Eating seemed pointless. I lost weight and read a lot of books and fell asleep on the couch to talking heads on TV discussing how the other presidential candidate was the antichrist and would damage our country forever.

o o o

Nancy Wynne Newhall once said, *"The wilderness holds answers to more questions than we have yet learned to ask."*

I think it's true.

I think it's in the zig zags we begin to catch painful glimpses of what's inside.

And painful as it may be, it's important not to look away. The internal soul work is crucial. *Especially* in the desert seasons.

See, the Israelites could have just went straight to all their circumstantial dreams.

And yet God took them a long way around by a weird road.

Ever been on a road trip with someone directionally challenged, and wondered, *wait, where are we going?*

That's this road trip. At least if you're in the wilderness. And let's be honest, it can feel like the road trip from hell.

We want to scream:

*God, why are you driving me in zig zags?*

*Why did you just take that detour?*

*Why are we driving through California from Florida to get to New York?*

*Are you kidding me? Is this thing in reverse?!*

Yet we trust the Driver. And when the car begins to smoke, we don't just keep plowing ahead, waiting and crossing fingers for life to get better. That's not a coping strategy.

Instead, while we're in the car, we're going to learn together how to shift our thoughts and hearts into the right gear, eat the right kind of snacks, use the right grade of fuel, fill the vehicle with the right kind of soundtrack, steer in the right direction, all that good stuff.

But we're also going to need reminding, and I suppose this is the gist of this chapter, sometimes in life we hit potholes big enough we need to pull over and check things out. Kick the tires. Assess the damage.

Sometimes the bumps and knocks get big enough and linger long enough that we need to *look under the hood*.

Have you done any of that lately? Mustered enough courage to lift the latch and squint inside?

To honestly evaluate what got you here, at least emotionally and spiritually?

Taken time for any self-exploration and perhaps even run your trembling hands back down the family tree to see what kind of past roots might be producing some current fruit?

Have you dared to peek behind any forbidden curtains of childhood to see what hasn't been healed or dealt with?

This stuff is not fun. I know.

And yet the greatest pain *and* power of the wilderness is God uses it to expose things in us, to cause things to surface so they might be healed and redeemed.

I am not saying you've caused the wilderness. I'm just saying God will use it as a gift. A gift you and I shouldn't waste.

And I'll be honest—under my hood, I've found a lot.

At times, I've been encouraged to find *good* underneath. To see some of the best in me come out under the squeeze, my fight or flight causing me to run forward, hard and fast, tackling challenges head on. To discover I really do love people and I really do love God. Glad that people who know me best would say I'm inspirational and strong and have God's favor and Presence on my life in a unique way. Happy that the people who know me best tell me I'm honest and authentic.

But....

I've found *ugly* underneath, too.

Maybe even more so.

I've discovered while I'm really strong, I'm also really weak. Weaker at times than I wish to admit.

I've noticed sometimes in pain I get stuck in my head and it can lead to self-absorption. This in turn disgusts me.

I've observed I have an addictive personality. I can run to God's Presence and find strength for the pain, but I can also be tempted to numb that pain away in the first place.

In my unhealthy modes, I lean deep into performance to scratch my soul's thirsty itch for value, drawing my sense of self-confidence from the applause of other people. If you're familiar with the Enneagram personality typing, this means I'm a "3," "the achiever," or "the performer."[2]

If I'm not careful where I draw my identity and source from, I will only feel as significant as my last good performance, be that a conversation, a well-delivered talk, or a meeting where I came across strong and put together.

I've learned when I'm weak and confused in the garden, I "take my question to Eve," instead of my Creator. I will draw the waters of my identity and meaning from the opposite sex and therefore, not surprisingly, rejection has left wounds far deeper than needed when the bucket comes up dry.

I've learned I'm not as consistent as I desire to be. Or as organized as I want to be. Or that if I'm not careful I can manipulate my charm to paint a picture that benefits me well.

Hope you're impressed.

o o o

Regardless of why we're in this painful place in life, it's a good time to look under the hood. A good time to lift the latch and let in some light, as we expose the deepest places of our souls to the love and wisdom of God.

As we get honest about how we feel.

As we process.

As we find a counselor or mentor and invite truth and openness into our soul in a new dimension.

As we walk past the Red Sea to red sand.

As we'll eventually be in the Promised Land.

These first couple chapters have been a basic preface to *what* might be going on. In the next section, I say we probe even deeper and ask *why*.

Welcome to the wilderness.

## WILDERNESS WRITINGS

(Notes from the Section—What stood out?)

_____

_____

_____

_____

_____

_____

_____

_____

_____

_____

_____

_____

_____

_____

## DESERT DECISIONS

(Future Applications—What steps are you going to take?)

_____

_____

_____

_____

_____

_____

_____

_____

_____

_____

_____

_____

_____

_____

*the*

# PURPOSE

*of*

# PARAN

## Chapter Three

### THE WHEEL OF PURPOSE

*"You don't understand now what I am doing,
but someday you will."–Jesus (John 13:7)*

*"I am certain that I never did grow in grace one-half so much
anywhere as I did upon the bed of pain."–Charles Spurgeon*

*"Can you trust God with a mystery?"–Clint Claypoole*

W h y ?

On this shore of eternity, it's the question of questions.

It's the question we ask again and again as kids, to the near madness of our parents.

And it's the question we ask again as adults when the pain and largeness of life turns us back into kids once more.

It's the question I asked nearly ten years ago as I left *Jason's Deli* one fall afternoon.

I had just paid for my turkey wrap and began working the complimentary food bar of sesame seeds, jalapenos and mixed nuts that I just found out last week isn't complimentary.

I turned to find a seat and spotted Lee and his wife, Regina, already seated, waving me over. I sat down and attempted small talk.

As my food arrived, though, I began to sense the weight at the table. I knew today had been a follow-up appointment for Regina. Gripping the sandwich in my hand, I asked meekly, "So how did it go?"

Her head had been down, facing her plate, and it bothered me she wasn't lifting it. The pause was too long. When she finally looked up, her eyes were beginning to color red.

"It's cancer," she whispered with a weak smile.

The sandwich I had been about to eat suddenly seemed useless. What do you do with food in that moment? And what do you say?

And *why* would this happen?

o o o

If you're holding this book, I can only assume you have a list of your own *whys*.

*"Why was I never good enough for my father?"*

*"Why can't I get past my past?"*

*"Why would they take me for granted?"*

*"Why can't I seem to get unstuck from this habit?"*

*"Why did she betray my trust?"*

I know too well what it's like for my soul to groan underneath the weight of that question, whether directed at myself or someone else.

I also know what it's like when the *whys* get so deep, so personal, they change direction. The arrows of inquisition stop pointing east and west and turn north, upward towards the sky, where we cannon the question towards heaven itself, hoping for a blast stirring enough to cause God to send down a reply.

*"God, why?"*

*"Why would you let my parents get divorced?"*

*"Why would you let me get sick like this?"*

*"Why would you let me be abused?"*

*"Why did you let me fall in love only for my heart to be shattered?"*

*"Why are you leaving me in this season for so long?"*

The question *"why?"* burns in us all.

It burned in our heroes of heaven as well.

Scripture sweeps nothing under the rug of Elijah, Moses and all the rest. We can eavesdrop even now on the raw, bare bones laments of King David:

> God, God. . .my God! **Why** did you dump me miles from nowhere? Doubled up with pain, I call to God all the day long. No answer. Nothing. I keep at it all night, tossing and turning.[1] (emphasis mine)

Have you ever felt this grieving of soul, this crushing disappointment?

Even Christ Himself, when the separation and wrath of our sin came down on him in pulverizing totality, cried out from deep down in His soul, *"My God, My God, **why** have you forsaken Me?"*[2] (emphasis mine)

Sometimes the question's rhetorical. A visceral, verbal reaction to what has gone so wrong. Other times we genuinely want to know, as if understanding would make the pain go away.

Now. If we can find our way around a Bible and basic theology, there are plenty of pat "why" answers to sift through.

Truth is, we live in a world tainted by sin, children of Chernobyl[3], subject to sickness and sadness. Until all things are restored, *"the rain falls on the just and the unjust."*[4]

Toss in humanity's free will. We damage and sow more harm for ourselves and others than we can calculate.

We also understand all the philosophical contrasts. We'd never fully appreciate light without darkness, joy without pain, spring without winter, and so on.

We even know the power *perspective* brings to our *whys*. We understand the 20/20 clarity of rearview vision, to reflect upon past seasons and realize what we considered a curse may have been a blessing. What seemed like a cruel denial is often a loving protection. What seemed like a setback could've been a setup. Yes, all that.

Yet, in the heat of an extremely painful wilderness, though, all those answers don't really help, do they? At the end of the day, there are just some things on this side of heaven we'll never understand.

That's life.

Here's the good news for every believer, though.

We may not always know why.

But we *can* always know God brings *purpose* to every difficult station of life.

For the child of God, there is reason embedded in every season.

There is purpose in the pain.

That simple knowledge alone can serve as a kind of triage for the soul as we bandage our wounds and husband our emotional resources to move forward.

o o o

Again, I can see God's people, having just crossed the Red Sea. They stand back and soak it all up, their wildest dreams taking shape right before their eyes.

They are free, their enemies float lifelessly in water, and ancient promises unfurl like a scroll as they sing songs about their brand-new future in a brand-new land. How the hearts of all their enemies will melt in fear as they enter the Promised Land.

But then they spend the next forty years in unbearable frustration. Wandering, complaining, and losing heart. From the Wilderness of Sin to the Wilderness of Sinai to the Wilderness of Paran. Just wandering and wandering, asking *"what is happening?"* And *"why?"*

We know it wasn't God's will for that first generation to spend *that long* in the wilderness and *die* before reaching the Promise.

But it *was* part of His divine will for them to spend at least *some time* in the wilderness.

But why?

I can't tell you why you've had to go through all that you have. I wish I could.

But I do know this: *There is no season without purpose in the life of a son or daughter of the King.*

*Especially* the wilderness.

There *is* a purpose in our pain.

I believe the greatest picture of that purpose, the purpose of the wilderness, is actually found in the book of Jeremiah.

About 850 years after Moses, his eerily similar counterpart arrived on the scene. Another prophet, this one named Jeremiah. An insecure man with a heart tenderized by the bleeding compassion of God for His people. In the eighteenth chapter of his book, we see God give the prophet a compelling picture of His heart for Israel:

> *This is the word that came to Jeremiah from the Lord: "Go down to the potter's house, and there I will give you my message." So I went down to the potter's house, and I saw him working at the wheel. But the pot he was shaping from the clay was marred in his hands; so the potter formed it into another pot, shaping it as seemed best to him. Then the word of the Lord came to me. He said, "Can I not do with you, Israel, as this potter does?" declares the Lord. "Like clay in the hand of the potter, so are you in my hand, Israel."* (Jeremiah 18:1-6)

God had a divine purpose for His people, and He longed for them to yield like supple clay in His hands, that He might prepare them for all He had planned.

And so He is with us.

Paul tells us in Ephesians 2:10 that, *"...we are God's handiwork, created in Christ Jesus to do good works, which God prepared in advance for us to do."*

God has unique designs for your life. Specific molding and shaping. All glorious. All good.

But how does He mold us and fashion us?

On the potter's wheel.

He takes us in His dexterous fingers and spins us. He breaks this piece off. He twists that shape back into form. He snips, relaxes, squeezes, presses.

And we *feel* it. Dear heavens and all it contains, do we feel it.

It reminds me of when C.S. Lewis wrote, *"We are not necessarily doubting that God will do the best for us; we are wondering how painful the best will turn out to be."*

The wheel of God is where we discover He is more concerned with our holiness than our happiness.

He is after His glory. He is after our full *joy*.

He is committed to who we're *becoming*.

He is, therefore, rolling us over and over until He can see His reflection staring back at
us through the vessel of our lives.

He is skillfully applying pressure until we're *"conformed to the image of His Son."*[5]

Do you feel empty?
If so, remember vessels have to be emptied and cleaned before they can be filled.

Do you feel vulnerable?
Consider that vessels must be transparent so the Owner can not only see through it but look at it and see Himself.

Do you feel shattered in a million pieces?
Whisper a reminder to your heart that God and God alone is the Specialist in taking discarded fragments and spinning

wondrous meals, works of art, glory and splendor that leave men speechless.

Those aren't soundbites; they're rib-eyes of truth about just how committeed God is to using the raw essence of everything we've been through to optimize our future and help us become everything we we were ever destined to become.

So, what is the purpose of the wilderness?

*The wilderness is the* **wheel**.

It is where God takes the shards and debris of our lives and transforms us into the image of His son. Preparing us for His work. Stripping us of all that hinders. Strengthening us for the blessings just around the corner.

I know all our wilderness seasons look different.

However you got to where you are now, know this: the broken seasons of our lives can be the great wheel on which God takes the most ugly that is *in* us, or that has even been done *to* us, and lets His fingers loose to heal, redeem and fashion unfathomable beauties.

o o o

The main problem with being on the wheel? We want *off*.

It can be terrifying to be on the potter's wheel.

Any wheel, for that matter.

Atlanta has a Ferris Wheel called *SkyView Atlanta*.

Calling it a Ferris Wheel is a bit modest, though. It towers nearly twenty stories above Centennial Park and boasts nearly four dozen sleek gondola carriages, all of which are uber-clean, enclosed, and climate controlled.

Nevertheless, people lose their minds.

When I lived in Atlanta and guests would visit from out of town, I'd take them for a little orbit. Always, one of the guests loved it. And one of them hated it. I mean, near-panic-attack hated it. And then hated *me* when I made it worse by jumping up and down like a five-year-old.

Honestly, I don't love heights, but I love *SkyView*. On account of it being so nice and well-financed, I just tend to trust I'm in good hands.

Not so with the Ferris Wheels at traveling carnivals, however. I'm sure they're fun and I'm sure this is not fair and please don't send me an e-mail, but I can't help but picture intermarried cousins putting it together while under the influence. Then, I picture it losing control while I'm in it. And then I picture me flying through the air with regret, screaming, finally being plunged to my death in a hot vat of funnel cake oil.

These are the things I picture.

Some of us know what it's like to be on some kind of wheel, screaming, begging for rescue.

But *all* of us know what it's like to be on God's wheel at some point or another, again, screaming, begging for rescue.

Whatever wheel of life I find myself on, the question is the same: do I trust the hands behind it?

Proverbs 3:5-12 says, *"Trust God from the bottom of your heart."*

When the very hands you're asking to heal you are gripping the surgeon's knife and cutting you open, it requires a rock-solid trust in the goodness of a Father's intentions.

Maybe this is why Charles Spurgeon once encouraged, "God is too wise to be mistaken. God is too good to be unkind. And, when you can't trace His hand, you can always trust His heart."

I must trust the Potter's hand.

I must remember the hands forming me have holes above the palm, scars that purchased my freedom.

When we remember whose hands we are in, we begin to do a little less *yelling* and a little more *yielding*.

Isn't that God's desire? Isn't that the longing He expressed through Jeremiah?

> *"'Can I not do with you, Israel, as this potter does?' declares the Lord. 'Like clay in the hand of the potter, so are you in my hand, Israel.'"*

Can we trust the glorious things God has planned for us?

He is better than any father we've ever known, to an innumerable degree. His generous heart towards us, reflected in the words of His Son in John 10:10, are unmistakably clear:

> *The thief's purpose is to steal and kill and destroy. My purpose is to give them a rich and satisfying life.*

Can we settle that reality in our heart? Those are His plans for us.

When we don't, when we refuse to trust, blinded by our pain and frustration, we tend to do one of two things while we're on the wheel.

First, we *run*. We throw in the towel and give up altogether.

Or second, we *aid our pain*.

We think, *Well, if I can't see how life's going to get better any time soon, I'm at least going to numb this agony...*

*I'm going to take an extra pain killer.*

*I'm going to drown myself in another relationship.*

*I'm going to busy myself at work.*

Either of those choices—run or aid—*make things worse, elongate our time in the wilderness,* and *keep us from growing in the ways God is trying to grow us.*

As odd as it may sound, there is maturity and a bittersweet beauty in learning to *sit in the pain.*

I don't mean to wallow in self-pity or to stay stuck in sorrow. I mean to choose joy in your heart the best you can with God's grace, but to say:

*"You know what? I'm not defaulting in this season. I'm not leaning back on my normal vices. I refuse to self-medicate. I'm going to learn how to sit with God in this pain. To cry in His Presence if I need to. To journal. To share openly with a friend.*

*But I'm not running and I'm not aiding my pain. Joy is just around the corner. I'm not wasting this season. If I'm going through hell, it's not going to be in vain. I'm bringing some treasure and experience and growth with me.*

*God is not responsible for all my pain. I know there's an enemy who attacks. I know people have done some horrendous things.*

*But I also know my life is in God's sovereign hands. And He is working it all out for my good. I'm on the Potter's Wheel. I'm in the wilderness. And while I'm here, I want to grow. I want to learn every lesson He has to teach me. I want to mature how I need to mature. I want to strengthen how I need to strengthen.*

*Lord, I'm asking You to heal me. I'm asking You for breakthrough. I'm asking You for everything in my heart.*

*But Lord, while You have me on this wheel, teach me how to yield to the influences of Your Spirit that I may become everything You have called me to be. Help me to become like the image of Your Son."*

That prayer, that posture, will make the difference between pots that shatter and pots that shine for the glory of the Maker.

We're all clay, after all. From the dust, just like Adam, with the breath of God animating us inside into living beings. Then as believers of Jesus, containers of the divine Spirit pulsing spiritual life now through our souls.

Clay.

Job acknowledged this when he said, *"Your hands have made me and fashioned me....You have made me like clay."*

Paul knew this when he referred to us all a few thousand years later as *"jars of clay."*[6]

Yes, if we stay on the wheel even when it hurts, if we adopt the prayer above, if we allow that to be the posture of our heart, we can receive Paul's exhortation to Timothy to become *"a vessel for honor, sanctified and useful for the Master, prepared for every good work."*[7]

o o o

So, will I trust the potters hand?

When it feels like the pressure of His grip is more than I can possibly bear, can I rejoice that He is lining the fundament of my life with the gold of endurance?

While blessings delay and my hopes despair, can I trust He's just filling in the final corner of the foot of the bowl?

Maybe we're only moments away. Rich Cabernet from Christ's hand is about to cascade in rivers until it fills the mouth, spilling over the rim of the bowl and splashing over and on everything around me.

Perhaps he knows there are yet fissures in the bowl. That if He were to fling open the windows of heaven and pour out the aged wine of Naples just yet, it would only seep through cracks.

Perhaps in His love He is taking His time, not only so you can become the vessel of honor He has planned, but so your life will have the substructure to hold all the blessings He is so eager to pour out.

Perhaps your tears are about to turn to wine.

As our Master once said, new wine cannot be put in old wine skins.[8]

There are things, even people, that you can't take with you into your Promised Land. But it's not because God has less for you. It's because He has more.

o o o

If I am clay, then more than once I have felt like a jar just dropped from the top of the Eiffel Tower.

I'm reminded of the famous nursery rhyme,

*Humpty Dumpty sat on a wall,*
*Humpty Dumpty had a great fall.*
*All the king's horses and all the king's men*
*Couldn't put Humpty together again.*

Ever felt that way? (What a horrifying *nursery rhyme* by the way....)

We feel, *I truly don't think I can ever be put back together.*

I wrote this book for everyone kneeling in the mud, staring uselessly at the broken shards of your life, wondering if things can ever be the same. If your heart can ever be repaired.

It can.

## Chapter Four

THE UNWANTED GIFT

*"What's past is prologue."–William Shakespeare*

*"I would have lost heart, unless I had believed I would see the goodness of the Lord in the land of the living."–Psalm 27:13*

*"Courage, dear heart."–C.S. Lewis*

I can still remember the worst gift I've ever recieved. At least the gift that made me *feel* the worst.

A few years ago, I was finishing up a Christmas dinner with my parents, aunt and uncle at my old house. We were all halfway into second helpings and our breathing had begun to slow, like bears who had just been shot with tranquilizer darts.

Amazingly, though, our topic of conversation still turned to food.

Besides my sister, I'm the only one in my family that's more of a city person. I'm also a diehard foodie. I love to eat foods I can't pronounce. The weirder the better.

Somehow, I found myself on a tangent about restaurant chains and gave a no-doubt-pretentious speech about how much I hated generic food locations, specifically *Applebee's*.

Everyone listened kindly and then we went to open gifts. I opened my envelope and took out the surprise for all to see, which, to my horror, was, yep, an *Applebee's gift card*.

My face turned pale as I stared at it.

"Yeah, sorry…I know you're not a big fan," my uncle started apologetically.

"No, no! That's not true…." I began, and then realized I didn't really have anywhere to go from there. I paused for an uncomfortably long time. My mom shot me a glance, nonverbally begging me to at least say *something*.

"I may not always *choose* to go there," I continued. "But for chain restaurants, it's actually one of my favorites!"

Out of the corner of my eye, I caught my dad putting his head in his hands.

Oh, the gifts we hate.

Socks. A boring book. Hideous clothes. A gift card to a restaurant that confirms you are a horrible person.

And worst of all…*pain*.

Yes, *pain*. James 1:2 (MSG) puts some teeth into the thought: *"Consider it a sheer **gift**, friends, when tests and challenges come at you from all sides."*

A gift.

Tests and challenges. Trials and pain. Wilderness and wheel.

All of it the great, *unwanted gift.*

Why is it a gift?

Here's the full context in the NLT:

*Dear brothers and sisters, when troubles of any kind come your way, consider it an opportunity for great joy. For you know that when your faith is tested, your endurance has a chance to grow. So let it grow, for when your endurance is fully developed, you will be perfect and complete, needing nothing.* (James 1:1-4)

As God plants His feet on the floor and leans over the wheel, the same eyes that wash meticulously over the clay are filled with a clear, compelling vision for your life. A vision of purpose and meaning.

God knows getting you to that Promised Land is going to require endurance, and pain is the gift that allows endurance the opportunity to develop.

James 1:4 promises if we allow our endurance to become fully developed, we will be *"perfect and complete, needing nothing."*

What an incredible, long-term reward for short-term pain.

Also, I love that phrase "so let it grow."

Cheesy as it sounds, can we just say that our loud?

*So let it grow.*

Perhaps that can be our motto while we're in the wilderness.

*God, if I'm going to be stuck in this desert for a little while longer, I might as well let my endurance grow.*

*God, I want out of this season. But while I'm here...*

*My character, God—so let it grow.*

*My prayer life—so let it grow.*

*My anointing and purpose—so let it grow.*

*My faith and dependence on you—so let it grow.*

*My patience and perseverance—so let it grow.*

Sometimes the worst seasons are the best seasons. The "cursed" seasons can be the "gift" seasons. And sometimes God won't let us get *out* of seasons because He is still trying to get things *out* of us.

*So let it grow.*

The pain on the wheel hurts, but it's leading somewhere. We're becoming somebody God can use in mighty ways.

Here's how Peter unwraps the same theme as James:

*So be truly glad. There is wonderful joy ahead, even though you must endure many trials for a little while. These trials will show that your faith is genuine. It is being tested as fire tests and purifies gold—though your faith is far more precious than mere gold. So, when your faith remains strong through many trials, it will bring you much praise and glory and honor on the day when Jesus Christ is revealed to the whole world.* (1 Peter 1:6-7)

May God give us grace to quit squirming on the wheel and declare instead, *"so let it grow."*

We can become crocks of gold, refined by the fire of trial, or cups of straw and hay that melt in the face of future challenge.

Here's the promise at the end of that passage from James:

*Consider it a sheer gift, friends, when tests and challenges come at you from all sides. You know that under pressure, your faith-life is forced into the open and shows its true colors. So don't try to get out of anything prematurely. Let it do its work so you become mature and well-developed, not deficient in any way….*

***Anyone who meets a testing challenge head-on and manages to stick it out is mighty fortunate. For such persons loyally in love with God, the reward is life and more life.*** (James 1:2-4, 12 MSG, emphasis mine)

There is wonderful joy ahead, and God wants us ready and solid, no matter how challenging that process may feel in the moment.

He is purifying us on the wheel; scouring our propped-up egos with his fingernails, pressing our pain points so we deal with our roots of sin, stretching us so faith might bud.

He is even cutting off the dead weight that keeps us from growing.

In fact, the most painful part of the wilderness and the wheel is when *people* we care about are being cut from our lives.

At times there are friends, acquaintances or co-workers ordained for one season of your life, but not the next.

Joshua (Moses' aid who would eventually become his successor) and Caleb (who we'll discuss in detail soon) were the only two from that original post-Egypt crew to cross the goal line. Meaning they lost *everyone* they had loved and held dear. People they'd traveled with. People they'd always imagined would be with them for the rest of the journey.

Now *that* is where life gets hard, isn't it?

We'll taste the joy of their victory later but consider for a moment life from Caleb and Joshua's perspective. Everyone they cared about or knew died off in that first generation. No one else continued with them to their future.

I'll never forget grieving over someone who left my life when a friend called one morning and said, *"Russ, one of the purposes of the wilderness is to determine who will go with you to the promised land."*

The truth is, not everybody can.

It took me a long, long time to get over Hazel. It just did.

She was my soulmate. We were meant to be. We were meant to change the world together.

For a good year and a half, I nursed a wound in my heart I thought would never mend.

Around the time of our breakup, the ministry in Greenville was exploding. Lee, my pastor and mentor, announced he was going to move back to Kentucky and plant a church in Lexington. He asked if I would go. I lied and said I'd pray about it, and then called back five minutes later to tell him I'm all in.

I dove in headfirst into the new adventure, but secretly, I was still mourning the loss of that relationship.

In fact, once I moved to Lexington, the sap of my heart began to ooze its way onto the keyboard. I'd ricocheted between a half-dozen writing projects my whole life but *this—this was it*. I'd been reading a lot of Donald Miller at the time and wanted to release all my thoughts on modern Christianity in a stream-of-conscious memoir of sorts that interlaced my story of heartbreak over Hazel with God's heartbreak over us.

My motives were questionable perhaps. It was good work, not great, provocative in parts but also sticky with sentiment, and it over-emotionalized God in a way I'm not sure He would love. Also, though therapeutic, I sensed it turning the corner to counterproductive.

Still hemorrhaging from the loss, the writing was a cathartic bandage, but once prolonged, the literary heart-space was simply giving too much oxygen to the wound.

In other words, I needed to move on.

I was finishing up a grilled sandwich at Panera with Lee around this time, him bouncing message ideas off me, when he mentioned a familiar verse from 1st Samuel, the question God asked the prophet after the king's downfall–*"How long will you grieve over Saul?"1*

The words nearly knocked the sandwich out of my hands. All of a sudden, Samuel's question was my question.

*How long will you grieve, Russ?*

Somehow, I knew I was supposed to stop writing the book. To stop secretly imagining what it would be like for her to read it. To see my side, feel my pain. But in a "mature, gracious" way, of course.

I knew I was supposed to *let her go.*

So, I did. And God healed the wound.

Crazy sidebar? Not long after I stopped writing the book she got married. Tall, handsome rich politician who ran a radio show back in the southeast some of my friends listened to. They had a kid. Perfect, beautiful family. The one I'd dreamed of having with her.

Fast forward a year or two. They divorced.

In the same way she turned on a dime with me, she had done the same with him. And inside, deep inside where I felt too ashamed to admit to anyone, I repented of the dark underbelly of satisfaction that threatened to break the surface of my flesh.

Fast forward a couple more years....

My first autumn in Atlanta. I'm about to head to the mountains for a student retreat when a message lights up my phone—her ex-husband has been arrested. For crimes too vile to repeat. The state Governor withdraws support of him immediately.

I'll spare the messy details of what transpired (and names have been changed, by the way), other than in an embittered, ongoing domestic dispute, his ex-wife—my ex-girlfriend—had leveraged dark, heinous accusations in order to obtain child custody and legal support so her and her new husband could move out of state.

Eventually, as proof emerged, charges against him were dropped.

During this time, I received a voicemail on my phone.

It was him.

I had a friend in similar legal trouble, and suddenly, we had a common enemy. He wanted to collaborate, to meet and discuss what we both experienced at the hands of this girl who had caused us both so much hurt.

These are the vindication moments movies are made of, no?

And yet, I never could get my fingers to dial the number back. The gentlest whisper of the Spirit was somehow louder than all the other shouts. The Voice that wanted me to move forward and choose forgiveness. The same Voice that had told me to stop writing the book. Yes, that Voice, whispering the same sentiment Sean Connery in *Indiana Jones and the Last Crusade* whispered to Harrison Ford as Indy is hanging by a cliff stretching dangerously down to retrieve the gold and glory of that Grail:

"Indiana…*Indiana*…let it *go*."

Definition of surreal?

A year later, I'm standing in my hometown Christian bookstore. I stop by a familiar corner. It was the corner where years earlier Hazel and I had stood, me reading to her my favorite portions of a book on prayer, looking up to see tears spilling out the ramequins of her brown, milky eyes, me dreaming all the more intensely what our life would look like.

Now, in place of that book and that memory was a new memory and a new book. His book. This man had written a book about my ex-girlfriend, his ex-wife and fatherhood laws. The Governor of a large, southern state had endorsed it with a forward.

Unreal. The book I started, he finished.

I write this with distance now, honestly not holding an ounce of anger or hurt towards her. I've collected enough years and mistakes of my own to wish her at least half the grace and mercy and thousand chances God has given me.

I also hold no judgment to the man for having written the book.

I just know I was supposed to let go. I was supposed to stop grieving.

And I'm so glad I did.

o o o

So how long *will* we grieve over Saul?

How long?

How long will we stay stuck in what wasn't God's plan for our future?

Perhaps for some of us, God simply allowed a relationship to fall apart so we would run back to the eternal things that matter most in the first place.

He knew the breakup or demotion would drive us to climb back on the Potter's wheel.

To again find ourselves in the center of His will, clay tender in His hand, moistened by pain, and ready for growth.

Even momentary sorrow can help purify and produce gold.

Ecclesiastes 7:3 states that, *"sadness has a refining influence on us."*

We can never fathom in the moment what a gift our tough seasons can be.

This was certainly the case for the children of Israel. As discussed, God didn't take them on the direct route. The wilderness was an act of mercy. God knew they weren't ready, so he sent them through a desert detour. He put them on the wheel.

Once they crossed the Red Sea and reached the other wilderness, He used *that* dry desert to deal with their internal giants so one day they could fight their external giants.

Oh, how unloving it would have been for God to send them unprepared.

Oh, the many disguised mercies enwrapped in the seasons we despise most.

I know you wanted a new car for Christmas. But I believe God and all of heaven are watching to see what you will do with the *unwanted gift*.

○ ○ ○

The *unwanted gift* arrives heavy, bearing many other gifts. Much like a great, reverse Trojan horse. And this wheel can accomplish far more than we ever imagine in the moment.

The unwanted gift of trials and pain produces *sibling gifts:*

*Power.*

*Perspective.*

*Compassion.*

*Healing.*

*Cleansing.*

*Preparation.*

*Purity.*

Some of what needed to be purified on my wheel involved escaping my pain.

Food. Relationships. Wine. Clothes. Travel. Music. Take your pick.

I followed Jesus passionately through my middle and high school years. I never really found myself in sketchy scenes or taboo habits. But in my early twenties, there were a couple cracks in my armor I didn't think were a big deal.

I didn't factor in that the enemy was setting me up. Then, some desert storms hit.

One Thursday night, hurting and broken, I felt the pain of God beginning to remove the sutures and prod around, digging into the wound to root out some weeds He'd been longing to deal with for a while.

Then, Sunday evening, one of the church elders called. He said while praying over me, he felt led to tell me this season was about God putting a new infrastructure inside me. Replacing old systems and defaults and installing new frameworks to support all the great things God had planned. He said there were things I had allowed in my life up this point that I could not take with me to the future.

These are the moments and transformations that only happen *in pain*.

Weeds are torn out *on the wheel*.

Preparation for the Promised Land happens *in the wilderness*.

A couple years later, I was free but still wrestling with disappointment. I sat down to lunch with that same elder who had called me Sunday evening. We caught up as we always would, and I began to open my heart about the discouragement I was feeling. He counseled and shared perspective to the best of his ability.

And then, almost mid-sentence, something shifted. The Presence of God seemed to gather like fog at the table as the elder leaned in, eyes ablaze. He began to speak directly to the insecurities I was privately wrestling with God about. He spoke by the Spirit, powerfully, prophetically, straight to my soul.

As tears collected at the corners of my eyes, he paused, smiled, and added,

*"Russ, there are just some things so precious, God takes his time. Like aged wine. The cheap stuff is no good. Russ, God is about to turn your tears to wine. And you are going to love the way it tastes."*

See, the Potter's Wheel is not just about what God wants to do *through* us, though that is true.

It's also about what He desires to do *for* us as a good, generous Father.

Yes, we're clay.

But we're not just His jars; we're His kids.

o o o

There is a centuries-old Japanese art of repairing cracked pottery called *Kintsugi*.

It dates back to the fifteenth century where shogun Ashika Yoshimasa supposedly sent broken bowls to China for repairs, only to be disappointed when they returned home, aesthetically displeasing.

Very little care was given to the mending process, many times the broken pieces only being fastened together with metal staples. This motivated an alternative restoration process to be devised.

Thus, *Kintsugi* was born. A method which utilizes a gold-dusted epoxy in the repair. It's breathtaking. Worth a pause, in fact, to google the image.

Kintsugi, or "golden repair," celebrates the history of each artifact by highlighting its fractures with ornate linings of gold instead of merely trying to hide the cracks. In this way, it values the beauty in the flaws, and then redeems the piece in a manner which makes it even more stunning than it was before.

And this is us.

Born broken. Brokenness reinforced through the brokenness of parents, environment and experiences of life.

But now, eyes opened by the Spirit to see Jesus. The renewing power of His Presence surging into the brokenness causing the clay to come to life. Royal blood, divine blood, more costly than silver or gold, redeeming us and giving us infinite value among the treasures of heaven. God breathing life and purpose into the scary, painful shadows of our souls.

Our scars making the story *more* beautiful, not less.

Interesting enough, the Israelites spent most of their forty years in the wilderness of Paran, a name which literally means "to glorify, beautify, adorn."

Can God really heal and redeem us?

Can He really turn our scars to stories, etched with the divinity-stitched splendor of gold from heaven?

He can.

His strong right arm is powerful. And His hand is sovereign.

I know God's sovereignty can be confusing. But it is comforting.

Charles Spurgeon once said, *"When you go through a trial, the sovereignty of God is the pillow upon which you lay your head."*

Why?

Because trusting God's love and sovereignty frees us from being the helpless victims of others.

How often, even if we don't verbalize it, do we at least *feel* it:

> *Oh, God, he ruined my life.*
>
> *Oh, God, if **she** wouldn't have left me, then my life right now....*
>
> *Oh, God, if **they** wouldn't have cheated me...lied about me....*

I'm not trying to sound preachy, but you need to remember as God's son, *your bowl was never in her hands.*

You're God's daughter, and *your cup was never in his control.*

You're a child of the Most High, and *your destiny never rested in their flimsy fingers.*

The pottery of our life rests securely in the sturdy hands of the Potter himself. And plaited into every square millimeter of the substance of our life is Romans 8:28:

*And we know that God causes everything to work together for the good of those who love God and are called according to his purpose for them.*

He knows what He's doing.

He's whistling and working.

Even while His Father's heart breaks for your sadness.

Even as Jesus wept for Lazarus, knowing He was about to raise Him, so He weeps with you.

Though He knows what He has prepared, His tears mix with yours in the clay while He continues to squeeze and sculpt.

Weeping.
Interceding.
But smiling.

Saying, *"Just hold on. I know what I have planned."*

Don't despair when the fingers press and push and prepare you. Don't climb off the wheel when the blade begins to slice. Your imagination is not big enough to picture the glory of what He's making.

Trust him.

There is a skilled and nimble hand at work. And that nimble hand is aware of every scrap. He doesn't waste a thing.

One of the philosophies that birthed Kintsugi, by the way, was the Japanese feeling of *mottainai*, which conveys "regret when something is wasted."

That is Jesus. He doesn't waste pain; He uses it.

Just ask Joseph from the Old Testament. Born with dreams of destiny. Only to live a life of disappointment. Rejected by his brothers. Betrayed. Rotting in prison, surely wondering where God was. Somehow keeping His purity, only to be lied about and punished. His most vital years languishing away in prison for crimes he didn't commit.

Oh, how he must have withered in disappointment. Oh, how all hope must have been leaking from his heart. God used him to interpret dreams and touch people's lives and again and again he is only forgotten, neglected and alone.

Until one day, all of the broken pieces, all of the gold epoxy, came together on the wheel, and he got to stand before his family, now elevated as the second most powerful man in the land and declare:

> *You intended to harm me, but God intended it for good to accomplish what is now being done, the saving of many lives.*[2]

Only then could he see: his pain had been leading somewhere. It had been building something.

None of his pain had been wasted.

Not. One. Ounce.

We can rarely trace God's hand in the moment, but He's gathering all the scraps. He's making Michelangelos out of messes. He's the great Alchemist, spinning gold from agony.

If we could just imagine we're old friends seated at a coffee shop right now, I'd want to encourage you, *trust God with your pain*. Trust where it's leading.

Let it turn to oil. Let it turn to power. Let it turn to godly change within.

Let it foster, above all, the greatest gift of pain on this side of life: an unrivaled intimacy with Jesus.

There are mountain heights of friendship with God never felt so tangibly as in the low valleys of pain. And many times, the greatest glory rests on the seasons of the greatest agony.

If, by the grace of God, I can choose to focus less on the pain and more on staying close to Jesus, if I can choose to soak in the sweet fellowship with God that comes along with tender brokenness, then my worst seasons can also become my best seasons.

The Psalmist tell us, *"He is near to the broken hearted."* It's not until I travel back through another broken season that I discover afresh just how true that is. It's when my face is in the dust that I most keenly taste His glory.

Sit in your pain. Don't numb it. Don't run from it. And while you're sitting in the stillness and pain, soak in His Presence.

Don't spit on what could be moments of sweetness.

It might be tough to picture the distant hills while in this valley. But even in the valley of death, your *"cup runs over"* as God *"prepares a table."*

Let Him set your plate. Look at His eyes through your tears. And linger long in communion therein.

○ ○ ○

It's healing to process. To be honest.

To confess like David:

*Day and night I have only tears for food….*
*My heart is breaking as I remember how it used to be….*[3]

But as purpose and hope begin to stir in our hearts, we can also, like David a few verses later, ask a different *why*. We can take the finger of our questions, press it into our soul, and say:

*Why am I discouraged?*
*Why is my heart so sad?*
*I will put my hope in God!*
*I will praise him again—*
*my Savior and my God!* (Psalm 42:5, 6)

Oh, the simple but potent power of locking our eyes on Jesus again. Even while we recoil on the wheel, we can rejoice in God. Not because of the circumstance, but because we trust Him *in* it.

And while we mature on the wheel, we can even begin to exchange our *whys* for *whats*.

The ninth chapter of the book of John contains a powerful example of this perspective Christ desires for us. Jesus and his disciples walk past a blind man and the disciples immediately break into *why*.

First, they ask if it was because of sin in the blind man's life, then they inquire about the possible sins of his parents. Jesus responds bluntly:

*You're asking the wrong question. You're looking for someone to blame....Look instead for **what God can do.*** (John 9:3 MSG emphasis mine)

Christ changed their *whys* to *whats*.

This is exactly what I witnessed in the life of Regina, whom I mentioned at the beginning of the last chapter.

I'm sure she and Pastor Lee wrestled with questions as they processed what the word "cancer" would mean in their lives. But I watched them take the platform that next Wednesday and announce their journey to 500 students, smiling through tears, making their pain an amplifier of the faithfulness of God. They clearly and bravely provided the facts but spent most of the time bragging about Jesus.

Later, Lee told me, "Son, they've spent years hearing me say how good God is when we were on the mountain. Now I get to tell them how good and faithful God is in the valley."

One of the moments Regina found most difficult, however, was the long journey down the hall of the hospital immediately after the diagnosis. She said she remembered wishing there was someone there waiting. A joyful, Spirit-saturated lady who had walked in her shoes, who could be there to listen, to cry, to pray, to process.

Months later when we moved to Kentucky to plant the church, she called UK Hospital and offered her services to do just that for other women.

She didn't wait to get off the wheel to be used by God.

She let her pain become her platform.

She embraced purpose in the midst of a difficult season.

She said, "even while... let it grow."

While I was asking "God, **why?**," she was looking for "**what God can do.**"

Lord, even while I'm on this wheel, may you leverage my pain as a gift for Your purposes. May I not only yield to Your work **in** Me, but may I be aware of mighty things You long to do **through** me. Give me grace, Lord, to trust in all the glory You have planned. No eye has seen, no ear has heard...

Yet you, Lord, are our Father. We are the clay,
you are the potter; we are all the work of your hand.
(Isaiah 64:8)

# Chapter Five

## DANCING IN THE DESERT

*"You can worry or you can worship, but you can't do both. Either your worship will be crippled by your fear or your fear will be crippled by your worship."*–Louie Giglio

*"Wait patiently for the Lord. Be brave and courageous. Yes, wait patiently for the Lord."*–Psalm 27:13-14

*"The silver waters of the Holy Ghost flooding up out of the redeemed and cleansed heart of the worshipping man is as sweet and beautiful to God as the loveliest diamond you can find."* –A.W. Tozer

Do you like to dance?

Better question. *Can* you dance?

My heart bursts with pride when I think of Kira, my niece. Best dancer I've ever seen. Call me biased, but her skill is unreal. She moved to LA a couple years ago and things are *moving*. Just last week, in fact, she was signed to go on *TLC*'s 25th Anniversary Tour, dancing, chasing waterfalls, all the things.

Maybe you can't dance. Or worse, maybe you're like me. You're convinced you have rhythm, but you really, really don't.

If you have two left feet, that's fine, at least for now. But sooner or later, I think God wants us to dance.

o o o

The original plan for the wilderness may surprise you. It did me.

I was already well underway writing this book when I felt God unveil in my heart what is perhaps obvious in the text. From the first moment God spoke to Moses about leading His people into freedom, His heart and desire was clearly stated:

> Then you and the leaders of Israel will go to the King of Egypt and say…"Let us take a three-day journey into the wilderness **where we will worship God**…." (Exodus 3:18 MSG, emphasis mine)

God wanted to deliver His people. Lead them out of bondage in Egypt to a beautiful land flowing with milk and honey.
But on the way He wanted to lead them to a dry, barren, uncomfortable place to… *worship.*

Now. I don't know your ideal worship environment, but I think I could've come up with something better than a desert. Maybe an auditorium packed to capacity, electric with energy while *Passion* or *Elevation* or *X Church Worship* (had to inject that) takes the platform. Perhaps my face in the carpet while *Bethel* leads spontaneous praise with candles in mason jars lighting the haze. *Housefires* or *Maverick City* leading an intimate chorus while we worship in the round. Some soul-filled gospel. Or maybe you're a hymns and grand choir kind of person.

Yet God's first order of business was to lead them to a painful place, surrounded by jackals and cacti, and lift their calloused hands to *Hillsong*'s new single.

Just to punctuate the point, God repeats this same desire multiple times over the next few chapters:

> This is what the Lord, the God of Israel, says: "Let my people go, **so that they may hold a festival to me in the wilderness**." (Exodus 5:1, emphasis mine)

> "The Lord, the God of the Hebrews, has sent me to say to you: Let my people go, **so that they may worship me in the wilderness**." (Exodus 7:16, emphasis mine)

> **"We must take a three-day journey *into the wilderness to offer sacrifices to the Lord our God***, as he commands us." (Exodus 8:27, emphasis mine)

This thought may seem simple, and even perhaps odd, but it's the first thing you need to know about the wilderness. And it will change everything if you get it in your veins.

You may be thinking of the desert as a torture chamber. A dry and weary land. Last chapter, we saw how the wilderness is a place of preparation, cleansing, and strengthening. Just for a minute, though, I want us to consider the first item on the wilderness agenda:

The wilderness is a place of **worship**.

I was thinking about this one night on a drive from Greenville to Atlanta. It didn't make sense to me. I knew the children of Israel would be ready to throw the block party of the decade those first few days, no matter where they were. Anyone can dance when 400 years of slavery ends, and God delivers you in mind-bending flair.

Yet their worship, much like ours, wouldn't last long. Why would God design the wilderness as a place to extricate praise? And doesn't it seem insulting? Some of us in this journey just lost loved ones. We've wept bitter tears. The first major suggestion of what to do in the most painful place of our lives is going to be to...*worship*?

I asked God to help me understand, and immediately sensed deep in my heart this simple answer:

"The wilderness is the true place of worship because you **can't** worship if you're still in Egypt, and it's **easy** to worship once you reach the Promised Land."

Egypt, as we know, is symbolic of our past. In the New Testament it represents our lives before Christ. No one in chains can lift their hands. No one in darkness can shine Christ's light. 1 Peter 2:9 says it this way:

But you are a chosen people, a royal priesthood, a holy nation, God's special possession, **that you may declare the praises of him who called you out of darkness into his wonderful light.** (emphasis mine)

Dead men can't celebrate. Unregenerated hearts can't worship. Those still shackled in sin can't shout the chorus of the redeemed. Those still in Egypt can't sing the song of the delivered.

Only thankful sons and daughters brought back to life can do that. Only heirs of a generous King. Only liberated criminals made new.

Let's be honest. If we only worship once we reach the Promised Land, how will we ever know if we love God just for what He does or actually for who He is? Wasn't that what Satan argued about Job?

> Then the Lord said to Satan, "Have you considered my servant Job? There is no one on earth like him; he is blameless and upright, a man who fears God and shuns evil."
>
> **"Does Job fear God for nothing?"** Satan replied. "Have you not put a hedge around him and his household and everything he has? **You have blessed the work of his hands**, so that his flocks and herds are spread throughout the land. But now stretch out your hand and strike everything he has, and **he will surely curse you** to your face." (Job 1:8-9, emphasis mine)

Anyone can praise God in the sun. Only a devoted heart can lift hands in the rain.

I have honestly come to believe the wilderness is the truest place of authentic expression. It is the place praise can shine forth, bright and high like the north star, because the hands of the worshipper are *freed from the bondage* but not yet *filled with the blessings*. It is in this bitter place that the sweetest idol-free adoration can ascend to the Almighty.

God, by the way, doesn't beckon our affection and focus because *He* needs it, but because *we* do. He's a divine Father, not a narcissist. But He's also self-aware. He's God. He's the source of life. And He knows that inviting our full trust, heart, and orientation into the oasis of that life is the most loving thing He could ever do.

So. Is your heart so broken you fear you may never recover? Are you floating on a bed of tears? Allow me, if you will, to provoke you with a bold thought: this is an opportunity. It is your great opportunity to worship. To worship like you never have before.

This is your chance, knowing one day you will look back and say one of two things. I *cursed* God in the wilderness, or I *praised* Him in the wilderness.

May I encourage you to mix your tears with the oil of praise? And may I stir you by telling you from experience that broken worship is the sweetest worship?

It is the place where the alabaster box, the treasures of our life, break succinctly at His feet, our tears falling hard against His ankles. When we, like that scandalous lady from the Gospels, leverage our pain for worship, the ends of the earth may one day catch the sweet scent of our tear-stained song for the God we love.

Our bones may be broken. But we can still dance in the desert.

o o o

I really should be a better dancer. Honestly, I should.

When I was in Elementary School, I lived in the world of *Nickelodeon* on Saturday nights. Right after *Are You Afraid of the Dark?* came an obscure show called *Roundhouse*. Still not really sure what it was about. I just know throughout the show they pulled off synchronized breakdances and flurries of aerial work that made my adolescent brain melt.

I watched in dizzied awe as they spun on their heads, mastered the beat, and rebelled against gravity.

As a passionate, easily inspired kid, this had an effect. I ended up spending a whole year choreographing, practicing, and filming my own dance routines to *Ace of Base*, *Duran Duran* and even Will Smith's early rap album.

*Bienvenido a Miami....*

It wasn't until I became older and painfully self-aware that I began to realize just how little rhythm I actually possessed. Survive ten somersaults in a row on my parents' carpet? Easy. Sway to music without looking sea-sick? Challenging.

Enter Cody and Amber's wedding in Charleston, South Carolina. Two of my best friends were getting married. The ceremony was held in one of the most beautiful locations in the Southeast, all white, dark wood, and ringed with coastal palms. A lot of my old friends from Greenville would be driving in in to attend, and of course, I would be expected to dance.

Of course, if you're like me and you can't dance, the only thing worse is the *pressure* to dance. I can't emphasize enough how much I didn't want to. I didn't know how, I wasn't in the mood, and I'm sure had the wrong shoes.

Sounds selfish, I know. I was excited for my friends, truly. But I was also single at a wedding, had gained a considerable amount of weight, was approximately six months overdue for a haircut, and had just come through a pretty tough breakup. In the moment, nothing had me particularly jazzed about life.

Have you ever felt that way? That you just don't want to dance?

That you've made up your mind?

You've made up your mind not to join the party. You've made up your mind not to smile. You've made up your mind not to engage with people in conversation anymore. You've made up your mind not to allow joy in. You've made up your mind not to forgive. You've made up your mind not to lift your hands. You've made up your mind not to move forward. You've made up your mind not to worship.

You've made up your mind not to dance.

There's only one problem for people like you and me.

Our God is the God of the dance.

May sound funny and bit trite, but it's true. And He's not just the Lord of the Dance; He's the Creator of the dance, the King of the Dance, and the Initiator of the Dance.

We were made in His image and anything good, no matter how much it's been corrupted, found its origin in Him. Laughter, smiling, eating, talking, singing, and yes, uninhibited, disequilibrating dancing.

The Persons of the Trinity have mingled in a mysterious Dance of community since time began, and so have God's people.

It's strewn all over the pages of Scripture, the very patriarchs and matriarchs of our faith leaping, twirling and stomping across the meadows of every millennium.

Even now, if you turn up the music, you can catch a glimpse of a rebellious and defeated son, hesitantly heading home to a teary-eyed father. The son expects a beating. Instead, he gets dancing. The father runs and tackles him into the grass in a fit of joy, kissing him with tears, and thanking the heavens above his son is alive again. They make a feast and before long the party's so out of control the religious, offended older brother can literally "hear the dancing in the field."

The music's getting louder now. I can see King David spinning wildly before the Ark, his cynical wife glaring from the window. He disrobes and dances with all his might. At her scolding, he informs her she hasn't seen anything yet. His best moves are just warming up.

Don't forget the first miracle Jesus ever performed was at a wedding party He brought back to life with the best wine. I don't believe for a minute He spent the rest of the night standing there, analyzing Leviticus.

And if you want to smile for days, consider that one day soon we'll be at Heaven's wedding. Marriage Supper of the Lamb. The Party of Eternity. Jesus Himself the Groom. Held in paradise. Cabernet and Filet. And dancing that will go on for centuries.

Well-known theologian and philosopher G.K. Chesterton once said the only thing concealed or perhaps held back in the personality of Jesus was His unbridled joy and laughter. According to Chesterton, the sheer force of it would have been too much for us.[1]

But I want to go a step further. If God's joy as expressed through laughter would be too intense for our human senses, I believe God's dancing would "break the roof of the stars."[2] The heavens themselves might would cave in.

I believe it with all my heart. Our King dances. And so do His children.

Sorry, I have to break it to you. There are no seated saints allowed at this Party. No wallflower nerds permitted.

Yes, that night at my best friends' wedding I danced. I sucked it up. I finally let loose.

I knew of no reason to dance. I wasn't good at it. I wasn't excited about anything going on in my life. And I was alone.

But you know what? I was alive. God was good. I had working legs. And that night I used those legs to get down.

I danced anyways.

I danced like crazy. I forgot everything else. Everyone else. Everything wrong. And I went for it.

And I have to tell you, it felt good. In fact, to be honest, I felt agile and smooth as I was letting go. I felt like Bieber, smoke and lights pulsating behind me, my peers looking on in jealous awe at my movements.

Upon further review when I saw the video, it appeared as if an elephant had lost a leg and was desperately drowning in the ocean. Some people looked concerned. I swear I saw one parent even check the punch bowl for alcohol.

The point is, I danced.

Sometimes the music makes us move. Other times we have to make ourselves move. Sometimes God gives us joy. Other times we choose joy. Sometimes life nearly jolts our hands up in the air because the circumstances are so wonderful. Other times we offer by faith "a sacrifice of praise."

Dancing is simply a decision we make.

And sometimes, as the theologians of LANY sing, we have to dance in order to survive and not die.

At first, the children of Israel danced. But quickly, as things didn't go their way, their merriment and whirling turned to moaning and whining.

We can choose a different path.

Even when the notes of the song aren't clear, we know the Songwriter is at work. When the last note sounds, He will have woven together a melody more masterful and magical than anything we could've ever dreamed. And trust me, we will wish with all our hearts we would have never sat it out.

We served the God of the dance. And He's invited us to dance, even in the desert.

I know it's tough. But I believe there's a militant joy God wants to put back into our souls. A steely resolve to groove even in grief. To dance even in the rain. While all hell breaks loose, to dip to the side. While enemies are at our table, to keep our feet tapping. While the wind screams against us, to spin with it in trustful surrender to a God who's still in charge and still holds every tune in His hand. While chains cut into our wrist like Paul and Silas in jail, to lift those clanking hands in joyful song that God Himself is in this hellish situation *with me*.

Will you dance anyways? You might be in the Promised Land before you know it. Will you be one of the brave few to keep clapping, even in the desert?

Even now will you worship? I say we should. We'll be in Jordan soon enough.

o o o

I do want to offer a word for the deeply depressed or bereaved.

As trite as it may sound, I think it's important, even just briefly, to state your worship may look different in the wilderness. Style and posture can vary from season to season as differently as they do from denomination to denomination.

I grew up in a very formal Presbyterian church. I don't think I ever even heard anyone clap. One day as a kid I gave a very satisfying and far-too-loud sigh after I downed my communion juice and the entire church, to my parents' horror, turned around and stared at me. Suffice it to say, my first time in a charismatic church was interesting. As a man in front of me raised his right hand in worship, I gently told my friend who brought me that I didn't think this was the best time to be asking questions.

Funny as it may seem, the pressure of praise and style actually discourages some people. They feel guilty for the way they worship in the midst of great pain. For what they feel. For what they don't feel. And I believe sensitivity is vital here depending on how severe a loss you may have just suffered.

Listen.

You can be sobbing for days over the death of your father, while holding on to the promises of God in your heart for peace to come. That's worship.[3]

You can be standing numb during a worship service, inwardly begging God to unthaw your heart and renew your joy and affections toward Him.

You can be walking through hell in your life right now but striving to the best of your ability to lean on God instead of temporary compromises that would make you feel better.

You can be nearly paralyzed with doubt, not even sure what faith looks like anymore, but muscling one foot in front of the other towards God anyway.

That. Is. Worship.

It may take various forms, but no matter where you are in life, I am believing with you for the grace to let worship rise in your heart.

There can be a grace-given gladness even in the midst of tremendous grief. "Sorrowful, yet always rejoicing," as Paul put it. A worshipful trust that "He is near to the broken heart." A trembling but secure hope that "sorrow may last for the night, but joy comes in the morning."

You may not be ready to bounce around like Brandon Lake. The truth is, you may be so immobilized by despair you don't even know what to say. That's okay. Like Hannah in the temple, he can listen when our lips move but sound is absent. Tears are a language He understands.

In fact, I love how David describes the preciousness of worship when our hearts are aching:

> *Going through the motions doesn't please you, a flawless performance is nothing to you. I **learned God-worship when my pride was shattered. Heart-shattered lives ready for love don't for a moment escape God's notice.*** (Psalm 51:16-17 MSG, emphasis mine)

○ ○ ○

In your wilderness season, one of the forms worship may take is "a song in the night."

> *But no one says, "Where is God, my maker, **who gives songs in the night**...."* (Job 35:10, emphasis mine)

I was so encouraged when I heard well-known Pastor and Passion Founder, Louie Giglio, speak with transparency of his battle with depression, and the cloud that would visit and disable him every morning at 2 a.m. Many things lifted him out, not the least of which was a "song in the night."[4]

It's the idea that God can personalize to us a song anchored in truth, that expresses our soul, as a way to index our hearts towards God in the midst of pain and confusion.

I was in an arena filled with thousands of teenagers when I felt God give me my own song in the night. Someone handed me a last minute ticket to *Forward Conference* in the Gwinnett Arena (Atlanta, Georgia), possibly the largest student conference in the world. At the time, I was in the early stages of my wilderness season but filled with much hope.

That Saturday night, as *Bethel Worship* took the platform to lead in song, the words and melody of "King of My heart" crashed into my soul like a tidal wave.

Steffany Gretzinger began the hauntingly beautiful verse, and my soul collected the words like rain. Words about God being the King of my heart. Words about Him being my fountain to drink from, my shadow to hide in, and the ransom of my life.

And then the line that makes the song. The simple truth that can affect our destiny and everything inside us. Our anchor for every storm. The anthem of the universe.

The simple declaration to God that He is *good*.

God is *good*.

It's the first truth the enemy attacked in the garden when He questioned our ancestors, "Did God really say?"

Our Creator, dripping in abundance, lavished every good thing upon Adam and Eve. But the serpent, in the darkest lie ever told, brought to question the goodness of God. He convinced Adam and Eve the Lord was holding out. That He was, in fact, not fully good. That He could not be fully trusted. And the insidiousness of that lie has curled its way into the human psyche ever since.

The problem is, the very health and future of our souls rests in how good and trustworthy we think our Father is.

Just that morning, before heading to the conference, I experienced one of those special, specific times where I could sense God wanting to talk to me. I grabbed my journal as the Holy Spirit began to pinpoint areas of disappointment in my life. Places I had refused to even pray about anymore. Desires I had long ceased to dream for.

To be transparent, God flipped a painful floodlight over the surface of my soul, and I realized—I had long ago stopped asking Him for a wife.

Layer by layer, like an onion, God began to peel back the reasons why.

> *Fear of disappointment.* Why get my hopes up again to only certainly be let down?

> *Shame.* After all my mistakes and imperfections, why did I think I deserved to even believe for that?

> *Selfishness.* The older I got the easier it became to be on my own and indulge self-focus.

As bittersweet conviction washed over me, I began to dream and trust again.

I wrote out prayers, desires and vision.

I even thought back to the hazel-eyed brunette at the church in Atlanta where I now worked. The one who had caught my eye. The one my hopes had been vacillating back and forth on.

I thought about all this as I raised my hands that night, tears in my eyes, to declare over my life the words of that song and that God truly is good, that my soul really can trust Him.
I thought about this as the anointed exclamation thundered down into my chest and Jeremy Riddle brought his rustic voice into the bridge, the declaration that God is never going to ultimately let us down.

That began a season of trusting, believing, declaring and journaling like never before. That song became the anthem of my days. Little did I know, it would soon become the song in my night. And little still did I know, God would soon use that song to test the purity of my worship in the wilderness.

A few months after that hope-filled night in the arena, the new but ancient thing I had begun to hope for in my chest seemed to be crystallizing before me.

I had started talking to someone. The hazel-eyed girl.
Brunette. Skin canvassed with freckles and spirit infused with an evergreen magic that cast a spell on anyone who came near.
Years before, after a toxic breakup with a girl I never should have dated, a friend reminded me, "Russ, you thought she was beautiful, and I get it. It had been a long time since you had

allowed yourself to date. But next time you pick, remember one day old and wrinkly and married, it's the *soul* you come home to."

It didn't take long for me to realize. This girl was the kind of soul I wanted to come home to.

Nearly a year before, she'd introduced herself after one of my Sunday messages and an unspoken bond cemented overnight. Over the course of the next year, we nursed that bond until it turned to a near maddening chemistry, something in the soul exchanged back and forth like lightning in a bottle.

It was everything, really. The companionship of doing ministry together. The thrill of running in the same lane. The banter and laughter and camaraderie that made me feel like I'd known her forever. The attraction and how we began ricocheting off each other in the most wonderful ways.

I found myself wanting to be near wherever she was and writing poems and all of those sickening things you don't think you'll ever do again.

I had spent ten years believing I'd never feel that way about a girl again.

Now I did.

Ex-girlfriends had accused me of not being intentional enough. But now, now I was walking into the back of an auditorium where a girl was sitting and sobbing in the confusion of her emotions, I was sitting down and taking her by the hands, looking her in the eyes and telling her softly, confidently, earnestly, that I'm all in, that I see a future with her, that *I want this*.

She sobbed harder. She wanted it to.

I was like a child with excitement. A new chapter had begun. The promise was almost here. The hopes had materialized.

I'll never forget the night months later when those new hopes crashed. They came tumbling down around me, cabins on fire, the promise seeming to collapse right in front of my eyes. And all I could do was watch the flames.

It was late at night when the call had come. I was pacing the church, trying to pray and prepare for a speaking opportunity in the morning. Though it may sound odd, I had sensed the Holy Spirit trying to prepare my heart for a setback of some kind, and yet the wind was still knocked out of me.

She'd had second thoughts. Something didn't quite feel right. She shouldn't have moved on so quickly from the previous man she'd given her heart to before.

This, of course, played into the wilderness already creeping up. The tumultuous years of church-planting, the two times a transitioning church had fallen on my shoulders, the warding off of past habits, the heartbreaks, the loneliness, the emptiness I felt at a church where the leader who hired me along with all my friends had left. And now, the second time I felt I'd found a soulmate and it had left me as disappointed as the first. The near-panicky level of pain I was feeling would usher in the wilderness that gave way to this book.

But back to that night.

You know, I've not always passed the Lord's tests. In fact, I would say I've failed more than I've passed. But that night I somehow knew I had a choice, and the choice was simple:

Would I still raise that song over my life? When nothing around me seemed good, would I still declare He is good? When I was so let down that I felt hollow inside, could I still declare He's never going to let me down?

It sounds melodramatic in review and I'm not trying to make a movie scene out of it, but I'll never forget walking outside around midnight to look at the stars, and then raising my hands as the saline stung my eyes, declaring towards the galaxies and a God I didn't understand that, "You are good. And You're never going to let me down."

o o o

I want to tell you something. If you ask God, He can give you a song in the night. Whether it's a song, a verse, a phrase, or simply a position of your heart, you can lift your hands in surrender and worship, offering your very breath and affection back to God. It's the reason you're alive. And it's the most powerful thing you can do.

Truth is, whole volumes have been written on the nature and power of worship.

While I desire to express worship from pure love for God Himself, I've also come to understand the benefits of what transpires when we choose worship in our darkest seasons:

- We give God something to inhabit
- Our perspective lifts
- The atmosphere of our life changes
- Our focus readjusts from our problems to His power
- A shift of responsibility takes place from our shoulders to His
- We invite His Presence and provision into the situation

- We exchange fear, dread and defeat for peace, joy and victory
- We declare to the world around us Jesus is enough
- God gets a lot of glory

So, what could happen if we shut down our pain-reinforcing music, books-to-cope and numbing distractions and turned up the volume of God's preeminence in our hearts? What would happen over the course of time, if not immediately, if we changed the soundtrack of our lives by conversation, music and focus from *our fears* to *His faithfulness*?

I want to extend an invitation. I want to invite you to close the book as this chapter ends, find a quiet place, and do what may seem insulting right now for me to suggest. Take your pain, your anger, and all your disappointments into God's Presence, and choose to worship.

I want to remind you God is bigger than our suffering. He is the King of the Universe who sits on a throne of glory amid unapproachable light. He owes us nothing and yet gave us everything. If He never did another thing for us, He gave up His precious Son to die in our place that we may have resurrection and be forgiven. Adopted into the family. Names written in the book of life, every coming eon to be spent in rapturous union with Him. And He intimately cares about you and knows what He's doing.

Remember Job who we mentioned earlier? God did, in fact, allow Satan to test the purity of Job's devotion. He lost almost everything. His wealth. His kids. His health. His reputation. And while He lay there, dying and miserable, his encouraging wife said:

*"Are you still maintaining your integrity? Curse God and die!"* (Job 2:9)

His response?

*"Shall we accept good from God and not trouble?"* (Job 2:10)

And then in Job 13:15 he declared defiantly:

*"Though He slay me, yet will I trust in Him...."*

We always have the choice—to be Job or Job's wife.

The wilderness was designed to be a place of worship. We don't have to demote it to a prison of worry. It is a place of praise. We don't have to downgrade it to a paralysis of panic.

You will get through this season. But while you're still disappointed, He's still deserving. While you're still angry, He's still will worthy.

*The Lord gives and the Lord takes away. Blessed be the name of the Lord.* (Job 1:21)

Can I encourage you in this way? Can I challenge you even in the middle of the pain to offer Him an expression of your love?

While angry tears roll down your face, choose to lift your hands.

While unanswered questions assault your mind, choose to raise your voice.

While all your worst moments flash across your mind, choose to shift your eyes back onto the Master.

Take up a song in the night.

I dare you to dance in the desert.

I dare you to dance anyways.

And I get it. I truly understand what it feels like to be doubled over in stomach pains of the soul. I remember one Saturday, I honestly wondered if I was going crazy. I woke up and within minutes was weeping and didn't really know why. I wept most of the day, and nothing would shake off the sadness. Nothing I did eased the emptiness.

Have you ever sunk in front of a mirror to your knees and looked up to see your own tears? It's a low moment. You think you should check yourself in somewhere. Even now, some of you are reading this and finally realizing you're not the only one that's crazy. That you're not alone.

I remember looking at my swollen, red eyes in the mirror and then looking up at the beige ceiling in sadness.

"God," I started. "I just don't know what else to do."

Have you ever been there?

"I've done everything I can think of. Lord, I'm trying to obey you. I've tried to take care of myself physically. I've watched every sermon I can. I've listened to uplifting music. I've buried myself in your Word. I've placed myself in accountability. I've recruited people to pray. I've done it all. There's nothing else I can do!"

As I began to softly sob again, I felt Him gently whisper, "Yes there is. You can worship."

I walked from my house on the hill down to the church. I approached the front of the platform. And I worshipped.

It doesn't happen this dramatically every time, but I can tell you that night as I began to penetrate the darkness over me with praise, everything shifted. The atmosphere of my evening and even the next few weeks altered. In His Presence, there really is fullness of joy.

I encourage you. Stop reading my words and take up a song of worship.

Dance a little bit in the desert.

*Then Moses and the Israelites sang this song…*


*"God is my strength, God is my song….*
*Who compares with you in power, in holy majesty,*
*in awesome praises, wonder-working God?*

*…Miriam the prophetess, Aaron's sister, took a tambourine,*
*and all the women followed her with tambourines, **dancing**…."*
(Exodus 15 MSG, emphasis mine)

# Chapter Six

## GRACE

*"I do the things I do because I don't understand anything about my life."* —Cory Matthews (Boy Meets World)

*"But in your great mercy you did not abandon them to die in the wilderness."* —Nehemiah 9:19

*"When God predetermined your destiny, he factored in your stupidity."* —Larry Randolph

Desert storms swept over my life in late summer of 2016.

Of course, that language implies I was a helpless victim instead of an active participant.

I suppose that's the thing about the "perfect storm" descriptions. Sometimes they *explain* it; doesn't mean they always *excuse* it.

The first half of 2016 felt like a promised land, actually.

I was breathing in the invigorating, spring air of *momentum*.

I was loving the city of Atlanta more than ever. I'd started my Master's Degree in *Passion City Global Institute*'s inaugural class. I completed my second round at *Financial Peace University* and was nearing that debt free scream. I got back in shape and shed thirty pounds in two months. I experienced a supernaturally peaceful, mutual break up and felt anticipation about what the future might hold. My leadership was thriving, my relationship with God growing, the ministry blooming.

And summer was whispering its secret promises of joy and love like it always does.

Life was on the up and up.

But.

I was also lonely and discouraged beneath the surface. All my best friends in Atlanta were now gone. My pastor had moved to another town and the direction of the church was shifting. My restlessness was growing. There were some hang ups I still hadn't crucified. Finally, at the ripe age of thirty-one, I was beginning to strongly desire my life partner. Then that brunette came along I mentioned last chapter. I fell in love for the first time in ten years, and then it fell apart.

Meanwhile, as also mentioned earlier in the book, the chemistry of depression from my dad's side of the family had been swimming its way into the limbic region of my brain for a while but was now tapping me harder and harder on the shoulder, demanding to be addressed.

Some "harmless" tendencies I'd never quite stomped out past the yard were looking for an open door back in.

It was all catching up. The exhausting, turmoil-filled years of church planting, and all the toll of ministry and betrayal and pain. Shame over past mistakes. Being left as interim Pastor twice, all the past heartbreaks, the emptiness and disillusionment I now felt in my current ministry context, the loneliness of not having a family in any of these cities to go home to on my difficult days. And now, the girl I had fallen in love with and then been rejected by was sitting directly across from me at work every day.

Yes, despite all my hubris and feelings of youthful invincibility, engine lights were starting to flash.

My soul had hit its pothole in the road.

One Wednesday night in August, we threw a big student event. I ordered all those *Bubble Bros* that wrap up students in giant, clear bubbles and allow them to run and roll and wrestle into sheer madness. It was a hit. More students showed up than we'd ever had before. I remember laughing and celebrating with the team and then getting into my car to drive. Drive and drive alone in circles around the city, my nightly routine.

The next evening, I decided to drive to a city nearby, one of those nice, quaint little city-towns where you can stroll the blocks under twinkling bistro lights and let the atmosphere get on your skin.

I decided on a restaurant and I ate.

And I drank.

And drank.

I poured liquid relief over all the agony of my heart and then got in my car, thinking I was good to drive.

I wasn't.

I hit a curb as I was pulling out and stopped to make sure my car was okay. Fortunately/unfortunately, an inquisitive officer was right there, right there to help me with the tire and then help me to the station.

I don't imagine I need to explain to you all the thoughts and feelings I experienced in the back of that police car, the cuffs harsh and cold on my wrists.

*Is this really happening?*

*I am not a criminal.*

*I am a good person.*

*I am a Christian.*

*Dear God, I am a Pastor….*

*What have I done?*

*What kind of person am I?*

*Is my future over?*

*Is my ministry over?*

*Even more importantly, I could have hurt or killed someone.*

*I could have traumatized a family forever.*

*I could have been killed myself.*

*What is wrong with me?*

*What will become of me now?*

It's true a sort of numbness can set in at the onset of tragedy.

But the first part of that numbness wore off pretty quickly the next morning. They had released me at dawn, and I caught an Uber back home and walked over to the church and began moving chairs around the auditorium like a Zombie.

A friend I used to work with stopped by. After some small talk, I broke down and told him what happened. That's when it hit me—I need to immediately call my pastor-boss and tell *him* what happened.

Over the phone he could tell something was up, and he rushed over to the church.

Emotions were gathering as I sat down on the other side of his desk.

"Russ…everything okay?"

"I need to tell you something."

o o o

My pastor could have handled it many ways. Any punishment, or immediate termination, would have been understandable.

I write this forever thankful he offered grace instead.

He offered a path of restoration.

In the office that morning, though, he wasn't sure what to do yet. He told me to take the weekend off as he prayed and processed.

That night I told my roommate. The next day I asked to meet with the girl I was working with, who was helping me run the student ministry. I told her what happened and said, "Whatever this looks like, I need both your help and support in this season." She was all in.

Then, I drove home to Greenville, took my dad out to dinner and told him everything over a cold, half-eaten salmon. I saw in his eyes both the disappointment and unflinching support I'd expected. On the way home, he uttered the terrifying words I'd already been thinking. "Now we have to tell your mom."

The next day I went with a friend to *Free Chapel*, a large multi-site church pastored by Jentezen Franklin, one of my heroes.

I stood there numb through worship, numb through the message. At the end of service, though, one of the first glimmers of hope broke through my new darkness. During a prayer time after the sermon, I heard God speak. Straight to my heart, for the first time in months, as clear as I've ever heard Him.

*"Russ, I am about to give you a supernatural strength for this season."*

That moment and those words shifted something in me. Sure enough, strength followed.

Driving back to Atlanta Sunday night, I knew—I can't take back what happened, but I *can* choose how I face and handle this season moving forward. And somehow, I knew that choice would determine my future.

Upon returning, I initiated tough conversation after tough conversation. I told all my co-workers. I met with elders. I called mentors. I sought counsel.

I *didn't* do a lot of praying.

I think spiritually, I still felt numb. And very, *very* ashamed.

I mean, what was there to say?

One night that first week when no one was there, I walked over to the church to do some mindless work in the auditorium and try to talk to God. While there, my phone rang.

It was my best friend, Logan.

I almost hit "Ignore." I hadn't told him yet. I was going to fly to Dallas the coming week to decompress and tell him and my former pastor in person.

I answered anyway.

*"Russ..."* he started.

I could tell he was emotional. That he had something to say but didn't quite know how.

*"You know I'm not one to throw out 'God said' or to have a lot of visions. And this is going to sound crazy.*
*But Russ, God gave me a vision about you last night.*
*I saw roots in your life. Weeds actually. They had been there a few years. Then I saw one giant weed come up to try to choke you and take you out in an instant.*
*Then I saw an even bigger hand. And I knew, that hand is the hand of God in this season. Reaching down. Pulling the weeds*

*up. Tossing them in the trash, commanding them to never grow again.*

*I saw you broken. I saw God running towards you. But not towards you as a prodigal son. Just towards a hurting son. Saying He was going to draw you away to Himself in this season and reveal Himself to you as a Father in new ways you've never known."*

I wept.

I guess weeds do only come out on the wheel.

o  o  o

I won't bore you with all the details of the following months and year.

I'll just say it was a long road. And that that season was both the worst thing and the best thing that ever happened to me.

Aside from all the court-ordered activities, I submitted to a path of restoration with my pastor that took several forms.

I took time off from all ministry duties. For a month, in fact, I didn't even step foot on church property. Instead, I rested and spent time with God, mentors and loved ones. I agreed to abstain from any alcohol. I met weekly with a professional counselor for pastors. I engaged weekly in a rigorous "freedom" curriculum with one of the church elders to discover and root out any buried issues in my life.

It was a long, beautiful, horrible, painful, wonderful, fruit-producing season. So stressful, I developed Shingles that didn't go away for months. So beautiful, it developed gold in me that won't go away ever.

I learned much about God and life.

I learned a whole new respect for healthy boundaries.

I learned to be cognizant what escape you reach for when you're in the wilderness.

I learned an eternal appreciation for the unwavering support and unconditional grace of the people in my life. People forever in my corner, who always see more in me than I do, and who simply refuse to let me define myself by my worst moments.

I learned how to dance in the desert.

And you better believe it, I learned a whole new dimension and understanding of the grace of God.

You know, I remember always seeing those lists of all the people in Scripture God used with their biggest sins right by them as a label. You know, the kind you always see on Facebook:

*Moses the murderer. Noah the drunk. Rahab the prostitute. Gideon the coward. David the adulterer and murderer.*

The list goes on.

I always appreciated the reminder of the humanity of my heroes.

But I suppose it wasn't until I came face to face with my own humanity that a new layer was added in me that will never go away. A new level of humility. A new level of compassion. A new level of gratitude that Jesus still loves and redeems even people like me.

That God doesn't hold my worst record over my head. Instead, He replaces it with the perfect record of His Son.

That God still gives second chances. And a thousand more.

And I guess Logan was right that day at the pool.

Right when he kept repeating the phrase "grace of God" over and over again, over every portion of the story as I finally told it.

Right when he felt in his spirit I would write out of this season.

Right that God would somehow use my story and pain one day to help other people.

At least I hope it's helping *you* as the words pour over your soul.

## WILDERNESS WRITINGS

(Notes from the Section—What stood out?)

_____

_____

_____

_____

_____

_____

_____

_____

_____

_____

_____

_____

_____

_____

_____

## DESERT DECISIONS

(Future Applications–What steps are you going to take?)

_____

_____

_____

_____

_____

_____

_____

_____

_____

_____

_____

_____

_____

_____

_____

*the*

# VALLEY

*of*

# SEEDS, GIANTS, & GIFTS

# Chapter Seven

## LIFE IN DEATH VALLEY

*"There's nothing so wrong with a desert that
a little rain can't fix."–Eugene Peterson*

*"God delights most in the prayers we pray in
times of dryness."–C.S. Lewis*

*"The Holy Spirit will give you water to sustain you through
the dry and barren times."–Bill Johnson*

There's hope in even the driest deserts.

Death Valley is certainly at the top of that list.

If you haven't been, just know it's a baked and moistureless national park straddling California and Nevada. Three thousand square miles of cruel sun, stunning panoramas, and tourists sobering up from Vegas.

Geography conspired to make it earth's oven as parts plunge up to two miles below sea level, the lowest point in North America. It shies away from any major body of water by a considerable distance and the Sierra Nevadas block any Pacific moisture from ever whispering its way into the basin. We're talking less than three inches of rain a *year*.

Officially, it's the hottest place on earth.

In fact, July 2018 saw an insufferable twenty-one days in a row of 120-plus degree temps. Can you imagine? The gold medal, though, goes to July 10th, 1913. A meteorologist there at Greenland Ranch clocked the day in at 134°F, the highest atmospheric temperature ever recorded on our planet.

The topology of Death Valley is almost as combative as the heat. A smattering of wildflowers rumor here and there, but plant life is spotty. It's all salt flats, sand dunes and rocky earth, making it a brutal place for things to grow.

A dry desert indeed.

However, occasionally, just occasionally, the perfect circumstances brew together to draw magic from the valley.

2016 was one such occasion. Heavy rainstorms in October dumped oceans onto the desert surface, optimal winds and temps nodded in their agreement and–*voilà*–the valley experienced what is known as a "Superbloom."
Almost overnight, a graveyard became a garden. Millions of wildflowers spilled out of the ancient earth and thrust their pedals and stalks toward the sun.
Tourists flocked. *National Geographic* went nuts.
This couldn't be real, could it? Field after field rioting with color and life.
Grown men laughed. Young husbands made picnics for their wives. Kids flew kites and danced under skies of spun gold, their feet floating over valleyed carpets of indigo, purple and rustic yellow.

Cameras clicked. Poets wrote. Enthusiasts of all kinds bought plane tickets to come take in sweeping vistas drunk with hue and bloom.

A promised land indeed.

Here's what's fascinating. Prior to a Superbloom, at least on the surface, the parched land of Death Valley appears an impossible place for life.

Yet we discover millions of seeds were in the ground all along. Just waiting and waiting, deep and dormant. Just waiting and waiting for rain to fall.

What a perfect picture of our lives, huh? We look out over an intolerable desert of loss and disappointment and weariness. Harvests of righteousness, happiness and goodness look impossible.

But I want you to catch a new glimpse of what's possible. If it helps, Google images of Super Blooms right now and sear the images into your brain. Embrace the potential.

See, here's what's exciting in discouraging times:

No matter how desolate the surface of your life may seem, you can plant seeds, and you can plant those seeds *today*.

God can kiss those seeds with rain tomorrow.

In the sun, tears will dry and new things will grow.

Erosion can turn back to Eden.

This is the image the Psalmist had as well. He reflected woefully on the plight of God's people through the wilderness, and then wrote:

*But he also can turn a barren wilderness into an oasis*
*with water!*
*He can make springs flow into desert lands*
*and turn them into fertile valleys so that cities spring up,*
*and he gives it all to those who are hungry.* (Psalm
107:35-36 TPT)

May your soul hear this: rain will come. With God, all things
are possible.

I believe it for you. I really do.

I believe as we walk with God, we can know our grays will
eventually turn to colors and our deserts will turn to gardens. I
believe promised lands whisper closely from just around the
bend.

I believe soon you'll say:

*[Some of us] once wandered in the wilderness like*
*desert nomads, with no true direction or dwelling place.*
*Starving, thirsting, staggering, we became desperate*
*and filled with despair. Then we cried out,"Lord, help us!*
*Rescue us"' And he did! He led us right into a place of*
*safety and abundance, a suitable city to dwell in.* (Psalm
107:4-7 TPT)

o o o

Your story probably looks nothing like mine.

However, regardless of what's happening around you, the garden of your life is before you. And you get to be downright choosy what types of herbs, spices, and English Ivy you want sprouting up or curling around the outside of your window.

That possibility alone should filter in some hope.

Rain will come. This season will end.

But as you look forward to the season beyond this season, an important question
remains:

What will you plant?

See, I can't always control the *season* I'm in, but I can control the *seeds* I sow.

So, what kind of seeds am I planting right now? What kind of emotional, spiritual, physical, mental seeds? What kind of words, actions, thoughts, and patterns?

And I get it. It can be really tough to wrap your mind and emotions around these questions while life feels so out of control. It's hard to grow a garden in the middle of a hurricane.
But we must lean in, full force, and pay diligent attention to our ways and our hearts, no matter the period of life we're in. Even if you're not a farmer, I'm sure you know, the seeds we plant now will be the harvest we enjoy later. And I'm sure you understand the trees will always be bigger than the seeds, the harvest bigger than the planting, and the fruit the exact same DNA as the substance sown.

So, let's get our fingernails dirty for a few chapters.

I want to look at the small things that become big things.
I want to look at the seeds that become oaks.
I want to look at the kids that become *giants*.

You know, for all the problems the Israelites experienced in the desert, giants weren't actually one of them. Giants didn't show up until the sequel, until the Promised Land. If anything, it was giants on the *inside* in the form of ten spies (more on that later) within the camp that prevented them from stepping into their destiny and ever conquering the *actual* giants waiting for them on the other side.

Same for us. Regardless of what we think, it's not giants on the outside that stop us from our future. It's giants on the inside.

It's the giants within me that continue to limit me from God's best. The giants in my thought life, patterns of living, emotional maturity, decisions, and relationships.

I say we go all David on them.

I say we fight the giants we were destined to slay in the Promised Lands ahead.

I say we plant healthy seeds now so we may live under the shade of some giant Sequoias later.

While we do, can I encourage you to have a notepad or your phone's Notes section handy?

See, in the first section of the book, we took time to look at *what* a wilderness is.

In the last section, we looked at purpose and the possible *why* of a wilderness in our lives and in the plan of God.

In this section, we're about to get uber-practical and look at *how* to navigate the wilderness while we're in it.

I agree with whomever said "note-worthy lives are lived by note-taking people." So, let's grab highlighters and pens for these next few chapters. I think they're going to change our lives.

# Chapter Eight

## GIANTS TO KILL

*"It was I who knew you in the wilderness,
in the land of drought."—Hosea 13:5*

*"Hope itself is like a star—not to be seen in the sunshine of
prosperity, and only to be discovered in the night
of adversity."—Charles Spurgeon*

*"You cannot shorten the wilderness God has designed for
you, but you sure can lengthen it."—John Bevere*

There's a lot of "culture" talk these days.

Buzzword aside, I tend to think it's a good thing.

Culture—the behavior, language, spirit, beliefs, and atmosphere of a place or person—affects *everything*. It is the thing that matters more than we know, the unspoken essence always *felt* even when not *said*.

And regardless of the domain—entertainment, business, church, home or just our lives in general—culture will form either by design or by default.

At its core, though, a culture simply forms by the values or "seeds" planted and fertilized.

In fact, the word "culture" comes from the Latin word *cultura*, an agricultural term. It literally means "to cultivate the soil."

Therefore, as we look at the soil of the kind of life we want to cultivate, it's just as important what *stays out* as what *goes in*.

So.

Let's start with the seeds to avoid.

In his second letter to his church in the city of Corinth, Paul didn't pull any punches reminding his people about the importance of the Israelites' story from thousands of years earlier and what we're to learn from it. He outlined the internal "giants" that prevented the Israelites from stepping into a rich future.

I think it's worth consuming the passage in its fullness:

> *I don't want you to forget, dear brothers and sisters, about our ancestors in the wilderness long ago. All of them were guided by a cloud that moved ahead of them, and all of them walked through the sea on dry ground. In the cloud and in the sea, all of them were baptized as followers of Moses. All of them ate the same spiritual food, and all of them drank the same spiritual water. For they drank from the spiritual rock that traveled with them, and that rock was Christ. Yet God was not pleased with most of them, and their bodies were scattered in the wilderness. These things happened as a warning to us, so that we would not crave evil things as they did, or worship idols as some of*

*them did. As the Scriptures say, "The people celebrated with feasting and drinking, and they indulged in pagan revelry." And we must not engage in sexual immorality as some of them did, causing 23,000 of them to die in one day. Nor should we put Christ to the test, as some of them did and then died from snakebites. And don't grumble as some of them did, and then were destroyed by the angel of death. These things happened to them as examples for us. They were written down to warn us who live at the end of the age. If you think you are standing strong, be careful not to fall.* (1 Corinthians 10:1-12 NLT)

No doubt about it, this is sobering. Yet if the power of its warning hooks into us, it's also strengthening.

If I'm honest, I can read passages like this and wonder how someone like me could ever make it, not to mention become discouraged by all the ways I've already messed up.

But I'd remind you for those of us who've linked our lives to Jesus, we are children of a Father of grace. We don't live under condemnation. And with God's hand on our lives, we can find restoration and help and become everything we're meant to become. It's not too late for us. Hear it clearly inside your spirit: *it's not too late for you to walk in God's best.*

I would also remind you the purpose of these passages is never to condemn, only to convict and protect. They are meant to instill a stabilizing reverence and godly confidence that lead us into better and more life-giving paths.

The people of Israel cheapened their own humanity by living beneath God's intention for their lives. They chose corruption instead of calling. The good news is God loved us enough to preserve their story so that we may learn and decide differently.

The choice is on the table.

○ ○ ○

Three specific giants levitate off the pages of that 1st Corinthians passage, and I want us to call them by name and ask the Holy Spirit to do some giant-killing work in our hearts.

In fact, for each giant I'm going to hand you a stone-and-sling weapon. By the Spirit's power, we'll go on a rampage.

The first giant is *Idolatry*.

This has to do with our *Affections*. (I'm going to stick with "A" words to satisfy the alliteration-giant inside me)

Paul said the first generation out of Egypt *"craved* evil things" and would "worship idols."

The first of the Ten Commandments given in the wilderness dealt with this inclination of our souls. Simply put, it matters to God who sits on the throne of our hearts. It was a passion in His heart then and it's a passion in His heart now.

Exodus 34:14 tells us why, *"You must worship no other gods, but only the Lord,* **for he is a God who is passionate about his relationship with you.**" *(emphasis mine)*

It's important we get that love is God's motive. Always. See, I know this is where some are triggered by memories of a strident preacher making them feel bad for thinking about their boyfriend sometimes more than God or actually wanting to excel in their job. You'll find no such guilt trip here.

The importance is where we place our trust and treasure. God, who loves us with tender compassion, knows any kind of well we draw our life from but His will leave us thirsty, or worse, poisoned. As my Pastor likes to put it, "idols don't usually come from a sinful desire; idols come from a sinful response to a divine desire."

In fact, not to skip ahead to the second giant, but I like how St. Ignatius of Loyola defined sin:

"An unwillingness to trust that what God wants for me is only my deepest happiness."

Point is, God's fired up about you, more passionate than you'll ever grasp. He's committed to you. Committed to your heart. Committed to your future. And His desires for our lives are always in sync with what's best for us and our truest joy.

Like lovers vowing fidelity at a chapel, though, passion demands purity. Fiery love begets and insists on fierce faithfulness. We've captured God's heart and He desires the reciprocation.

If you read those first few dense books of the Bible, and listen past religious, familiar wording, it's obvious that the Lord longed, downright ached, to meet with that ancient tribe of travelers in rich and meaningful ways.

Unfortunately, their restless and idol-ridden hearts just never would make space for it.

If we leapfrog over the Red Sea deliverance, we'll find that Moses and the people immediately began to experience frustration and lack. They also began to encounter God in brand new dimensions. Made-for-movie miracles to meet their needs on almost every page.

However, when moments came for the people to experience their own intersection with God, the rendezvous never happened. They really liked His blessings. They just never fell in love with Him.

We see this play out in real time in Exodus 32. Moses was up on Mt. Sinai, basking in some face-to-face with God. Matted to the dust, glory and majesty weighing over him. The only problem was he'd been gone a while. He'd been gone so long, in fact, the children of Israel decided to entertain themselves with a substitute while Moses experienced the real thing.

The sad tale reads like this:

*When the people saw how long it was taking Moses to come back down the mountain, they gathered around Aaron. "Come on," they said, "make us some gods who can lead us. We don't know what happened to this fellow Moses, who brought us here from the land of Egypt."*
*So, Aaron said, "Take the gold rings from the ears of your wives and sons and daughters, and bring them to me."*
*All the people took the gold rings from their ears and brought them to Aaron. Then Aaron took the gold, melted it down, and molded it into the shape of a calf. When the people saw it, they exclaimed, "O Israel, these are the gods who brought you out of the land of Egypt!"*

Several chapters earlier, they had eagerly sworn to obey everything God told them. But it's a month later. In the absence of leadership, vision, and God's tangible Presence, they threw together something they could manage and control to soothe their flesh and make their hearts feel better. They took their woes to their own bronze-aged version of a beer bottle or Netflix binge instead of the Maker on the mountain.

I can only imagine how this broke God's heart, especially after all He had done to show His kindness and commitment toward them. The tragedy can't be understated.

They even called their man-made shrine "Elohim" which means "the Lord" and attributed God's glory and faithfulness to something inanimate and temporary.

A golden calf. How easily we trade eternal things for earthly things.

A *calf*....

Yes, in their restless impatience, they took gold and fashioned it into their own bondage. They made a *calf* and treated it like *Christ*.

After all, God had seemed absent and inactive, so they had to stoke their affections *somewhere*. For this act, though, they paid a high price. Not just then, but in coming generations where the seeds of their idolatry bore future fruit.[2]

As always, our lives always affect more than we know and longer than we know. Wherever we place the wings of our worship will have a butterfly effect on every place our life touches. Whoever we seat on the throne of our hearts will impact every subject of our kingdom.

o o o

Maybe you're reading this and feeling kind of bad about now. Maybe a lot currently competes with God for what fires you up and gets you out of bed.

Welcome to the club of humanity.

Puritan author John Calvin once wrote, "the human heart is a factory of idols." None of us have arrived in our unfocused devotion to God.

So, what's the sling-and-stone weapon to defeat idolatry in our lives?

Is it to feel really bad, drink some spiritual *Red Bull*, slap ourselves in the face, and memorize nine large chunks of the Pentateuch[3] by Tuesday?

*Maybe if I can just force myself to pray more....*

Yes, dive deep into Scripture, talk to God a lot (why wouldn't you?), fast, go to church. Of course. But all of that should really only point to the main goal of *falling in love with Jesus*.

That's the weapon and it's so simple it might make you angry: *fall in love*.

Before you get miffed, that was the response of Jesus, too, when asked for the secret, when asked to sum up all the religious obligations they were under for the Old Covenant.

*"Teacher, which commandment in the law is the greatest?*
*Jesus answered him, "Love the Lord your God with every passion of your heart, with all the energy of your being,*

*and with every thought that is within you."* (Matthew 22:37 TPT)

Falling head over heels in love with God is the cure to a million ails.

How do we not become enraptured by lesser things? We stay mesmerized by glorious things.

How does a man not cheat on his wife? He stays in love with her.

He lives to serve her instead of receive from her. He chooses to delight in her and focus on her beauty and the goodness of her best qualities. He's intentional to set aside quality time to listen, look in her eyes, watch horrible romcoms, go on dates, buy flowers, keep his mouth shut when she drives, make love, and just sit and be present when she's sad.

If you've ever been in love, you know this is true. No distance is too long, no chore too arduous. Washing dishes even becomes a joy. Your world is tilted, your heart is full, and you're so stone in love that duty becomes delight. We turn into Wesley from *The Princess Bride*, rolling down the hill, saying even as it hurts,

"As...

You...

Wish...."

When it comes to romance, we want the real thing, not lip service. So does Jesus.

Through the Apostle John, the Spirit of Jesus spoke prophetically to the church in Ephesus some dire, heart-rending words:

*"I know all that you've done for me—you have worked hard and persevered. I know that you don't tolerate evil. You have tested those who claimed to be apostles and proved they are not, for they were imposters. I also know how you have bravely endured trials and persecutions because of my name, yet you have not become discouraged.* **But I have this against you: you have abandoned the passionate love you had for me at the beginning.** *Think about how far you have fallen!* **Repent and do the works of love you did at first.**" (Revelation 2:2-5 TPT)

Jesus applauded all their endurance and great religious accomplishments, but their love had grown cold. They were sitting at the kitchen table but not really there. They were in their Bibles, but just flipping pages, expectation long lost to hear God's voice. They were participating in worship but had ceased singing *to* God and now only sang *about* Him, not actually engaging with soul and body to enter His Presence. They were a *"people who honored Me with their lips but their hearts were far from Him."*[4]

Jesus told them to repent. To let their hearts become soft again in His Presence. To even cry and confess how far they'd strayed. To get honest. To do the "works of love you did at first."

To buy flowers again. To go on dates.

To truly pray and put heart into it and stop repeating meaningless words. Maybe to fast and stimulate spiritual senses to become alive and tender again. To worship and go after God. To get away with Him. To watch some Spirit-anointed messages at night instead of *Hulu*.

Whatever it takes, Jesus misses the passionate love affair you once shared. Or if you've never experienced it, He'd love to get started.

Just be honest with where you are in this moment and watch Him draw near.

o o o

The second giant to kill is as old-fashioned as your grandmother's hideous wallpaper. It's a killer, though.

I'm talking *sin*.

The kryptonite5 to our race. The arrow right through the Achilles of the human soul.

Sin. Missing the mark, falling short of God's glory, doing what we shouldn't and not doing what we should. We've all done it and we're all too well acquainted. "All have fallen short of God's standard...."6

It's the thing we all have. It's just the thing we need to make sure doesn't have us. If it does, it will derail and rob big time.

Jesus said in John 10:10, *"The thief's purpose is to steal and kill and destroy. My purpose is to give them a rich and satisfying life."*

Jesus is always a giver. Sin is always a taker.

As we parachute back into 1st Corinthians, we continue reading that,

> These things happened as a warning to us, so that we would not crave **evil things** as they did, or worship idols as some of them did. As the Scriptures say, *"***The people celebrated with feasting and drinking, and they indulged in pagan revelry.***" And we must not engage in sexual immorality as some of them did,* causing 23,000 of them to die in one day. ***Nor should we put Christ to the test,*** *as some of them did and then died from snakebites.*

Again, sobering. I've never seen this verse tattooed on a shoulder.

But God is serious about our joy and He is serious about our future. He is therefore serious about everything that steals and chips away from who we are. And as we see above, immorality and disobedience lower the ceiling on our potential and waylay our humanity.

The first giant was idolatry, or what we labeled as misplaced *Affections*. To keep up the alliteration, we'll name this second giant *Actions*.

Continued actions of sin and disobedience must be dealt with seriously in the desert before they deal seriously with us. It's been said before, but we first form our choices and then our choices form us.

Unfortunately, as we just read, the Israelites chose lives of "revelry" (wild living with over-indulgence of substances), "sexual immorality" (impurity and sexual impropriety outside the healthy, God-given parameters of marriage), and "putting God to the test" (sin, unbelief and disobedience).

Whole books have been written on disobedience and iniquity, and you have your Bible handy day and night, so let's expedite the giant-killing and get back to some good news.

Before we kill any giant, though, we must first see it as our enemy. We'll never confront what we don't perceive as a threat.

So, let's etch it in stone: sin's a killer.

We coddle it, excuse it, wink at it, rename it and justify it. In short, we underestimate it. We shouldn't.

It ushered in the fall of humanity and every ounce of pain and sickness ever since. It put nails through the throbbing wrists of God's Son. It's responsible for every death and agony we experience.

And it always starts small and harmless.

To my regret, the first time I ever drank alcohol I did so illegally and underhandedly. I was a sophomore in high school. I was following Jesus at a pretty distant clip. And I was curious.

I convinced a friend to convince his mother to buy us a pack of *Fuzzy Navels* (yep, that's the real name). The plan was to sneak them in his backpack on Friday and we'd spend the evening in my parent's basement playing pool, talking brunettes, and drinking some cheap, fruity version of spiked Kool-Aid. Wild ones, we were.

The night before, God gave me a dream. I say it cautiously, as I'm not crazy, nor the kind who casually makes those kinds of boasts. God doesn't usually speak to me in that way. To my memory it's the only dream like that I've ever had. My dreams usually consist of weird planets where peanut butter doesn't exist, and I'm being chased in my underwear by the *KGB*.

In this dream, though, we got the drinks as planned, the middle is hazy, and it ended in a car wreck with police all around us. I woke up knowing in my "knower" this was a warning from God.

Judge me hard, but I didn't listen.

I must have really wanted that *Fuzzy Navel*.

The next night we partook as planned and fell asleep downstairs. At 3 a.m., a thundering crash jolted me upright in the spare bedroom, my head still floating slowly around the room. My mother rushed downstairs and told me to come hurry and look outside. I sat halfway up and looked around, squinting towards the dusty window and the marriage of moon and tree painting their way inside. Everything felt dark, static and unreal. I must have thought I was dreaming, so I went back to sleep until my buddy shook my shoulders hard enough to fling any last fuzzy out of my bloodstream.

I took the steps by two as I ran upstairs and rushed outside and to this day the scene from my front porch feels like its own dream. There before me lay my car, my parents' car and a stranger's car, all terribly wrapped around each other like branches, cop lights circling around it all the way I imagine crows would circle around a broken nest.

The dream flashed before my eyes. I was seeing now what I saw the night before.

Somehow, a *sober* driver momentarily took his eyes off the road and hit my car so hard it folded around mine and my parents' and sent them all into our front-road ditch. By an apparent miracle no one was hurt (with the exception of my car, which was totaled).

I don't call it judgment. I call it mercy.

I don't think for a minute God caused the wreck to happen. (Nor do I think it's wrong to have a drink in moderation if you don't have a problem). I think God saw into my present and future and wanted to summon my best, while putting his arm in front of my calling and protect me from falling over guardrails and bloodying my soul on hidden cliffs in years to come.

I also think the sweaty preacher was right. Sin always costs more than we know.

Those *Fuzzies* just weren't worth it.

o o o

It's red pill, blue pill.

God's way, or my way.

Sin really is on a degradation campaign.

The Puritan John Owens exhorted his people to "always be killing sin, or sin will be killing you." It's only as we put to death greed, lust, addiction, unrighteousness and all the fruits of the flesh that the vine of our spiritual life receives breathing room to grow lush with vitality and ripe with the fruit of the Spirit.

If we want to set ourselves up for success here, we must start killing sin while it's small, before the "small foxes spoil the vineyard." (Solomon 2:15)

We also must realize the best defense is always offense. We need to lean forward with such intentionality in our new, explosive journey of changing the world for Christ that we're too busy to be dragged down by lesser ways.

Afterall, the best way to defeat something is to replace something. Paul told his church in Ephesians not to get drunk on wine, but *instead* to be filled with the Spirit.[7]

However, if you're nagged at the moment with some lingering, infectious junk in your life, I have good news. The deathblow to something as old-fashioned as *sin and compromise* is something just as old-fashioned: *confession and repentance.*

Confession. Admitting to God, and others (not everyone), where you've gone wrong and need His mercy and help.

> *Finally, I* **confessed** *all my sins to you and stopped trying to hide my guilt. I said to myself, "I will confess my rebellion to the Lord." And you forgave me! All my guilt is gone.* (Psalm 32:5 NLT)

And,

> *...***confess** *your sins* **to one another** *and pray for each other that you may be healed.* (James 5:16 NLT)

Repentance. Changing our minds about our ways and choosing to walk in God's ways.

*Now **repent** of your sins and turn to God, so that your sins may be wiped away. Then times of refreshment will come from the presence of the Lord....* (Acts 3:19-20 NLT)

Proverbs 28:13 states, *"People who conceal their sins will not prosper, but if they **confess** and **turn from them**, they will receive mercy."* (emphasis mine)

Confession and repentance. They both matter.

Also, these two come from kindness and conviction, *not* shame and condemnation.

The latter aren't from God. Shame and condemnation say you *are* a mistake and there's no hope.

Kindness and conviction say you *made* a mistake and there's incredible hope.
Conviction says there's a better way, so let's change our minds about our old ways, receive grace, and allow Jesus to stand us back on our feet.

*Before I confessed my sins, I kept it all inside; my dishonesty devastated my inner life, causing my life to be filled with frustration, irrepressible anguish, and misery....*
*My strength was sapped, my inner life dried up like a spiritual drought within my soul....*

*How happy and fulfilled are those whose rebellion has been forgiven, those whose sins are covered by blood. How blessed and relieved are those who have confessed their corruption to God! For He wipes their slates clean and removes hypocrisy from their hearts.* (Psalm 32:3-4, 1-2 TPT)

I'd like to end this section with prayer, with a time of confession and repentance. You might even want to find a private place to spend time with God after. But I deeply sense before we move on, there is soul work God wants to do to get some of us unstuck. He wants to free us.

*"Father, I come to you as I am. I'm asking You to search my heart. Lord, you know me even better than I know myself. Would you reveal those things in me that trip me up, that keep holding me back.*

*I repent, Lord, for everything I've allowed in my life that's not of you. Every thought pattern, behavior, action, heart issue, compromise and sin. Forgive me and cleanse me completely, I ask. Create in me a clean heart and fill me with a fresh desire to walk in your ways. Fill every empty and weak space in me with Your Spirit, I pray.*

*Heal and set me free from any addictive or immoral areas in my life. I confess those specifically now…and I ask you to break those chains over me by the power of Your Spirit.*

*Thank you, Lord, that the Cross has enough power not only to forgive me but to deliver me and to empower me to walk in a newness of life. Make old and dead areas in me alive and purify me by the washing of your holy blood. Revive me. Change me. Restore to me the joy of Your salvation.*

*I declare old ways are gone. I'm a new creation in God.*

*No more trips around the mountain for me in these areas. In Jesus' Name I pray, let it be!"*

o o o

Ready to call out the final giant?

It's been a long, murderous chapter, I know. Hopefully you snuck a sandwich break in there somewhere. But we got this.

Let's crush the third colossus from the passage:

"… **And don't grumble as some of them did**, *and then were destroyed by the angel of death."* (emphasis mine)

Grumbling and complaining.

So far, we've taken up a sling and stone against idolatrous *Affections* and disobedient *Actions*.

The final and great wilderness sin that threatens to keep us from the Promised Land is a wrong *Attitude*.

We'll land even deeper blows later as we look at the life of Caleb, but let's go ahead and throw something at this bitter behemoth.

I can remember hearing little attitude sermonettes as early as third grade. Each July, my dad ran a summer basketball camp, and every morning would rally a hundred elementary kids into a huddle to teach us how our "attitude determines our altitude" and tell us all about making lemonade from lemons, that sort of thing.

The Israelites must have missed that summer camp.

Here's the thing. Life can be hard. We all have bad days. We all wallow in bad moods and go through tough seasons. We all need a safe place to pour out our frustrations.

But all of that is different than letting *a spirit of complaint* overtake your life.

Nothing will keep us stuck in life more than a poor attitude.

In fact, I'm pretty sure my dad even taught us the cheesy metaphor about the busted tire. I'm sure you've heard it: "A bad attitude is like a flat tire—until you change it, you won't go anywhere."

Oh, so cheesy, and oh, so true.

Our attitude matters.

It is vital to maintain a sweet spirit even in bitter places.

If we pick the Israelite journey back up from chapter two, we find the shoreside party has quieted down.
Klieg lights on the whole crew now. They're waking up, happy and hung over from the miracle. Moses' sister, Miriam, is rubbing her dance-sore legs with a contented smile, pulling a few pesky strands of algae from her hair from where she'd ventured for a midnight dip.

Give it a couple hours.

The dopamine of the celebration is fading, and the vibe is devolving into something a
bit more primal—thirst.

So, Moses leads them out from the Red Sea and into the desert of Shur where they travel three days without water before finally, *finally*, coming to an oasis.

Ah. You know the feeling. Going through a tough time, but then—*bam*—that sweet nectar of relief when things finally yield your way.

Yet with the first lap of water, they discover it's *bitter*. So bitter they couldn't even drink it. In fact, they decide then and there to define that place by the pain it evoked. They name it "Marah," which, yep, means "bitter."

Ever defined a time or space in your life by the pain you felt?

Safe to say, this people did *not* maintain a sweet spirit in their bitter place, and of course, they waste no time finding someone to blame.

"Moses, how could you?! This is all *your* fault."

Oh, how they complain. In a pattern we become all too familiar with, they whine, Moses cries out on their behalf, and God answers. In this instance, God graciously converted the waters from bitter to sweet.

Then they traveled to the oasis of Elim and journeyed on to the halfway point between Elim and Mt. Sinai, a wilderness called the Wilderness of Sin.

There, a month out of Egypt we read:

*There, too, the whole community of Israel complained about Moses and Aaron. "If only the Lord had killed us back in Egypt," they moaned. "There we sat around pots filled with meat and ate all the bread we wanted. But now you have brought us into this wilderness to starve us all to death." (Exodus 16:2-3 NLT)*

Again, this is only days after God snatched them like fish out of the pond of misery and slavery. Only days after He supernaturally met every need they encountered in the desert.

And yet this people allowed temporary emotions to grow so large it blotted out all perspective. They allowed momentary grievances to overshadow every ounce of thankfulness and joy for what God had done for them.

A little bit of pain and delay caused them to conclude God's promises would not come true, after all. That they had been brought out here to die. They even began to speak of how good *Egypt* had been.

Just so we remember, Egypt was hell. There they were enslaved, beaten, and most likely tortured.

It's sad we can relate to their tendency, though, isn't it? We've almost all gone rogue on God before, idealizing past seasons we'd begged God to get us out of.

Amazingly, God showed complete patience. He rained down buffets of hearty quail and flaky manna for them to eat.

*Then the Lord said to Moses, "I have heard the Israelites' complaints. Now tell them, 'In the evening you will have meat to eat, and in the morning, you will have all the bread you want. Then you will know that I am the Lord your God." (Exodus 16:11-12 NLT)*

God let Moses in on a secret, though. This provision was actually a test. How they handled this blessing would reveal the condition of their hearts and whether they would follow God or continue to go sideways when things got tough.

They did not pass this test.

We could fill the Boston Public Library with the documentation of all their grumblings. Here's just one more example from one book later in Numbers 21:4-6:

> *Then the people of Israel set out from Mount Hor, taking the road to the Red Sea to go around the land of Edom. But the people grew impatient with the long journey, and they began to speak against God and Moses. "Why have you brought us out of Egypt to die here in the wilderness?" they complained. "There is nothing to eat here and nothing to drink. And we hate this horrible manna!"*

They not only failed the provision test; they grumbled about the provision God was giving them. They spoke against God. They spoke against their leaders. They grew weary of the length of the season.

Their impatience gave way to an embittered spirit.

I once heard John Bevere say, "complaining is such an offense to God because it's me saying, 'God I don't like the way You're doing things and if I were you, I would do them differently.'"

Ouch.

You may be thinking, *I am literally reading this book because I'm going through the hardest time in my life and I have a lot of complaints, okay?*

And that *is* okay. That's called the human existence. Our spiritual heroes had complaints, too. In fact, I love that large portions of Scriptures, like the Psalms, give voice and prayers to our complaints.

God understands and knows our pain. He doesn't ask us to throw a mask over our deepest grief. He doesn't scold us for our disappointments. Instead He hurts with us and longs to draw close to us in our questions and frustrations.

The question isn't, is it okay to have complaints?

The question is, how do I have complaints without complaints having me?

How do I make sure I don't get trapped, tortured and tripped up by a *pattern* of pessimism or a *spirit* of grumbling?

How do I keep a grip on perspective? How do I steer my heart intentionally to ensure it doesn't get moored in "Marah," bound up in a bitter place that ultimately becomes difficult to escape?

First, it matters *where* we take our complaint.

Some people are stuffers. Maybe you're one. You keep your deepest turmoil tucked inside. The processing system only cycles *internally* and under pressure spins faster and faster, louder and louder, an eventual explosion inevitable.

Others, on the other hand, trundle through life like a complaint vending machine, full vent-mode spilling out of the delivery bins of their mouths and on to everyone they come in contact with. Or even worse, they find kindred bitter spirits so they can commiserate together, dining on mixed cocktails of shared resentment.

Neither are healthy.

Our stickiness inside needs to be processed *somewhere*. I'd posit a couple vendors.

First and no surprise, God, the maker and the expert on all things *you*.

David said in Psalm 142:2, *"I pour out my complaints before him and tell him all my troubles."*

What a great habit.

God knows what we're feeling anyway. He'd rather us process our pain in His Presence where He can strengthen and help us. Plus, have you ever had someone complain behind your back and you wished they would just bring it to *you*? I have a hunch it's the same with God. He can handle our angst and anger. We just need to take it to His Presence. I have found when I don't know what else to say to God, even my anger can be an offering if I'll just bring it to Him.

Then, *each other*. We need a small circle of trustworthy friends with whom we can be completely raw and vulnerable.
Safe because they love us, are for us, and can take our unfiltered truth.
Safe because they'll always speak words of life to our spirit and in the right timing help lift our perspective. Friends who, when done listening, will add words of wisdom and light that create space for God to do something in our soul. Friends who will sympathize while remaining advocates for our future, not accomplices in our frustration.

Bringing our wounds and worries to the Presence of God and the presence of faith-filled friends—this practice is a good tonic for our emotional well-being.

But the ultimate sling-and-stone to a grumbling spirit is *the power of thanksgiving.*

It's the "Finish Him" moment from *Mortal Kombat,* and it might single-handedly be the most dangerous weapon against a bad wilderness attitude.

A grateful posture is an almost immediate elixir against a grumbling, downcast heart. Mix it in daily and it becomes power-gel to help you run the distance.

o o o

I wish you could've met Brother Pfaff before he died. I met him as a youth leader right out of high school and immediately knew—this is the happiest human I've ever been around.

I could have sworn he was 137 years old (they claimed he was 80-something). He joined the youth staff, and though hopelessly out of touch, was the hottest item on campus. Students hung all over him. When upbeat songs kicked off worship, he jumped higher than all the dignified adults and too-cool-for-school teenagers.

He was always smiling, always laughing, always gleaming.

I had to know his secret.

One night I found it like candy in a drawer as he was leading a bible study in someone's home. He read a verse stating we should be thankful *in* all things and then another verse stating we should be thankful *for* all things, then laughed heartily like he'd just heard a joke from outer space we'd all missed. We looked at each other and then back at him and smiled nervously.

"Well! We're to be thankful *in* all things and *for* all things! I think that about sums it all up, don't you?"

He went on to tell his story of living in Africa as a missionary much of his life. He told us how he was teased and attacked. He spoke of the lonely years, and of the lack of basic amenities. He spoke of his wife dying later on in life.

And then he looked up and smiled past the ceiling and gushed about how good God is. How he couldn't help but burst into thanks all through the day.

He said after living in Africa he never takes a shower without stopping and blessing God for hot water, nor uses the restroom without thanking Jesus for *running* water, never looks at a plate full of food without earnest gratitude spilling off his lips to God, and so on.

He told us a thankful heart is the secret to a great, happy life.

I believed him.

To this day, whenever Thanksgiving rolls around I think of my aunt Gail's baked macaroni and cheese casserole, my sister's old place in Virginia under all those marigold-leafed trees where we used to visit in the fall, *Boy Meets World* reruns, and Brother Pfaff.

o o o

I'm convinced one of the biggest obstacles to keeping my heart thankful is my spiritual amnesia.

If you have time later, read Psalm 106, a forty-eight-verse, power-packed summary of that first generation out of Egypt and their wilderness journey. Miracles, promises, praises, downfalls, it's all there.

And it won't be difficult to note the causal relationship between their *forgetfulness* and their *faithlessness*.

The passage starts with an appeal to *"give thanks to the Lord, for he is good,"* and then notes *three different times* how *"they forgot"* the goodness and miracles of God. It even goes so far to say their *"ancestors in Egypt were not impressed by the Lord's miraculous deeds."* Then, halfway down we read:

> The people refused to enter the pleasant land,
> for they wouldn't believe his promise to care for them.
> Instead, they grumbled in their tents
> and refused to obey the Lord.

There's TNT-power strength and instruction in this passage, but here's the gist: an Egyptian army didn't stop them from entering the promised land; a spirit of unbelief and grumbling did.

And we see one of the things that continually injured their *faith* was their *forgetfulness*. They were quick to forget just how good God had been to them.

We all tend to, don't we?

I like how the beginning of Psalm 106 says, *"Give thanks to the Lord....Who can **list** the glorious miracles of the Lord?"*

I like this because I'm a list guy.

I love lists. Lists make me happy.

And if forgetting how good God was yesterday tanks my faith for tomorrow, I think lists might also make great, standard wilderness equipment.

When I was a student pastor in Atlanta, I hosted a monthly "Team Night" at my house for the adult volunteers. We'd stuff our faces potluck style, talk, play games, cast vision, and then I'd share a brief (they'll laugh when they read that descriptive word) devotional.

I started something on the first one which ended up a staple. I told them we were going to kick off every Team Night making a "POS" on the whiteboard.

They looked at me the same way you're probably looking at that sentence. I think they imagined a phrase with some sort of profanity tucked inside.

You too?

For shame.

I told them "POS" stood for "pile of stones."

I reminded them how God always instructed His people in the Old Testament to build monuments or altars out of stones to commemorate something special, not because God really loved rocks, but because He knew we're prone to forget and would soon need reminding.

A few months later during a particularly tough week, I was complaining—er, *sharing*—with a friend just how tough my life felt. Without an ounce of compassion, she replied, "sounds like you need to journal your own POS this morning."

I think that's when I actually *did* use profanity.

I made the list, though. Once I was done, my spirit was different.

In fact, I've taken my own medicine and onboarded this as a regular practice over the last few years.

Not when I *feel* grateful or am in the mood to do it. Quite the opposite.

Every few months, when I'm starting to knock on the door of my own pity party or allow clouds of discouragement to float near my neighborhood, I'll pull out a pen and journal and make a POS. Everything's going on the list. Everything from breath in my lungs and food on the table, to the people in my life, to the last three prayers God answered, not to mention my name being written in heaven and Jesus dying on my behalf, and me receiving mercy instead of judgment, and the fact I have a dynamic relationship with the One, true, living God, and am on my way to an eternity to walk on golden streets with Him, and have destiny-laced, promise-packed days ahead, and, okay…I think I may have needed this again myself.

Anyways, might be worth it for you to give it a shot.

Might even be worth it go for it *now*.

The blessings, the answered prayers, the mercy, the grace, the promises, everything you can think to thank God for—see if you can fit it all on the lines below.

"POS"

_____

_____

_____

_____

_____

_____

_____

_____

_____

_____

_____

_____

_____

_____

_____

o o o

Affections. Actions. Attitudes.

Which giant or giants do you feel God speaking to you about?

Whichever it is, I'm believing for God to grace your hands for battle.

And as you pick up your sling, I'm praying this over you concerning every giant in your life:


*You provide a broad path for my feet,*
*so that my ankles do not give way.*
*I pursued my enemies and overtook them;*
*I did not turn back till they were destroyed.*
*I crushed them so that they could not rise;*
*they fell beneath my feet.*
*You armed me with strength for battle;*
*you humbled my adversaries before me.*
*You made my enemies turn their backs in flight,*
*and I destroyed my foes.*
(Psalm 18:36-40)

# Chapter Nine

## RHYTHMS

*"Don't judge each day by the harvest you reap, but by the seeds that you plant."–Robert Louis Stevenson*

*"Listen—the fingers that weaved the rainbow into a scarf and wrapped it around the shoulders of the dying storm, the fingers that painted the lily-bell and threw out the planets, the fingers that dipped in the mighty sea of eternity and shook out this old planet, making the ocean to drop and the rivers to stream—the same fingers can take hold of these tangled lives and make them whole again."–Gypsy Smith*

*"Observe the Sabbath and keep it holy."*
*–Exodus 20:8 GNT*

We've talked giants to defeat; now let's talk gifts to receive.

Beautiful, refreshing jewels straight from God for the dry times.

In life, there are seeds that become giants which need to be *choked*.

Then there are seeds that become gifts which need to be *grown.*

Let's turn our attention now to the latter.

Let's make a greenhouse in the Gobi.

In Exodus 16, when the people complained and cried out in hunger, God sent a rodizio of fresh quail that night and poured down bread in the morning.

The thing is, the bread looked a bit different than what they'd been using for their avocado toast. In fact, they called the bread "manna," literally meaning "what is it?"

And, let's face it, this is kind of par for the course when walking with Jesus, isn't it? We learn He is full of surprises. We learn He meets our needs in unexpected ways. And we learn there will always be seasons where we want to say, "what is *this*?!"

Here's what's interesting. The bread actually existed in the form of *seed.*

We read, *"it was white like coriander seed and tasted like wafers made with honey."*[1]

So, it wasn't just a gift to eat; it was a gift to *apply*. They had to work it.

Later, we read some of the things they did with it:

*The manna was like coriander seed and looked like resin. The people went around gathering it, and then ground it in a hand mill or crushed it in a mortar. They cooked it in a pot or made it into loaves.*[2]

It was a gift they would gather, grind, crush, mold, cook, and mix.

The manna was *gratis*, but it required participation and application. They had to put it into play and practice.

The same is true of the gifts we're about to discuss.


○ ○ ○


We discussed the three A's of wilderness giants: wrong *affections*, *actions* and *attitudes*.

Now we'll push into the three R's of wilderness gifts, and I'll go ahead and give them to you in advance: *rhythms*, *ropes* and *revelations*.

First in the dew: *rhythms*.

The first time Moses went up the mountain in Exodus, God gave him several chapters worth of laws and policy and rules and guidelines. It's a lot to scarf down on your daily Bible-reading plan if we're just going to be honest, and it feels a little negative in vibe.

That is, until you realize what a gift for God to provide normalcy, structure and instruction to a people fresh out of chains who'd had no prior training or purpose other than to be someone else's property.

Now God was making them legit. He was making them a people. He was giving them healthy practices and boundaries and cultivating them into an actual society. He was showing them right from wrong, and how to love and interact with each other.

He was teaching them how to *live*.

Since they'd been in Egypt their whole lives, He had to *de*program a lot of their default settings so He could *re*program them for life in Him and life in Canaan.

One of those first program adjustments dealt with *rhythms*.

They'd had one rhythm their whole life: work. It's all they did and all they knew. Sunup to sundown. They weren't human beings. They were human doings.

So, God sought to humanize them towards their original design to flourish through an archaic-sounding concept called "sabbath," a word that literally just means *"to cease."*

He commanded them to start a new rhythm: take one day a week and *rest*. Don't talk about work, think about work, scheme about work, or do work.

Their agenda was to have no agenda. Their to-do list? To tear up the to-do list.

Their God-given goal was simply to rest and delight in God. To unplug the WiFi of their over-worked system one day a week to help heal the glitches and make the stream run better the other six.

This command even made the Big Ten. In fact, it's the longest one on there. God harkened it back to the very beginning, the creation account, where God "rested" on the seventh day, the day *after* making the universe, and the day *before* making sweet tea.

*"And on the seventh day He rested."*[3]

God is immutable in strength and power, so He wasn't wiped out from a 9–5 back-bender at the construction site. He was setting an example.

And yet, in mystery you can knock your head against a wall about later, the word used for "rest" here whispers something even deeper. The word is *vayinnafash* and it means "to refresh one's soul."

Think about that for a second.

God.

Refreshed.

His.

Soul.

It's wild, honestly.

Perhaps even wilder is to think God would do that, but I don't need to.

Curiously, over time, especially in the uber-fast-paced, post-modern, achievement-intoxicated, FOMO-laced, mammon-serving, options-drowning culture of today, the concept of sabbath has been almost all but lost besides a trending re-emergence over the last few years in certain evangelical subcultures.

There's even been a secular version of this resurgence in the form of digital sabbaths and a counter-resistance against social media and the untethered hurriedness of modernity.

A resistance is underway, nonetheless.

A spirit of rest against a spirit of slavery.

A spirit of striding instead of a spirit of striving.

A spirit of freedom in lieu of the spirit of Pharoah.

A spirit of *shalom*, or "wholeness," instead of a spirit of unrest, frenzy and anxiety.

This is the spirit and purpose of *Sabbath*.

Sabbath in Scripture is synonymous with health, rest, peace, healing, justice and restoration.

I don't know about you, but I think we could use some of that. Oceans of it, in fact.

I've been on a personal journey to reclaim the sabbath, and I'll just go ahead and say I hope you do, too.

Sure, we're no longer under old-covenant law. But that doesn't mean the principles have passed away. We still seem to think the rest of the Big Ten are good ideas: don't lie, don't cheat on your wife, don't go around killing people, you know, that sort of thing.

Just like the principle of first fruits or the tithe, the principle of Sabbath is threaded throughout all of Scripture, and it's one of the most beautiful, loving invitations God has ever extended to this weary world.

Famous rabbi Abram Heschel wrote, *"the Sabbath is the most precious present mankind has received from the treasure house of God."*

I know it has been for me.

Five years ago, I was in Charlotte, coming down from a cocktail of heartbreak, burnout and a bad decision or two.

One of my best friends and I were there for a few days to attend the famed Code Orange Revival at *Elevation Church*. My pancakes grew cold one morning at *the Flying Biscuit*, being pushed uselessly around the plate by my restless fork when my friend broke the silence.

"I know you think this season has to do with your mistake or this girl you're so broken up over. But it's not. I don't claim to know what it is, but I think the thing God wants to talk to you about in this season is not the thing you think God wants to talk to you about."

That's when I almost threw my restless fork at his regal face.

If I had heard that once in the last few weeks, I'd heard it a hundred times. Why did everyone keep saying that?

Yet it turned out to be true.

Did God want to develop and seal up any character leaks? Of course.

Did God want to heal the places in me disappointed by another love gone sideways? I believe He did.

Did God finally want me to pause and take a look under the hood at the damage from the last few miles? I'm sure.

Did God want to talk to me about my addictive personality and occasional tendency to avoid pain? Oh, I bet.

But through prayer, great friends, introspection, and counseling, it became clear—God wanted to put His finger on my *rhythms*. My rhythms and the broken places in me that fueled them.

All of a sudden, I could hear my mom through childhood, then adolescence, and then on into adulthood, saying, "Son, you just can't stay still."

It's cute when you're four, I suppose, but not so cute when thirty-four.

French philosopher Blaise Pascal once said, "all of humanity's problems stem from man's inability to sit quietly in a room alone."

Ugh. Leave me alone, Blaise.

But why?

Why couldn't I stop? Why couldn't I be still? Why couldn't I rest?

Why was my value so tied to my performance?

There are plenty of self-discoveries I could unfold here specific to my neurotic, Enneagram-3, Type-A wiring and personality. But the same light hits all of our different shadows, even if in different ways.

And it connects deeply to whether or not we ever step fully, not only into the words and beliefs of Jesus, but into the *ways* and *rhythms* of Jesus.[4]

Over four years ago, in that painful season, I began to re-discover this ancient principle called *Sabbath*.

I realized I had trusted God with a *tithe*, had trusted Him financially to bless my other ninety percent and make it go further.

But I had not trusted God with my *time*, had not trusted Him with a sabbath, with taking my six days blessed by the kiss of a rest-soaked *shalom,* and believing Him to spread the rest of my week further than it could have ever gone without honoring Him with that day.[5]

I'm only sharing my journey.

But I can tell you Sabbath has changed me.

It has forced me to slow down. To stop running at the speed of mania. To stop skimming across the surface of life.

It's brought healing. It's brought an even greater depth. It's allowed my weary heart to begin to recover.

"To keep a sabbath is to give time and space on our calendar to the grace of God," says A.J. Swoboda.

Practically, for me?

I set aside one day a week, almost always Saturday. I delete social media and news off my phone and don't let myself think about work. I rest in, no alarm clock set. I go slow in the morning. Real slow. I water plants. I let silence soundtrack my devotional time instead of Hillsong. I make a deep, strong pour over from coffee beans shipped in from Columbia. I go to Skillet, my favorite brunch spot, a family-owned, menu-changes-everyday gem right in the gritty heart of German Village. I sit at the bar and yack it up with Patrick (love that guy) and order their lamb sausage and omelet of the day, don't even care what's in it. Then I coffee shop hard, letting the environment begin to massage away the tight edges of my mind. I keep a relaxing sabbath playlist reserved only for Saturday, so AirPods go in. I read and journal and even make myself just stare and think. I'll go for a run. Later that night, even if I feel like isolating, I'll force myself to end the day with community. And when I say community, I don't mean any context in which I'll be pouring out. I mean the kind of community that's life-giving and filled with good food, a painful amount of laughter, and the kind of conversation that will fill up and minister to the human inside of *me*.

For others?

It's always going to look different. I have a good friend in Dallas with a wife and kids, and they make it something, as it still is in Jewish culture, that's looked forward to by the whole family all week. On Friday night, everyone kills their devices and the kids help mom make bread from scratch while dad finishes up any loose ends and goes to the store to buy the cookies and wine. As a family, they eat long and slow over candlelight, and say blessings over the kids. The next day on the actual sabbath they sleep in before entering into a fun, divine, blundering experiment of pancakes, bike rides, long naps, adventures and just an overall day of moving luxuriously slow without the entrapment of obligations and that ever-beckoning smart phone.

For most people?

The first time considering the concept, it seems over-ideal and highly unrealistic. And I get it. Maybe you're a single mom or you travel like crazy for your job or you have nine kids or you currently work seven days a week. The idea of one full "off" day a week is on par with salsa dancing alongside a rhinoceros.

Either way, may I suggest you at least close your eyes and *imagine* a life where you built weekly margin in for your soul? Can you picture yourself, how much fuller you would be to love Jesus and those around you well?

What if you just started taking baby steps towards this with a few hours a week to start, or even a half day? May I suggest all our excuses are just different variations of the same ones people have had since God introduced the idea thousands of years ago?

If I have at least piqued your interest, I'd love to suggest a few resources that do a really excellent job of teasing out the theological, historical and practical sides to this beautiful gift. In no specific order: *Subversive Sabbath* by A.J. Swoboda (Pastor of Theophilus Church in Milwaukie, Oregon), *Sabbath* by Abram Heschel, *Ruthless Elimination of Hurry* by John Mark Comer (a Pastor at BridgeTown Church in Portland, Oregon), and *Take the Day Off* by Robert Morris. They're all gems in their own right.

This sabbath journey, my desert-friend, is a journey from which I've never seen any regrets.

o o o

Pastor Robert Morris says the most important thing about Sabbath is not what you do but what you *don't* do: work. Pastor Chris Hodges (Pastor of Church of the Highlands) says the most important thing about it is a *change of pace*, to be intentional not to be in a hurry. I think A.J. would say the most important filter on Sabbath is to *only do those things which replenish* and fill your tank and nothing that depletes it.

I try to incorporate those three main concepts and just keep trusting God to bless my feeble efforts, knowing I'll never get it "perfect."

If I'm honest, I still have to fight my performance mindset because most of the time I feel I'm not very "good" at sabbath. I'm still probably on my phone too much, and I still tend to "hurry" from one delight to another, and at times I still get oh-so-antsy.

It's funny, though. About halfway through the day when I do a "sabbath" (or what my Pastor calls his "soul day"), there's usually a moment where I feel a subtle, invisible *click*, when something internal begins to catch up. It's like the shoulders of my soul finally begin to loosen. God's voice becomes nearer. I feel my love for others deepen and my frustrations begin to seem silly. I relax. At times I even begin to dream again.

It's like I'm stepping into this multi-millennia invitation from God's heart. An invitation of peace, grace, and rest.

And that invitation is on the table today for *you.*

*"Are you tired? Worn out? Burned out on religion? Come to me. Get away with me and you'll recover your life. I'll show you how to take a real rest. Walk with me and work with me—watch how I do it. Learn the unforced rhythms of grace. I won't lay anything heavy or ill-fitting on you. Keep company with me and you'll learn to live freely and lightly."* Jesus (Matthew 11:28-30 MSG)

The unforced rhythms of grace. I love that.

A great prayer during this time might be, "God, teach me your rhythms for this season."

I know I've personally been praying that prayer often these last few years.

○ ○ ○

God wanted to teach that early group of people new rhythms.

But not just for one day a week.

He wanted new rhythms integrated into every aspect of their lives.

Let's go back to that gorgeous word, *vayinaffash*.

God used this provocative imagery of Him refreshing His own soul. Catching His breath.

Then, He introduced a rhythm to make sure humanity always caught their breath too.

One day a week to inhale.

But these new breath-catching rhythms weren't confined to just Sabbath.

Or just humans, for that matter.

God even introduced practices to make sure the land itself would catch its breath every seven years, refresh itself in order to keep the soil healthy and fruitful—a practice still implemented to this day.

See, here's a great principle for life. Any area of my life that's *out of rhythm* will eventually get *out of breath*.

If I breathe in far longer than I breathe out, I'll get out of breath. It's a rhythm thing.

If I consume more calories in burgers than I expend in exercise, I'll get out of breath. It's a rhythm thing.

In life, if I consume more than I contribute, I'll get out of breath.

In other words, if there's not a healthy dance of input *and* output, of receiving God's Word *and* serving others, of hearing messages *and* putting my faith into sacrificial practice, of being encouraged *and* being an encouragement, I'll get out of breath. I'll become like the Dead Sea, a self-feeding body of water with no outflow. This is why Proverbs 11:25 informs us that, *"he who refreshes another will himself be refreshed."* It's a rhythm thing.

If I *receive* forgiveness but then don't *extend* forgiveness, or if I receive God's grace and let it come *to* me but then don't let it flow *through* me, I'll become out of breath. I'll lose spiritual circulation and nerve ending, resentment and hard heartedness choking God's life out of me and I won't know what happened. It's a rhythm thing.

Same is true in our stewardship. If I receive a paycheck with the talents God gave me but then have no flow of generosity, I'll get out of breath and not be the conduit He desires. My soul will get knotted up in self-focus, my closed fists blocking the flow of what He'd love to get *to* me if only He could trust it would also get *through* me. It's a rhythm thing.

Same is true in our daily patterns and routines. I've heard it said, "win the morning, win the day." If I start the morning by inhaling ten minutes of social media and email and news before

I even exhale a minute's worth of my soul in God's Presence and Word, I'll be out of breath. Say it with me—it's a rhythm thing.

Wherever I'm *out of rhythm*, I'll be *out of breath*.

In those desert years God wanted to reprogram some new rhythms in His people.

I wonder what new rhythms He'd love to program in you and me?

And since I haven't said it yet, I'll say it again. I hope you consider giving your soul the gift of deep, rhythmic recovery and rest each week. I hope you grow the seed of sabbath in the soil of your life.

Who knows? It could be just the oasis your soul needs in this desert.

Eugene Peterson, author of the *Message Bible*, encourages us:

> *One day a week stop what you're doing and pay attention to what God has been doing and is doing. Be reverent and worshipful and grateful for the Genesis world we are placed in. Remember in gratitude and worshipful adoration. Hallow this day. Keep this day holy.*

# Chapter Ten

## ROPES

*"If you embrace the promise without the process,
you are living in a fantasy."–Kris Vallotton*

*"When you abide with God in Sabbath, an unshakable
confidence shines from the inside out, enticing others toward
the gift of rest as well."–Shelly Miller*

*"Is any pleasure on earth as great as a circle of
Christian friends by a good fire?"–C.S. Lewis*

"Give a man enough rope and he will hang himself," claims the idiom.

The second "R" claims enough of the right rope can help a man *save* himself.

That "rope" is *people*. More specifically, the inner circle of friends you choose to be in your caravan through this desert road trip.

Why call it "rope?"

One, we've established I like alliteration. Two, Scripture seems to like the analogy as well.

Solomon draws the parallel between ropes and people in thick, warm language:

> If it is cold, two can sleep together and stay warm, but how can you keep warm by yourself? Two people can resist an attack that would defeat one person alone. **A rope made of three cords is hard to break**. (Ecclesiastes 4:11-12 GNT emphasis mine)

We see a basic reminder here that life is lonely and cold when lived alone.

Pre-universe, God existed in the context of (Trinitarian) community and He placed that same DNA in us. Even before the fall, He declared it unhealthy and incomplete for us to walk alone.

This is a needful reminder in the cold desert evenings. If you're anything like me, I tend to isolate when I feel sad. And yet I've found out the hard way when I want to be alone the most is usually when I should be alone the least.

Remember, solitude is getting away to be alone with *God*.

Isolation is getting away to be alone with *yourself*.

The litmus test is simple. If our souls get better, healthier, and more connected to God when alone, then that's a viable option.

On the other hand, if I tend to draw in on myself in pity and depression and succumb to my customized vices when alone, or begin spinning wild narratives and connecting dots that are't there, then it's *not* healthy for me. That's when I need the protection and support of friends, particularly a faith-filled community, surrounding me, covering me, letting God pour through them *into* me.

We are a body.

We are a family.

That's God's design and idea for our humanity to flourish.

God heals, comforts, speaks, and instructs us primarily *through* each other.

You and I were made for community. We can't just head for the hills when things get tough or disagreements creep in.

I'll be honest, there've been weeks of my life where I've calendared out life-giving community for every evening because I knew my soul shouldn't be alone and tempted by despair or sin.

I don't think that makes me weak. I think it makes me not an idiot.

In fact, if you need to, I'd encourage you to stop reading, get out your calendar and phone right now and do the same before you come back to this chapter.

The verse in Ecclesiastes goes on to say *two* people can resist an attack that would defeat *one* person.

I love how simple and yet profound the Bible can be. There are some street fights you won't win alone. Hunters pick off lone targets and so does the enemy.

Don't be caught alone in the dry seasons. Coyotes look for it.

But what's even better than two?

Three.

*A rope made of three cords is hard to break.*

This is the verse you usually only see at bridal showers, painted in cascading pink and grey letters on some Chip and Joanna Gaines kind of shiplap for the living room.

However, it should also be the wilderness cry for bands of brothers and sororities of sisters who choose to fight for each other's future, intercede for each other before God, and cover each other in their weakest moments.

We just need to make sure we have the right ropes.

We need to secure the kind of ropes that pull us *forward* through the desert, not backwards or sideways.

*"Don't be fooled by those who say such things, for 'bad company corrupts good character,'"* Paul reminded his people.[1]

The wrong company corrupts us, poisons us, and sidetracks us.

On the other hand, with the right people Solomon reminds us, *"As iron sharpens iron, so a friend sharpens a friend."*[2]

The people we're closest to, for better or worse, will infect our mindsets, viewpoints, attitudes, patterns, beliefs, and overall direction.

The difference between wrong ropes and right ropes is the difference between a noose and a rescue.

Yes, love *all* people. Does this really need to be clarified?

But your inner crew, your squad, the people you do life with and smash tacos with three days week, those you open up the deepest places of your heart to and allow to speak into your life—these need to be people with aligned values, healthy attitudes, eternal perspectives, and relational tracts with God that know how to hear His voice and intercede on your behalf when you need it most.

Deep down we know this, though, don't we? We all recognize we're shaped and influenced by those closest to us. We eventually pick up their sayings, favorite tv shows, and even the way they talk and think.

In fact, the stats have been in for a while: we're all becoming a representational amalgam of the five closest people to us. It's not even a question.

The question is, does that *encourage* you or *discourage* you?

The question is, are those you're roping the caravan of your life to rolling in the direction you want to go? Are they distracted by everything in the desert, on their way back to the things of Egypt, or are they focused heart and soul on God and the Promised Land?

The answer to that question, especially in the desert, is more of a tide-changer than I think we realize.

For me, I honestly don't know what I would've done over the course of my life without loyal, truthful, wise and Spirit-filled friends. Friends who were willing to stick with me through the thick and thin, continually speaking past my feelings and to my soul. Speaking to who I'm becoming and what God still longs to do in and through my life.

Not long ago I was on my usual Saturday sabbath, coffee in hand, trying to enjoy the day and read a good book, and yet haunted for no rhyme or reason by the shame of something in my past. I woke up with it on my mind and couldn't shake it out. I was even starting to roll down the train of thought that God couldn't still use my life in great ways. Maybe my best days *were* all behind. And then the phone rang.

A good friend of mine said he was watching a message about the grace of God, how God lavished it so richly on Moses, and how He didn't deal with him in proportion to his mistakes or even write his story with his lowest scores recorded against him.

*"Russ,"* he started, *"I felt strongly that God told me to call you and tell you the same thing. He's dropped your lowest scores, Russ. He does not hold your past against you. Nothing you've ever done needs to factor into your mind today as you dream about the future."*

I dropped my head and the tears slipped through my fingers and salted the coffee. I journaled every word so I wouldn't forget.

And here's the thing. I'm spoiled. Straight up. This is a somewhat regular occurrence within the circle of a few friends of mine.

I may not be wealthy economically, but I'm wealthy beyond measure in these sort of relationships, and I believe God desires the same for you.

You need people in your life that make you better, not just make you *feel* better.

Seek them out. Pray for them. Lean into them. Dive into community whether you feel like it or not, and when people let you down, remember they're human and flawed just like you, and don't bow out.

o o o

Not long into the road trip from hell, Moses discovered the power of ropes.

Rumors of this traveling caravan had reached a group of people called the Amalekites. These people were bad news in every way, and they decided not to wait for this new nation to come possess their so-called promised land. They decided to bring the thunder first. There at Rephidim, while the Israelites were most vulnerable, the men of Amalek attacked.

Moses provided Joshua with a strategy and fighting instructions. Then, he let him know he'd be standing on the top of the hill with the staff of God in his hands while they were in the battle down below.

Brave, Moses.

His trick worked, however:

*So, Joshua fought the Amalekites as Moses had ordered, and Moses, Aaron, and Hur went to the top of the hill. As long as Moses held up his hands, the Israelites were winning, but whenever he lowered his hands, the Amalekites were winning.*

I want to pause briefly and point out how entertaining it is to imagine how it slowly dawned on Moses this was happening. Think about it. You'll start laughing.

*When Moses' hands grew tired, they took a stone and put it under him, and he sat on it. Aaron and Hur held his hands up—one on one side and one on the other—so that his hands remained steady until sunset. So, Joshua overcame the Amalekite army with the sword.* (Exodus 17:11-13)

Take note of two powerful principles here.

First, as long as Moses had his hands up, the posture of surrender and worship, the victory was his. This truth applies to every generation, every circumstance, and every season. Worship and surrender bring breakthrough and victory. It is the posture that must be maintained, not just in the sunshine, but in the heat of battle.

Next, Moses got tired and couldn't do what he needed to do alone. It took three of them, *a rope of three strands*, to make it through and be successful.

Moses got tired. Maybe you feel that way right now. You're just exhausted. Weary from the battle. Perhaps sick of even trying.

You're going to want an Aaron and Hur on each side during those moments. To hold you up when you feel faint. To keep your arms in the right posture. To speak encouragement when you're unsure. To cover you constantly in prayer. To keep your hands steady.

*A rope made of three cords is hard to break.*

The people you've tied yourself to will be the ropes that either pull you forward or keep dragging you back.

There are tough mountains ahead. Let's ensure the right ropes for the journey.

## Chapter Eleven

### REVELATION

*"Find your tribe, for that's how you will find your future."*
*–Erwin McManus*

*"Blessed are you, Simon son of Jonah,*
*for this was not revealed to you by flesh and blood,*
*but by my Father in heaven."–Jesus (Matthew 16:17)*

*"Why are we all continuing to play this game*
*when we all know it has moved to the next stage?"*
*–Mikhail Bakunin to Sayid and Kate (Lost)*

·

R hythms. Ropes. The third wilderness gift is *revelation*.

This isn't a reference to that grand, terrifying book at the end of Scripture.

Here I'm referring to truth *revealed by God* that travels from *head to heart*.

A promise whispered by the Holy Spirit, a verse you've read a million times that finally takes on an interior meaning, a side of God you experience in a new, tangible way. A prophetic assurance or confirmation that becomes a weapon for your battles in life. The voice of God becoming personal and relevant.

See, I believe God is always speaking. Sometimes the noise in our lives is too loud, or we're tuned into the wrong frequency, but He is speaking, nonetheless.

I believe He's been speaking since the foundation of the world. He's been speaking through prophets and men and women. He's been speaking through creation. He's been speaking through His Spirit. He's been speaking through the pages of His eternal Word.

However, there are two Greek words for "word of God" used in Scripture.

*Logos* and *rhema*.

*Logos* refers to the constant, written word of God in Scripture. *Rhema* refers to the instant, personal speaking of God to us as individuals.

*Logos* is the words on the page. *Rhema* is the Spirit that gives them life.

*Logos* is wonderful. But God never intended *logos* to stay trapped in mere ink and page. *Logos* can be the words tumbling off a preacher's lips and hitting your heart in the same way the scientific name of an insect would in junior high. Trapped in *logos*, the soil never becomes wet and the wood never becomes aflame. God's ways remain rules. The heart is not stirred, the life is not changed. The concepts are theories with which to be familiarized, but the ideas are not yet living, not actually transforming the interior of our life, emotions and soul. The truth remains far away "out there" and not a burning, unavoidable, present reality.

Rhema, on the other hand, is where theory turns to theophany. This is where the sharp points of Scripture lift off the page and hook into the soft flesh of your heart. It's where the Spirit highlights a passage and impresses it distinctly and specifically to your situation. These are the moments a trusted friend shares a God-inspired insight that lines up with Scripture and resonates with your inner tuning. *Rhema* is where *the* Spirit whispers a reminder or warning to *your* spirit. Where a truth about God's Word or character you've always known mentally metamorphoses into a personal, meaningful reality.

*Logos* is reading all the stats about Italy in a textbook. *Rhema* is walking the streets and tasting the cheese.

*Rhema* is *revelation*, God Himself revealing something new to you about who He is or who you are in Him.

And revelation, important to note, tends to happen frequently right *before* and *during* the wilderness.

o o o

Immediately upon entering the desert, the children of Israel began to experience this kind of revelation, divine glimpses of God they could never have received in any other season.

Fresh from the Red Sea, they traveled to the Desert of Shur, there encountering three straight days of thirst and no water, only to arrive at Marah, the place with bitter water we discussed earlier. Grumbling and crying ensued. Camped there in a bitter, painful place, God revealed Himself for the first time as *Jehovah Rapha*, "the Lord who heals you."

They went from Marah to Elim, a Bronze Age Los Angeles boasting twelve springs and seventy palm trees. From there, however, they road-tripped to the Desert of Sin, stopping shy of Sinai. They moaned of thirst and hunger at that pit stop, wallowing in pity about how it would've been easier back in Egypt. But God graciously intervened, catering warehouse amounts of meat and bread, right there in the middle of nowhere. Thus, in the Desert of Shin, in a season of scary, excruciating lack, God revealed Himself as *Jehovah Jireh*, "the Lord who provides."

Two chapters over, we arrive again at the story of Aaron and Hur holding up the hands of Moses as the Amalekites are soundly defeated before the posture of worship and surrender. It's there Moses builds an altar, a memorial of sorts, and calls it *Jehovah Nissi*, "the Lord is my banner."

Are you seeing the pattern?

In each dark moment, God takes the opportunity to shine a spotlight on a dimension of who He is in a fresh, experiential way.

I can attest this has been the pattern in my life too.

Not long after I moved to Lexington, Kentucky, on my own for the first time, my good and trustworthy Jeep Grand Cherokee began to break down.

Who am I kidding? It was already in rehab. But I entered one particular week with a keen awareness it was now on life support and I was very close to trudging through the snow to get to work.

Over coffee one morning, first day off my retail job in a while, I knew I had to do something. Money was low, but life was good, and faith was high. I called a car salesman friend and asked if he knew anyone. He said to bring it by the parts shop connected to his dealership.

Before I left, I got on my knees and prayed. Oh, how I prayed. I asked God for a miracle. I hadn't been perfect, I reminded Him, but I had honored Him with the first fruits of my paycheck for as long as I could remember, and I took the morning to remind Him of all His promises to be my Provider.

I arrived at the dealership and met my friend Brandon, the car salesman. He had started coming to our new church plant just months ago, and it had made my year to watch his life and countenance change by the week, the vines of all his past seeming to unravel from him with each step he took towards God. Tatted from head to toe, he'd become a teddy bear on the inside, and he was beaming in front of all those Toyotas with a new-to-Jesus joy that seemed to have chased away all of yesterday's ghosts.

He smiled as I walked up.

"What seems to be the problem?"

"My professional opinion would be *a lot*," I said. I said it because it was true. I also said it because I know next-to-nothing about cars and can't even begin to fake the Tolkien languages of mechanics and car enthusiasts. "For starters, the brakes seem to be catching a lot. Also, the engine."

Almost on cue, a thin, reserved man walked up and held out his hand. Brandon introduced me and the man motioned for us to take a ride in my jeep. As we rode, he humphed and grunted at the breaks and I think mumbled something about a G9 defibrillator that was castrating a carbonara.

I nodded knowingly, "As I suspected."

After a peaceful, albeit bumpy ride, we parked back at the dealership. Out of the car, he looked at me, paused, and said, "You know what? I know what it's like to be young with bills. Your brakes need completely replaced, but don't worry, it's on me. No charge."

"Oh, sir," I started.

"Don't say another word," he interrupted. "Let me take care of this."

"I don't know what to say....I—"

"You do, however, still need to get that engine of yours checked out so don't get too excited. That's what's gonna *really* cost ya."

"Oh. Where do I do that?"

He pointed to the other side of the lot. We shook hands again and he walked off.

Well. One miracle down. *God, any help with this engine?* I whispered towards the sky.

I was halfway across the lot when a passing car slowed down, the window rolling down with it.

"Pastor Russ!"

A jolly, country voice began yelling from a jolly, country face.

"What are you doing here?"

I walked over, met by the smiling, eager countenance of a man I had baptized just a few weeks ago. He'd only been coming to our church for a couple months.

"Well, having some car trouble. I think we have a plan for the brakes, but apparently I need to get the engine checked out so I'm on my way over." I pointed in that direction as if he didn't know, then noticed his work tag.

"Hmmmm."

He stared at me for a long second like I knew the secrets of North Korea.

"Well, once they tell you the issue and the price, let me know before you do anything."

"Umm, yes sir."

"Promise me now."

"Okay. I will."

With that he drove off. Several hours and a few more castrated carbonara conversations later, I learned the engine repair would cost a full $800.

I texted the jolly man and let him know. He arrived within minutes and informed me he would be taking care of the tab.

"No, no, no..." I began protesting, but the jolly man turned and looked at me as if he might seriously punch me and said, "I've always been told not to block a blessing, brother. So don't you do it, neither."

I could tell he meant it, so I quieted myself a little and then began to thank him profusely.

I couldn't believe it. Brakes and engine, over a $1,000 worth of repairs, all taken care of by two different men. Just like that.

"Thank you, *Jesus*," I whispered.

I left that day on cloud nine, having just watched the Red Sea of my financial/vehicular obstacles part miraculously in front of me.

But the next morning was the best part.

I arrived back at the dealership to pick up my good-as-new car, but the jolly man and his screeching car blocked me on the way to the door.

"Get in!" he yelled.

Oh no. *What did I do?*

"Uhh...."

"I said, get in!"

Reluctantly I got in. The moment I closed the door, he sped off. I looked over at him nervously. His face was flushed, but I couldn't yet tell what emotion was reddening his cheeks.

Then, suddenly, he let out a "Whoooooooooo!"

I ducked as he violently pumped a single fist of victory into the air.

"Well, good morning," I started, but he just kept woo-ing. He'd try to start talking but was beaten back again and again by his own excitement.

I felt uncomfortable.

"Son," he finally said, having gathered himself, "I haven't sold a car in months."

"I'm so sorry."

"Just listen!"

"Okay."

"Honestly, because I haven't sold anything lately, things have been a little tight financially. But when I saw you walking across the lot yesterday, I heard God speak to my heart clear as day. He said, 'I want you to go take care of that young man.'"

At this he started to get emotional.

"Pastor Russ, after I paid your tab, I walked out and immediately sold a car to a family, and then another this morning."

That's when I started woo-ing (on the inside at least).

It's in those moments the reality of God and the kingdom gets back into your skin, and deep down you hope the sensation never wears off.

It does at times, of course. Truth is, I've not experienced many manna-from-heaven moments quite as dramatic since then.

I also know not every story ends with a nice, straight-to-home-Christian-movie red bow like that.

But the reality is, miracles do occur in the seasons and situations we hate or at least try to avoid. Yet new dimensions of God are unveiled primarily in the crucible of pressure.

And here's where disaster can become adventure—if we can choose to go beyond *survivors* of the desert and become *students* of the desert. In that posture we will discover and experience things about God we never knew before.

See, prior to this, I had heard, read and perhaps even taught about God's provision. Yet it was here when I was forced to trust in a new way, down in the hot valley of broken engines and red-inked bank accounts, that I had a revelation of *Jehovah Yireh*, the Lord who provides.

I had believed mentally God was my provider, but now I'd experienced it. The principle had become personal.

The desert is the residence of revelation. And revelation, you may want to write this down, tends to travel predominantly through *pain*.

I wish it weren't so. But it is. Pain is the carrier oil to get things from our head to our heart.

o o o

The moments of intervening, revelation-miracles are fantastic.

However, the gift of revelation, no matter when or how it comes, is no different than the other gifts. It's a gift to be applied and cultivated, and how we open ourselves up to revelation and steward that revelation is crucial for how we walk in victory through the wilderness.

There's no magic formula here, but there are some trail crumbs we can follow.

For starters, *personal* revelation begins in God's *written* revelation.

The Scriptures are the primary watering hole of God's timely words and perspective to our souls.
They're alive and breathing.[1] They're sturdy and dependable. And they provide an inner strength for these weak months under the sun.

David wrote, *"My soul is weary with sorrow; strengthen me according to your word."* (Psalm 119:28)

Gleaning *rhema* words begins with gleaning from the *written* Word. It is, after all, the *"more sure word of prophecy."*[3]

It is through reading prayerfully, humbly, over God's *Word* each day we slowly learn to hear His *Voice* each day. It's from being in the pages of His written Word that we grow our listening ability to get "a word" we know is just for us.

Revelation also comes from God's Presence.

We see this in story after story in Scripture. Wherever God is near, His voice and words aren't far behind.

Adam and Eve were hiding from God in shame. Then they heard His footsteps come near, and from that nearness God spoke.

Moses was hiding in the wilderness. Then God's Presence consumes a bush in burning fire, and from that fire the voice came.

Elijah, David, Abraham, all experienced the same.

We see this in the four hundred years of silence between Malachi and the New Testament where the glory of God had departed the temple. We see this in the call of Samuel, where *"the word of the Lord was rare"* but *"the lamp of God had not yet gone out."*

We live in a new day and a new covenant now. A beautiful one. A day and age where God now speaks through His Son, through His Word, through His Spirit in us, and through the lives of prophets and apostles gone by.

The principle remains. Wherever God's Spirit flows in abundance, revelation follows in tandem.

To best hear His voice, we must learn to enter and live in His Presence.

How do we do that? We don't walk by feelings. We learn that *quickly* in the desert.

But we *should* make it a daily habit to enter His Presence "with thanksgiving."

To approach Him with faith and boldness. *"Let us draw near to God with a sincere heart and with the full assurance that faith brings,"* wrote the author of Hebrews.

We do it through a life of constant worship, knowing He *"inhabits our praise."*

We do it through a desire and pursuit of the Holy Spirit, His Presence here on earth.

We do it by constantly drawing near to Him and becoming aware of him, even in the most mundane of activities.

James 4:7 tells us to *"draw near to God and He will draw near to you."*

Get in His Presence, get around other people filled with his Presence, and watch—you'll begin to hear His voice in ways you never have.

Side-note travelers tip? Try this with Scripture, too. Last week one of the girls on staff opened up about how hard it is for her to read her Bible. I could tell she felt guilty about it. "It just feels like reading math problems sometimes...."

I have a hunch it's the same for many. Our devotional life can seem mechanical and dry, and there will be days we experience that. It's called being human.

But if that's your constant experience, can I encourage you in the same way I encouraged her? When you come to your Bible in the morning, don't approach it "cold." Warm yourself first with the heat of worship. Enter God's Presence by faith with a song from your heart. Put on some soft music and quiet yourself before Him.

For me, sometimes I'll simply dwell on a favorite psalm or promise until a sense of His nearness settles over me. When I finally am ready to read, I ask God to speak to me. I ask Him to open my eyes to see treasure. I ask the same Holy Spirit that inspired this book to come and visit these moments and illuminate this book. And then I get out pen and highlighter, expectant for Him to draw near and speak.

After all, His Presence and His Voice go together.

All this instruction may seem a bit sophomoric for some, but allow me to encourage you on one more practical note: As things pop out to you from Scripture or you sense God speak to you through his Presence, write down what you see and hear.

In other words, learn to *steward* the revelation.

Robert Morris, Pastor of *Gateway Church*, released a book and sermon series five years ago that changed my life. Called *Frequency,* it focused on how to hear from God by tuning in and *stewarding* the voice and words of God.

"Why would God speak to you about this current situation," he posed, "if you still haven't done the last four things He told you?"

Ouch.

This is another reason writing down everything God speaks or impresses on our hearts through His Word or Spirit is so powerful.

Before that *Frequency* series, I had dabbled off and on with a journal for a decade or so. Since that day, I've kept one nearly religiously. I look at it as one of the most powerful tools to document and "steward" what He speaks. The practice has changed my life.

If this has never been a rhythm or even a thought before, why wait?

Let's make a list together.

Record below the last few things you believe God has revealed to you or spoken to you to remember, to hold on to, or to do:

_____

_____

_____

_____

_____

_____

_____

_____

_____

_____

_____

_____

Powerful exercise, huh?

Now, every few months or so, I will go back over "words" in my life. Words spoken over me by people I trust, things I believe

God's called me to do, revelations from His Word, promises whispered to my heart by the Spirit.

I don't want to fall into disobedience by my forgetfulness, and I don't want to fall into fear or discouragement by it either.

The practice has changed my life.

In fact, there's something I used to feel weird about. I experience a deep, nearly overwhelming sense of God's presence when I read back through my journals. Seems almost wrong how much anointing and strength I draw from reading them. After all, it's mainly just my own words and rambling, right?

Yet I've found it true that "the ark of the Presence rests on the word of the testimony."[4]

My journals contain my testimony. They contain the record of God speaking and working in my life. They document his words to me.

My journal is the written intimacy of our relationship, highs and lows and all.

It's a novel of rescue. A movie of revelation. A song of faithfulness.

It's a box of promises.

Yes, Moses and his people put all of God's most precious words and promises in a box.
I just put them in a journal.

Where are you putting yours? And how often do you take them out to consider and pray over?

I love Mary's response to everything spoken to her. After all the dreams and visions about Jesus's birth, and the shepherds coming and spreading the word, we read, *"But Mary treasured up all these things and pondered them in her heart." (Luke 2:19)*

I love that. One translation records, "and she thought about them often."

I hope you have a place both on paper and in your heart where you visit, treasure and ponder all of God's plans and promises for your life.

You'll find yourself supernaturally comforted, strengthened, and directed as you do this.

As an added bonus, by the way, the kingdom principle remains, "those who are faithful with little will be given more."

As you steward and walk in what God has already revealed, you can count on it that more will come.

Finally, go to battle with the revelation you receive.

Look what else Paul told Timothy:

*"This charge I entrust to you, Timothy, my child, in accordance with the prophecies previously made about you, **that by them you may wage the good warfare.**"* (1 Timothy 1:18, emphasis mine)

Paul knew Timothy would battle in this life and didn't want him unequipped. Paul knew prophecies are part of the spiritual material of God's weaponry.

So, he told Timothy to take the prophecies over his life and use them for battle. He expected Timothy, as a young soldier in the faith, to wage warfare against the enemy with the prophetic revelation entrusted to him.

It's sad how much God revealed and desired to do with the first generation out of Egypt only for them to continue to allow circumstantial "reality" to loom bigger in their hearts than the wonderful things God had revealed and promised. Unfortunately, that first generation did not use the prophetic revelation they had to build their faith and make it through. They left those weapons in the dust.

But not Jesus.

When Jesus was in the wilderness, he flashed the sword of the Spirit against each enemy attack. Every time the devil assaulted Jesus with lies and temptations, Jesus responded with the revelation recorded in God's Word and burned in His own heart.

*"It is written…"* He responded.

Ask God to speak to you like never before. Then document it. Journal it. Keep a file of life-giving words.

Obey what He says.

Read the words often.

Speak them out loud over your life.

o o o

As I close not just this chapter, but this entire section, I want to rally once more around the power of a seed.

We get to plant seeds in the desert. Then, we get to reap the crops for years to come.

Giants *and* gifts. That's what's crazy. Both golden calves *and* manna show up in future generations. The good and the bad.

The other day I was pushing through 1st Kings where King Rehoboam was in a pinch. It's hundreds of years after the exodus story of Moses and his people. I nearly caught my breath when I read:

> *After seeking advice, the king made two golden calves. He said to the people, 'It is too much for you to go up to Jerusalem. Here are your gods, Israel, who brought you up out of Egypt."* (1 Kings 12:28)

Wait, *what?* We're back to golden calves? Seriously?

Yes, because the generational iniquity of idolatry was passed down to… well, generations.

It's the same with alcohol, promiscuity, anything. Doesn't matter. Whatever isn't healed is handed down.[5]

On the other hand, manna also keeps showing up years and years later.

In fact, many varieties of manna are supposedly still around *today*, dotting the Middle East and even parts of Italy.

Take the beautiful area of Castelbuno, for example. Located in Sicily, the town lives up to its name, which means "good castle." It has one, replete with all the medieval beauty and rawness, missing guardrails, and haunted corridors one would hope for. The sidewalks of the town are painted with shops, exotic sausages, home-made sorbets, and dishes cooked and consumed with time and respect.

Perhaps dreamiest of all, the town has manna.

The manna tree has grown wild in the region for centuries and the manna is taken from its sap, sap which flows so generously in the months of July and August it literally drips off the branches and crystalizes like icicles hanging off the trees.

Local experts know just how and when to harvest, cut, and glean. Local consumers boast extravagant claims about the benefits and properties once consumed. Also, it apparently tastes pretty dang good.

Crazy, huh? This mysterious white stuff showing up on the ground thousands of years ago, provided by God for a starving, desperate caravan in the desert. Now, scarfed down alongside ravioli in northern Italy.

The seeds and gifts you sow and grow in the desert––they won't just get you through the desert. I've found they live long into future seasons as well. They become trees that give shade to others as they walk through their own dry times. They become meat and treasure you provide for future travelers.

You may be in the middle of Death Valley.

Why not plant some wonderful things?

*Moses said, "This is what the Lord has commanded: 'Take an omer of manna and keep it for the generations to come, so they can see the bread I gave you to eat in the wilderness when I brought you out of Egypt.'"*
*So, Moses said to Aaron, "Take a jar and put an omer of manna in it. Then place it before the Lord to be kept for the generations to come." (Exodus 16:32-33)*

## WILDERNESS WRITINGS

(Notes from the Section—What stood out?)

_____

_____

_____

_____

_____

_____

_____

_____

_____

_____

_____

_____

_____

_____

_____

_____

## DESERT DECISIONS

(Future Applications—What steps are you going to take?)

_____

_____

_____

_____

_____

_____

_____

_____

_____

_____

_____

_____

_____

_____

*the*

# SPIRIT

*of*

# CALEB

## Chapter Twelve

# THE MOST IMPORTANT THING ABOUT YOU

I want to tell you the most important thing about you.

That may sound dramatic or hyperbolic, but it is not. It is the single most important thing about who you are. It is the number one factor tied to your life, your future, and specifically, this wilderness season you are in.

Honestly, the topic in this section is why I wrote the book. And I am praying the words bypass information straight to impartation and combust like hydrogen in your heart.

For me, the impartation came like lightning in the middle of a dark, October afternoon. My spirit was heavy that Sunday morning. I had worn my best church outfit, a little too city for the town as usual, and hosted the service with plastic smiles and forced jokes about the return of Pumpkin Spice Lattes. I leaned into handshakes in the lobby, high-fives from students, and the wearisome work of being engaged in other human voices, all along carrying heavy disappointment in my heart.

I had just returned from my mandatory leave-of-absence/sabbatical of sorts and was navigating life the best I could. Inside, though, my soul felt as though it were still withering away.

Service completed. I hurried through artificial interactions and drove to a nearby town to huddle in a corner booth and hide in my thoughts. I ordered their Mexican eggs Benedict and gripped my coffee for comfort, letting the warmth of the cup in my palm ease some tension out of my spine.

Knowing I would be back at church in just a few hours for leadership meetings, I opened my Bible and asked God to speak.

He did.

And it shifted everything inside me.

The power I experienced poured from the life of a character in Scripture named Caleb. Though lesser known than Moses, he's a legend in his own right, and was an integral part of the wilderness journey, especially the second half.

Caleb was the son of Jephunneh from the Kennezites, one of the tribes mentioned in the covenant God made with Abraham, and one of the nations living in the land of Canaan.

This man Caleb, forty years old at the time, was a spy. An original *007* for God's people.

Now. Enter the *Skyfall* Files of Israel.

In Numbers 13 of our journey, the children of Israel have left Sinai. A lot's happened. Traveling, hardship, miracles, and mistakes. A lot of God-encounters for Moses and complaint sessions for the people.

Not to mention commandments given; laws, policies and festivals introduced; a tabernacle (church building) created; and a priesthood (church staff) installed. All deeply gritty and human, yet prophetic and profound.

More imminently, God positioned this people to advance into all He had promised, specifically the location of their future home. To prepare them, He instructs Moses to dispatch able men to spy out the land of Canaan and gather intel. To return with an *Excel* report detailing what the towns are like, the geography, the people, the livestock. Again, this business trip was not to determine whether or not to close the deal, but simply to gather real estate data for the leaders and post a few tropical Instagram Stories for the people. Promised land time was here!

However, when the twelve return, we read this:

> *At the end of forty days they returned from exploring the land....They gave Moses this account: "We went into the land to which you sent us, and it does flow with milk and honey! Here is its fruit.* **But** *the people who live there are powerful, and the cities are fortified and very large. We even saw descendants of Anak there."* (Numbers 13:25-28, emphasis mine)

They testify God's promise is in fact true, but they insert a "but" right after, and begin to describe the giants in the land as bigger than the God who promised to give it to them.

Right in the middle of their report of retreat, this fiery, no-nonsense spy named Caleb decides he's heard enough. Out of nowhere, he speaks up:

Then Caleb **silenced the people** before Moses—

I like this guy already...

—and said, "We should go up and take possession of the land, for **we can certainly do it.**" (Numbers 13:30, emphasis mine)

One voice of faith speaks into the pessimism.

Yet the negative spies are insistent:

But the men who had gone up with him said, "**We can't** attack those people; they are stronger than we are." And they spread among the Israelites a bad report about the land they had explored. They said, "The land we explored devours those living in it. All the people we saw there are of great size. We saw the Nephilim there (the descendants of Anak come from the Nephilim). **We seemed like grasshoppers in our own eyes**, and we looked the same to them." (Numbers 13:31-33, emphasis mine)

Except the two with the can-do spirit, Joshua (Moses' future successor) and Caleb, the ten naysayers outnumber the voice of faith. Since nothing is more contagious than attitude, the discouraging report spreads like an infection to the rest of the camp. By nightfall, the entire Israelite community has a full-fledged meltdown. Courage dissipates. Faith melts into fear.

In holy frustration, the Lord tells Moses He's had enough and is about to wipe them all out with a plague. Moses reminds the Lord of his own compassionate nature and God responds with mercy and forgives. Yet not without judgment and consequence:

> *The Lord replied, "I have forgiven them, as you asked.* **Nevertheless**, *as surely as I live and as surely as the glory of the Lord fills the whole earth,* **not one** *of those who saw my glory and the signs I performed in Egypt and in the wilderness but who disobeyed me and tested me ten times—not one of them will ever see the land I promised on oath to their ancestors. No one who has treated me with contempt will ever see it." (Exodus 14:20-24, emphasis mine)*

God says *"I'll forgive them. However, their journey stops here. They'll never enter the Promised Land."* Sobering words. And a sobering warning for those today walking through any kind of wilderness.

Then, the next verse begins with another "but," and this "but" contains what I believe is the secret to making it powerfully through any wilderness season. This "but" was the lightning bolt that imparted fresh strength into my heart that discouraging October day. And it is the most important thing about you.

God has just announced in verse twenty-three, that the million or so adults miraculously delivered from Egypt will all die in the desert. They will never see their dreams come to pass. None of them.

Except in the very next verse we read:

> **"But because my servant Caleb has a different spirit** and
> follows me wholeheartedly, I will bring him into the land
> he went to, and his descendants will inherit it." (Exodus
> 14:24, emphasis mine)

Roughly two million people die in the wilderness. Only two survive.[1] And God only gives one reason—a different spirit.

Caleb didn't survive because of position or fame. He didn't succeed because of wealth or resources. It wasn't his giftedness or charisma or skillset. It wasn't his background or upbringing or heritage. One thing and one thing alone got Caleb not only *through* the wilderness but *to* the Promised Land:

*He had a different spirit.*

Ten spies, reflective of rest of the community, had a wrong spirit. They were negative Nancys. Fearful Freds. Doubting Dans. Anxious Andys. Worried Wes's. And whatever other cheesy alliterative label you can find.

But not Caleb. While the children of Israel were fixated on the size of their problems, Caleb was fixated on the size of God. Their eyes were fixed on their smallness and inability; Caleb's focus was fixed on God's greatness and supernatural capability. They were shrunken with fear; Caleb was enlarged with faith.

Both experienced the same *season* but both cultivated a different *spirit*.

Caleb's spirit made all the difference. It determined his destiny.

So will yours, and so will mine.

In the last section we discussed *how* to manage the wilderness. In the next two sections I want to look at what will see us *through* and *out*. And the crux of it is *the spirit you choose.*

At the risk of repetition, it cannot be highlighted, boldened, italicized, underlined, screamed, or emphasized enough. The most important thing about you is not your money. It's not your looks. It's not your connections. It's not your gifting.

The most important thing about you is your *spirit*.

o o o

Everyone has a spirit.

I'm not referring here to the eternal soul, but to the aura one possesses. The spunk, the pluck, the moxie. The emotional atmosphere or *essence* a person carries with him or her. We all instinctively feel this, whether we verbalize it or not.

Have you noticed the people who walk into a room and the vibe sours? Their mood trends towards the gloomy, with more grievance than gratitude in their words. Pessimism discolors their outlook. And this spirit goes with them into every scenario they walk into.

On the other hand, I know a girl who seems to have a heaven-connected IV of Starbucks and joy in her veins. Bubbly doesn't describe it. Every intonation of every word bristles with energy and a smile. Exuberance spills into every interaction. People seem to smile more when she's there. Even hard shells crack and laughter finds its way in.

I used to work with a red-blooded leader with the confidence, testosterone and intensity you would imagine of Winston Churchill. I would not have been surprised, in fact, to have found him bareback on a horse in the church parking lot, face painted, firing flame-kissed arrows into the forest. It was just his spirit. And you wanted to be around him. His boldness was refreshing, his zest for life invigorating.

I've been around people whose spirit made me want to walk holier and set apart for the Presence of God. I've sat in meetings with people whose wise words brought mental energy, clarity and focus to the discussion. I've been around stolid souls whose mere presence in the room suffused calm and peace to any situation. I've been inspired around hearts that dance with innovation and creativity, who remind me God is an ingenious, beautiful, and awe-inspiring Artist.

I've also witnessed Jezebel spirits of intimidation and manipulation, Saul spirits of inferiority and Delilah spirits of seduction and deception. I've been around cynical spirits eager to find fault and arrogant spirits eager to praise and show themselves off.

Some people have *championing* spirits while others have *critical* spirits.

Some have *aggressive* spirits while others have *apathetic* spirits.

Some have *hospitable* spirits while others have *haughty* spirits.

Some have *empowering* spirits while others have *controlling* spirits.

So, here's the question—what kind of spirit do *you* have?

We all have different personalities. God makes introverts and extroverts alike. But there's a difference between *the personality you have* and *the spirit you choose.*

The core of you, your faith and attitude—how would people describe you?

Here's a good test for myself. How do people feel in my presence? How do they feel when they leave an interaction with me?

Does my spirit make people thirsty for God? To believe larger and greater that anything is possible? Or to be careful and settle for the known?

Does my spirit cause people to believe in themselves and the greatness God has planned? Or does it cause them to feel small about themselves and focused on their faults and inabilities?

Pastor Brian Houston, of the global *Hillsong Church* based out of Australia, reminds me of that courageous, can-do Caleb spirit. Early in his ministry, before his platform was large, he was asked to speak at an influential conference. It was an incredible opportunity for him and one he accepted gratitude. He thought it interesting, though, that the man who invited him had never heard him preach. Finally, he asked the pastor one day why he took a chance on him. The reply was simple. "Because I liked your spirit."

Our spirit can take us places.

Just like Daniel of the Old Testament. Young, inexperienced, and up against the odds as a servant in Babylonian captivity. Yet we read:

*Then this Daniel became distinguished above all the other high officials and satraps,* **because an excellent spirit was in him.** *And the king* **planned to set him over the whole kingdom.** (Daniel 6:3, emphasis mine)

Another translation says this happened because "he possessed an **extraordinary** spirit."

I don't know about you, but I want a spirit that attracts power with God and favor with man. Even in the middle of doubtful times, I don't want a doubting spirit.

I want to burn with a "Caleb spirit." I want fire in my eyes and faith like dynamite in my heart.

o o o

So, what was it, specifically, that distinguished Caleb's spirit?

That's the question I whispered to the Lord in my heart that October Sunday. I nursed some of my emptiness with a latte and flipped from Numbers 14 over to Joshua 14. The answer surfaced off the page like braille.

Joshua 14 takes place forty-five years after Numbers 14. The first generation died out and the new generation under Joshua's command had crossed the Jordan and begun the conquest. Now the leadership of the children of Israel is dividing up the land. Caleb's eighty-five at this point, an old man. We read:

*Caleb said to Joshua, "Remember what the Lord said to Moses, the man of God, about you and me when we were at Kadesh-barnea. I was forty years old when Moses, the servant of the Lord, sent me from Kadesh-barnea to explore the land of Canaan. I returned and gave an honest report, but my brothers who went with me frightened the people from entering the Promised Land. For my part, I–"*

Here comes the word…

*"–**wholeheartedly** followed the Lord my God."* (Joshua 14:5-8, emphasis mine)

Unlike his other fearful, half-hearted contemporaries, Caleb followed and served God with a whole heart. And I believe that is what informed, guarded and fueled his spirit.

As if to hammer home the point, the word repeats two more times in that chapter alone:

*So that day Moses solemnly promised me, "The land of Canaan on which you were just walking will be your grant of land and that of your descendants forever, because you **wholeheartedly** followed the Lord my God."* (Joshua 14:9, emphasis mine)

Again…

*Hebron still belongs to the descendants of Caleb son of Jephunneh the Kenizzite because he **wholeheartedly*** *followed the Lord, the God of Israel.* (Joshua 14:14, emphasis mine)

If we return, in fact, to Deuteronomy 14, we see the divine, symbiotic relationship:

*But because my servant Caleb has **a different spirit** and follows me **wholeheartedly**, I will bring him into the land he went to, and his descendants will inherit it.*

A different spirit.

Wholehearted.

I sat there in the booth, rolling the word on my tongue over and over.

And I began to remember a life-messages from my former pastor:

Partial.

"Partial is the enemy to your destiny," he would tell us.

A partial heart instead of a whole heart.

The stories and Scriptures began to flood my mind.

Saul, smug in his victory over the Amalekites, battle songs thumping through his chest, smelling God's favor in the air. Confident. Marching.

God, as an immediate king over his people leveraged the armies of Israel to punish the accumulated wickedness and sin of Amalek, and the punishment was to be absolute. Nothing left breathing. And Saul complied. Mostly.

Samuel arrived on the scene. Seeing the prophet coming, Saul called out enthusiastically with a religious, self-assured greeting, only to have his victory cigar snuffed out by the prophet's piercing rebuke:

> *"Then what is all the bleating of sheep and goats and the lowing of cattle I hear?"* Samuel demanded. (1 Samuel 15:14 NLT)

Saul backpedals, acknowledging they did, in fact, spare the king and some of the best animals, but they intended to use those animals as a sacrifice for God.

Samuel sees through the religious smokescreen of Saul's excuses. He bluntly asks why he didn't obey the Lord. After a few more justifications from Saul, Samuel drops the anvil on the king's ego and error, gives a sermonette about obedience over sacrifice, and then goes for the throat:

> *"So, because you have rejected the command of the Lord, he has rejected you as king."* (1 Samuel 15:14-23)

God had instructed Saul to wipe out everything. And he did. Almost.

He kept the king alive as a trophy along with a few animals *"to be sacrificed unto the Lord."* There was even a spiritual-sounding reason behind his action.

He was ninety-five percent obedient. But God called his partial obedience disobedience.

He was partial in his passion and service to God, and it cost him everything.

I think of the obscure story of King Jehoash approaching Elisha right before the prophet died:

> *"My father! My father! I see the chariots and charioteers of Israel!" he cried.*
> *Elisha told him, "Get a bow and some arrows." And the king did as he was told. Elisha told him, "Put your hand on the bow," and Elisha laid his own hands on the king's hands. Then he commanded, "Open that eastern window," and he opened it. Then he said, "Shoot!" So, he shot an arrow. Elisha proclaimed, "This is the Lord's arrow, an arrow of victory over Aram, for you will completely conquer the Arameans at Aphek."*
> *Then he said, "Now pick up the other arrows and strike them against the ground." So, the king picked them up and struck the ground three times. But the man of God was angry with him.*
> *"You should have struck the ground five or six times!" he exclaimed. "Then you would have beaten Aram until it was entirely destroyed. Now you will be victorious only three times." (2 Kings 13:14-19)*

At first glance, the prophet's anger seems arbitrary and unfair. But bottom line, the king's response and action was compliant, not courageous. It was passive, not passionate. It was half-hearted, not whole-hearted.

And if we don't feel the heat of God's intensity on our face just yet, let's bring the flames a little closer with the words of Jesus to the church in Laodicea:

*"I know all the things you do, that you are neither hot nor cold. I wish that you were one or the other! But since you are like lukewarm water, neither hot nor cold, I will spit you out of my mouth!"* (Revelation 3:15-17 NLT)

Jesus is not okay with lukewarm. He is not down with partial.

He doesn't ask us to adore the Lord with some of our hearts or the majority of our life. When asked for the *SparkNotes* summary of all the laws and prophets of all the ages, Jesus said it like this:

*"'Love the Lord your God with **all** your heart and with **all** your soul and with **all** your strength and with **all** your mind'; and, 'Love your neighbor as yourself.'"* (Luke 10:27, emphasis mine)

All our heart. All our soul. All our strength. All our mind.

Wholehearted.

If you can't tell by now, God is a passionate, leaned-in, all-out kind of God. And He desires for His people to reflect the same intensity.

"Partial is the enemy to your destiny," my mentor and pastor told me.

A partial heart will keep us stuck and sabotage a great destiny.

A whole heart, on the other hand, will fuel a full, robust, Caleb spirit. One that honors God and pushes us forward.

2 Chronicles 16:9 declares:

*"The eyes of the Lord range throughout the earth to strengthen those whose hearts are **fully committed** to Him." (emphasis mine)*

o o o

We'll take the next couple chapters to discuss the benefits of a Caleb spirit and how to fuel it.

However, as you read and contemplate these Scriptures and truths, my prayer is you would turn down the volume to any potential condemnation or discouragement from the enemy, along with any unhealthy pressure to somehow "try harder" or "perform better."

Instead, we should turn up the passionate, loving voice of our Father.

The invigorating conviction of His Spirit that simply longs to lead us into the abundance found in whole-hearted surrender. The fire of His Presence that alone can burn away the apathy and lesser things. The hot water of His love, washing His bride with His word.

He is a God of all mercy, grace and compassion.

And He is a God of all zeal. An all-consuming fire. Even in the midst of troubling times, He longs to touch our damp half-heartedness with white-hot coals from His altar.

Do you feel a shift inside even now? Even while all hell screams against us outside, God can create new landscapes on the inside. New scenery and atmosphere of the soul. Greys turning to colors and deserts turning to streams. Confidence returning. Hope stirring. Joy bubbling.

You know, as I continue to reflect on the journey of God's people, I have to believe some of Caleb's essence was imparted from his leader, Moses.

We know Moses had many faults. A lack of full-hearted zeal was not one of them.

I'll tell you a secret desire of mine. At the end of my life, I want my spirit to be that of the spirit of Moses at the end of his.

Do you remember?

*Moses was 120 years old when he died. His **eye was undimmed**, and his **vigor unabated**.* (Deuteronomy 34:7 ESV, emphasis mine)

I don't believe that just described his physical condition. I believe that described his soul.

He lived long and endured much, but his eyes and spirit were still full. He burned with vision and overflowed with vitality.

*Oh, God, I pray, let it be for me as well. And for everyone reading these words. We know it starts with a full, whole-hearted zeal for You. Stir us now, we ask.*

○ ○ ○

Much like any series worth watching, the story and treasure of Caleb's journey is too much for a solo episode. We'll put a ribbon on this chapter and tear into the next one like Christmas.

Why that kind of excitement? Because chances are, if you're reading this book, you would not have chosen the circumstances you're currently in. You would have never chosen the divorce. You would have never chosen the struggle or addiction. You would have never chosen the demotion. The setback. The depression.

You would have never chosen this season.

But.

You can choose your spirit.

And that will make all the difference.

*But because my servant Caleb has a different spirit and follows me wholeheartedly, I will bring him into the land.* (Exodus 14:24)

## Chapter Thirteen

A DIFFERENT SPIRIT

*"Only 30 verses in the Bible about Caleb. But those 30 verses can change our lives."–David Jeremiah*

*"Optimists are those who go after Moby Dick in a rowboat with a bucket of tartar sauce."–Zig Ziglar*

*"We cannot always choose what happens to us, but we can choose what happens in us."–John Maxwell*

Have you ever heard of John Wesley Powell?

The man's a legend.

Born in New York in 1834, he was the son of poor immigrants, and a man cut from a different cloth. A rugged, iron-spine with grit in his blood.

By age twelve, he was plowing and planting crops on his family's 60-acre farm. For leisure, he spent his youth in the revelry of outdoor adventure. Walking across Wisconsin for four months. Exploring the Mississippi River and eventually conquering its tributaries in Ohio, Illinois, and Des Moines.

Throughout his life, he served as a major in the Civil War, professor at Illinois Wesleyan University, second director of the U.S. Geological Survey, and the first director of the Bureau of Ethnology at the Smithsonian Institution.

The man had an insatiable hunger for life, adventure and knowledge. Even during the war, he spent his spare time studying whatever rocks were in his vicinity.

He is perhaps most well-known for his exploration of the Grand Canyon via the Colorado River. At the time, this spot on the American map was simply labeled "Unexplored." He thought it an embarrassment so little was known and discovered in his own country so he gathered nine men for a mission to cross that great unknown, despite being warned he would never come out alive. An extremely dangerous and difficult terrain, and none of his crew had ever even run a rapid.[1]

Another caveat to this death mission, if you ever visit the National Portrait Gallery in Washington, D.C., you'll notice something else interesting about John Wesley Powell. He only had one arm.

He suffered a wound in battle and underwent several amputations (before returning to war only a month later and then teaching himself how to write with his weak hand). Thus, he couldn't row or swim.

His father tried to stop his foolhardy adventures once he saw he was a "maimed man" but one biographer described John as being as "singled-minded as a buzz saw." This fearless, 5' 6-1/2", 120-lb man's man with one arm would not be deterred.

He and his team went, and they conquered.

John Wesley Powell refused to live life any way than fully alive. Fully leaned in. Wholehearted.

The rest of this book could be filled with his adventures and accomplishments. Yet we know it wasn't natural gifting that landed him in the annals of history. It certainly was not physical stature or ability. It had nothing to do with resources or family wealth. He possessed no tangible advantages over anyone around him.

One thing and one thing alone fueled his actions and set him apart from his contemporaries.

He had a different spirit.

o o o

Paul, in his letter to the Philippian church, wrote:

*It is no trouble for me to write the same things to you again.*

Repetition is powerful.

So, allow me to keep spinning the drill onto this one point: nothing is more important than our spirit.

A Caleb spirit, fueled by a whole heart, will direct our destiny.

Specifically, it will achieve several things.

First, it will:

### #1: Get you through the wilderness.

To recap, roughly 600,000 men died in the wilderness. Between 1-2 million people total of that first generation, and only Joshua and Caleb made it.

I believe one reason is because a *whole heart* yields *clear vision*.

We'll bite deeper into the veal of vision next section, but Proverbs 29:18 makes it clear that when it comes to vision, we will either thrive with it or die without it.

If Caleb was anything, he was a man of vision. It pulsated through his soul like torrents of fire. When everyone else was paralyzed in self-focus and doubt, convinced they couldn't go on, convinced God had left them, convinced they didn't have enough a, b, or c, Caleb rose with alacrity and moved forward. I think He must have remembered what God had spoken.

All the way back in Exodus 3:17, while the children of Israel were still in captivity, the Lord told Moses:

> "I have **promised** to bring you up out of your misery in Egypt into the land of the Canaanites, Hittites, Amorites, Perizzites, Hivites and Jebusites—a land flowing with milk and honey.'"

Caleb had a promise. He had a vision.

Therefore, he knew, "I'm not dying in this wilderness; I'm walking *through* this wilderness. To a land flowing with milk and honey."

God had been faithful to deliver. He had performed no shortage of miracles. He had proven to be true to His Word.

And God had painted a picture of a future bursting with promise and provision. Liberated from all enemies. Teeming with abundance and produce and local, raw, antibiotic-free, non-GMO honey. Acres of custom houses already built and lavishly furnished. God's blessing, Presence, and government over His freshly redeemed people. A nation of supernatural origin and pregnant promise.

This sight of the future, promised by the Engineer of existence itself, was seared across the retinas of Caleb's eyes. It had been set like cement in front of him, never to be removed by any seeming obstacle or setback.

Thus, while the children of Israel were cursing about the present, Caleb was whistling about the future. While they complained the giants were too big, God's promise emboldened Caleb with power.

Giants? What do giants matter if God is in the equation?

If you have a Caleb spirit with a God vision, giants just make the story more exciting.

It just inspires shepherd boys to walk by grown men with toddler faith and cry out, "Who is this uncircumcised Philistine who dares defy God's people? Who does he think he is?"

"But David, do you see how big he is?"

"I do. And he is dwarfed like an ant against the Swiss Alps at the vision I am staring at right now. A throne of unapproachable light where God dwells. Creatures and angels scream and cover their eyes at His unbearable majesty. Mountains crash to bellow out songs worthy of His glory...oh yeah...Goliath. Here, I'll just grab some stones. His taunts will turn to blood and silence. God is with me."

Giants make the story more exciting for sarcastic, ill-mannered prophets like Elijah. A man zealous for God's glory. Willing to challenge the idol-riddled nation to a competition on a mountain and savor the odds. To go on and mock the competing athletes, stack the deck against God with Aquafina-drenched firewood, and then watch the Lord showcase the whole thing with flames from heaven.

If we give God the faith-rich soil of a Caleb spirit and vision, then *giants just give God more glory.*

The children of Israel were half-hearted, stuck in their rearview-vision devotion. They believed when they could see it or after it had come to pass. Their faith was calculated, careful and convenient.

But Caleb cast his whole lot in with God and put his shoulders head-on into the vision promised for the future. He knew every syllable from God were dollars on a check he could take to the bank.

See, vision tethers to faith not only to get us through the wilderness, but to the *more* God has in store for us.

That's why a different spirit will also:

## #2 : *Get you to the Promised Land.*

For Caleb, that meant he eventually passed through the dry middle eastern deserts and entered the plush and fertile land God had promised.

For you, the promised land might be the sweet, tall grass of freedom from addiction. It might be the date trees of love come true. Perhaps the spiced meadows of reconciled relationships. The honey of healing from heartbreak. The mountain heights of lifted depression. The riverbanks of financial relief.

Whatever Canaan represents for your life, a Caleb spirit can infuse you with the fortitude and favor to make it through to the other side.

When all the other spies shrank in fear from their God-given land because of the opposition, Caleb responded matter-of-factly, "We can..."

He was a man of faith. The promises, or "tickets" as we referred to them in Chapter 1, were in all their pockets. But only Caleb cashed his in.

We are told plainly in Romans 4:16, "...*the promise is received by **faith**.*"

If we keep the promises before our eyes of what's to come, trust and expectancy will grow. Vision for the future magnetizes faith into the cold, metallic recesses of the heart and causes it to warm, burn, and energize.

The power of faith cannot be overstated. In fact, when we read through the Gospels, there is simply one thing above all else that causes Jesus to be amazed, grieved or moved—the presence or absence of faith.

*"Let it be done to you according to your **faith.**"* (Matthew 9:29 emphasis mine)

*He marveled at their lack of **faith.*** (Mark 6:6 emphasis mine)

*"When Jesus heard this, he was amazed...'I haven't seen **faith** like this in all of Israel.'"* (Matthew 8:10 emphasis mine)

As Pastor Wendall Smith once said, *"Faith is what honors God the most and it is what God mostly honors."*

Faith.

Even when it looks and feels like all hope is gone.

I remember sitting on the third story deck of an apartment in Lexington, Kentucky. A broken mess in the middle of the day. Sitting numbly above the chipped parking lines below. Spirit so low, hope so bleak. And as I was reading through a book, holding back tears, some light broke through in my soul as my eyes fell on this verse:

Yet I still **dare to hope** when I remember this:
The faithful love of the Lord never ends!
  His mercies never cease.
Great is his faithfulness;
his mercies begin afresh each morning. (Lamentations 3:21-23 NLT emphasis mine)

I think I only got halfway through the words before my face collapsed in my hands.

I wept as I remembered His mercy and goodness and compassion. As I considered the possibility that I could still dare to hope.

Truth is, there are things people have dared me to do that took a lot of guts.

I still remember the time my grade-school friend dared me to peek down a rattlesnake hole by our old church.

I remember when my parents convinced me to fly in a plane for the first time even though I was terrified of heights.

And I remember the moment my friend challenged me to walk into the other room, take a girl by the hand, and tell her how I felt.

But nothing, and I mean nothing, takes more guts than to hope. To choose hope in the midst of heartbreak and despair. It feels unnatural and counterintuitive and even cruel in the face of contrary evidence. It takes courage and grit and the grace of God.

Yes, the bravest moments for any of us are when our souls have been hollowed out, yet we still choose to shut the door on fear and despair.

We choose to keep believing. We choose to keep holding on.

*Let us hold tightly without wavering to the hope we affirm, for God can be trusted to keep his promise.* (Hebrews 10:19)

I dare you to hope.

And don't let go.

○ ○ ○

It's odd how much thought I've put into my funeral.

I think about the obvious, who will be there, what will my impact have been, all that. But if I'm honest, and I probably shouldn't admit this, every time I'm at a funeral I also find myself making a mental list of what I don't want my funeral to be like.

Truth is, I am a detail-obsessed tyrant when it comes to atmosphere. But seriously, must we escalate an already somber moment by meeting in drab, outdated, uninspiring environments, only to add melancholy elevator music, hunter green wallpaper and hideous flowers?

If you are reading this and have anything to do with my funeral (don't worry, it's actually already in writing), I want my funeral to build like a modern worship experience, intentionality embedded in every sight, sound and color.

I want life. I want pop-up banners and surprise guest elements. I want gastropub-level appetizers and my most recent *Apple* playlist bumping in the background and too many other specifics than space would allow here. And feel free to add moving lights and haze while you're at it.

I'll be in heaven after all. Please don't make it feel like the other place.

Okay. Tirade over.

There are also many things I would love said at my funeral, and near the top is a sentiment expressed in one of my favorite pieces of literature, *The Great Gatsby*.

Nick Carraway struggled for words to describe his endearingly delusional friend, James Gatsby. "Jay" was a complex figure. Deceptive and broken and hopelessly, irredeemably optimistic. My favorite line is when Nick describes Jay as "the most hope-filled man I've ever met."

I love that.

I confess, I want that to be said of me.

And the thing is, James Gatsby's hopes were groundless, strung by tinsel string of wishful thinking and illusions of self-grandeur.
But not ours.

Hebrews 6:18-19 declares:

*It is impossible for God to lie. Therefore, we who have fled to him for refuge can have **great confidence** as we hold to the hope that lies before us. This hope is a **strong and trustworthy anchor for our souls**."* *(emphasis mine)*

Our hopes are secure, firm, and anchored with reinforced titan steel. Secure in the Person of Jesus. Kept taut behind the veil. The promises unbendable.

Promises like Jeremiah 29:11:

*"For I know the plans I have for you—plans to give you a hope and a future and not to harm you."*

Promises.

A guarantee life will be a bed of roses and we'll get everything we want? No, we know better than that.

But we do know God has promised beautiful things:

- to leverage the good and even the bad for our benefit and His praise
- rich mercy and forgiveness through the blood of Jesus
- whatever we could ask or imagine, He can do immeasurably more
- to never leave us or forsake us, no matter what
- grace and power for every season
- a future home, inheritance in Him, ineffable glory and inexhaustible riches
- we will be overcomers in the end

Promises like 1st Peter 5:10 (ESV):

*And after you have suffered a little while, the God of all grace, who has called you to his eternal glory in Christ, will himself restore, confirm, strengthen, and establish you.*

Promises. Like the ones He has whispered to your heart. Concrete assurances that spill over and out of Scripture like a flood. Promises that are all "yes and amen in Christ."

I dare you still. With giants in the land and doubters in the camp, I dare you to believe God. To trust He's able. To be fully convinced He'll come through.

Everything around you may seem bleak and black. But a full-hearted faith connected to God's nature and promises will sustain and carry you.

Yes, before springs begin to crack through in the external, faith will be the watering tool for springs in the internal. In fact, for most of us, God is looking to call us out of the wilderness on the inside before He calls us out of the wilderness on the outside.

*That all sounds wonderful. But just to be honest, Russ, I don't have much faith right now.*

Great. Your honesty can be good soil to start tilling from. You can cry out like the centurion did to Jesus, *"Lord, I believe. But now help my unbelief!"*[2]

From there you can break up the soil, pull the weeds, and douse water onto whatever little seeds of faith you possess. God will bring the sun and rain.

*Faith comes by hearing and hearing by the Word of God.*[3]

Soak yourself in Scripture. Immerse yourself in anointed books, teaching and worship. Then, watch your faith grow. And don't get discouraged when you don't *feel*. We walk by faith, not by sight or emotions.

You just need to know, no matter where you are in your journey, there is hope.

David. Moses. Abraham. All were given promises early in life that took a long time to come to pass. Yet during the painful wilderness season of all their confusion and crushing disappointments came faith that would yield the spiritual fathers of future generations.

Be fully convinced that God is able. He trumps your circumstances and will complete what He began. His Word is forever settled. And when we choose to trust, something even better than "the promised land" happens: *we bring glory to God.*

The ten spies were men of fear. Caleb was a man of faith. And it took him the distance.

Thus, the vital offspring of faith is patience.

> *If we already have something we don't need to hope for it. But if we look forward to something we don't yet have, me must wait* **patiently** *and* **confidently***.* (Romans 8:24-25, emphasis mine)

Caleb was confident of God's promise when he stood up to the other spies. Yet it would still be forty-five years before he received and walked in it.

His faith produced patience, a perseverance sturdy enough to endure storm, doubt, and dryness.

Same with Abraham. He waited over twenty-five years. Yet he allowed that painful waiting room to become an incubator for his faith instead of an incinerator.

James encourages us in the same manner:

> *Consider the farmers who patiently wait for the rains in the fall and in the spring. They eagerly look for the valuable harvest to ripen. You, too, must be patient.*

*...For examples of patience in suffering, dear brothers and sisters, look at the prophets who spoke in the name of the Lord. We give great honor to those who endure under suffering. For instance, you know about Job, a man of great endurance. You can see how the Lord was kind to him at the end, for the Lord is full of tenderness and mercy.* (James 5:7-8,10-11 NLT)

Faith and patience. It's the powerhouse combination and the key to receiving all God has promised.

That is what I am believing for you. I am believing you won't grow weary, bitter or sinful. Instead, as the writer of Hebrews put it, I am believing,

*You will follow the example of those who are going to inherit God's promises because of their* **faith** *and* **endurance**. (Hebrews 6:12 emphasis mine)

Let vision be the windshield. Faith and patience the two hands on the wheel.

Before you know it, Jordan will be under your tires.

o o o

So. A different spirit, backed by a whole heart, will get you through the wilderness. It will get you to the promised land. And finally, it will:

### #3: Cause you to run TO the future, not FROM IT

Forty-five years after that first spy mission, Caleb found himself in the second generation out of Egypt. This time, God's people had passed the test. Under Joshua's leadership, they moved into the land of promise and began their conquering spree. Kings from the north, south, east and west of the Jordan were all defeated.

Now, to divvy up the acres.

At this point, Caleb took a delegation from his tribe to see Joshua and reminded him what he already knew, that Caleb stood for faith when his peers stood for fear. That because of his whole heart and different spirit, God preserved Him and saw him through. That it's now time for him to inherit the land Moses promised him.

At eighty-five years old, Caleb concluded the speech with his trademark bluntness:

> So give me the hill country that the Lord promised me. You will remember that as scouts we found the descendants of Anak living there in great, walled towns. But if the Lord is with me, I will drive them out of the land just as the Lord said. (Joshua 14:12 NLT)

I can see him now. Staring longingly at the hills. Looking past Joshua even as he spoke:

(Cue the bag pipes and blue painted face of William Wallace from *Braveheart*.)

*"I have lived a long time. I have seen my fair share of ups and downs. I have known betrayal and disappointment. Delays, defeat and devastation.*
*I have known the burn of desert heat in the day and the cold shivers of night. I have fought off jackals and snakes. I have known hunger and thirst.*
*I have waited a long time. But I've trusted God. And He has seen me through.*
*Now…Give me my mountain."*

Most of us mellow as we get older. Not Caleb. Fire in his eyes just danced brighter.

At nearly ninety years of age, Caleb says, "I still have hills to take."

So do you, by the way.

A couple details here continue to reveal just how intense Caleb truly was.

First, a leader as aged and highly honored as him could have left the fighting to younger soldiers. But Caleb? Not a chance. He wasn't afraid of the Anakites or anything they could do to him. He knew God was with him.

Also notice what he says:

*"You will remember that as scouts we found the descendants of Anak living there."*

The descendants of Anak.

Anakites.

*Giants.*

The hulks so big they caused the spies of the first generation to *feel "like we were grasshoppers in our own sight."*

And now it's been forty-five years, so they've had children most likely even bigger.

Oh, and they are living in "great, walled towns."

"Yeah, you see that town?" Caleb says, shoving his gnarled finger towards the east. "The one that's heavily fortified and has the genetic monster freaks living in it? I want **that one**."

Caleb intentionally picks the land with the largest giants, and then he intentionally decides to take it on himself.

Have I mentioned I love this guy?

The man's fierce. Bear's blood boiling in his veins. A touch of crazy, for sure.

But Proverbs 18:14 tells us, *"...a healthy spirit conquers adversity."*

And conquer he did.

We can't miss this. His whole heart kept him in a future-facing mode, no matter what was behind him or before him.
The spirit of Caleb is a spirit of offense, not defense. It is a posture of leaning forward, not back.

"My righteous one will live by faith. And I take no pleasure in the one who **shrinks back**." But we do not belong to those who shrink back and are destroyed, but to those who have faith and are saved. (Hebrews 10:38-39, emphasis mine)

A whole heart will cause you to run towards the future with faith, facing the problems, dealing with the pain, and moving forward in the midst of frustration.

A Caleb spirit will stop the pity party, will shut down the self-medicating. It will inject zeal and strength in your bones, ready to face new giants, and take new mountains in the name of the Lord.

o o o

To be honest, there are many situations in life I could have handled better. I could fill up this book with all the moments I missed it.

But when my world came to a crash in the late summer of 2016, something in me activated. Even as the flames of my life were licking higher and higher into the sky, dazed or not, I sprang into action.

As mentioned in the *Grace* chapter, I somehow intuited a tangible awareness of the importance of the decision before me. Face life and the future head on or stick my head in the sand and shut down. To avoid, ignore, postpone, or even numb my pain.

Somewhere in that process, I flew to Texas to spend time at Gateway Church, to re-set my soul with a mentor and close friends.

On the second or third night in Dallas, I found myself at the home of a precious older couple from the church. They're known for the power of their intercessory prayer ministry and had adopted my friend Logan as a spiritual grandson of sorts. He held no small admiration for them and their unique ability to hear from God. They are that unicorn in the church world, deeply spiritual and prophetic and yet healthy and normal.

I walked into their home with the sensation of *Novocaine* on my soul. Yet, even in my benumbed state, I remember taking in the sights and smells of pink curtains and china everywhere, big green plants, coffee and cookies and thick, perfumed fragrances. I remember how spry and lively and hospitable they were for their age and how even as I sank into the 1950's couch, listening to them catch up with Logan, I could feel in my bones the sweet Presence of God that resided in their home.

Gail motioned and gestured with the eagerness of a child, Pat right beside her, watching his wife with silent, gentle amusement. Logan engaged naturally and it felt like we had all known each other for years, even though I just sat there in silence. Broken but content. Feeling a childlike comfort as I let their warm voices swirl around and envelop me while I stared at the floor.

After hours of what felt like a mini family reunion, Logan asked if Gail would mind praying for us. I didn't pray. I just hung my head and postured my palms towards heaven.

But as she laid her hands on me and began quietly praying in the Spirit, my insides became hot and every defense melted. I felt the serrated sword of God's Spirit and Word begin shaving off fear and agony and lies. I felt God wrap His arms around me as I shook. To this day, it remains one of the most intense encounters with God I've ever experienced.

She began speaking prophetically, blindingly accurately, into my life. Things she nor Logan would have any way of knowing. She even spoke in intimate detail about people I knew. I still have her words treasured like gold in my journal and would not trade a million dollars for one syllable.

When I had finally picked myself up off the floor, I felt like I had just traveled back from outer space. Such holy awe. I didn't speak for the rest of the night even after we left, and I think Logan understood.

Before we headed to the door, though, as I thought all my tears were dry, I saw something flash in Gail's eyes. She pointed her finger at me with sharpness and said:

"You have just been through something traumatic. But you have not run from it. You have run **towards** it. You have faced it. And the way you have handled this, God wants you to know it is a precious gift in His sight."

My head could not handle the pressure of the emotion and it dropped again as I fought back tears. But she wasn't done. She hurried out and then back into the room, now gripping an object. It was a glass crystal shaped like an apple.

Great. Maybe she *is* crazy.

"This is a gift from a dear friend," she started back. "It's glass formed from the ashes of a volcanic eruption. And I feel like God wants me to tell you, He is about to take the ashes of your pain and make something beautiful. Your pain in this season will be the platform for the next."

I want to encourage you, not on the authority of Gail's word, but on the authority of God's Word, you can move forward in His strength. His grace is enough to get you through this season and face everything in front of you. God can use even great tragedy to bring great glory.

Just look at the Cross.

And as you trust Him with your pain, embrace Isaiah 61:3:

> *To all who mourn in Israel,*
> *he will give a crown of **beauty for ashes**,*
> *a joyous blessing instead of mourning,*
> *festive praise instead of despair.*
> *In their righteousness, they will be like great oaks*
> *that the Lord has planted for his own glory. (emphasis mine)*

## Chapter Fourteen

### WHOLE HEARTED

*"As long as your heart is beating in your chest, there remains hope of a better tomorrow."–Levi Lusko*

*"Oh, give me back my joy again."–David (Psalm 51:8)*

*"Of one thing I am perfectly sure: God's story never ends with 'ashes.'"–Elisabeth Elliot*

That rainy October day really did change everything.

The revelation in that coffee booth is something I will cherish all my life.

I walked back into the office that day with the same *surroundings* but a different *spirit*. And it changed how I experienced my *season*.

Those who interacted with me could tell. That's the beautiful thing about your spirit. You carry it with you wherever you go.

See, choosing a "right spirit" means what's *inside* of you starts affecting what's *outside* instead of what's *outside* always dictating what's *inside*.

*You* start happening to *life* instead of *life* just happening to *you*. That alone is paradigm-shifting territory.

Interesting again, isn't it, that it wasn't the giants *outside* in the distant towns of that first generation that caused defeat; it was their giants *inside*. Giants of fear, doubt and sin.

God had promised, but they had panicked. They were consumed with the great walls of their enemy, when they should have given heed to the sagging walls of their spirit:

> *Like a city that is broken into and without walls is a man who has no control over his* **spirit**. (Proverbs 25:28 NASB, emphasis mine)

> However, *"A* **healthy spirit** *conquers adversity."* (Proverbs 18:14 emphasis mine)

o o o

My friend Joel once told me he's not encouraged by encouragement. He's encouraged by a new perspective.

It's not a pat on the back he needs during tough times. He asks God to give him a new mindset. A new purpose and point of view for the circumstance he's in.

As we get ready to leave this subdivision on Caleb, I pray you've been given that gift.

I hope from now until the day you die, you carry the perspective that you can't always choose what happens on the *outside*, but you can always choose what happens on the *inside*.

And *that* eventually changes *both*.

o o o

Your spirit is a choice. Plain and simple. And it will determine everything.

This truth has transformed my life.

A few years back I even paid a tattoo artist a couple hundred bucks to cut and ink "A Different Spirit" onto the flesh of my inner arm so that for the rest of my life I'd have the visible reminder that I won't always be able to choose my *season*; but I can always choose my *spirit*.

And yet, as we round this cul-de-sac and continue on into vision and towards the Promised Land of this book, we're about to shift gears. And as we shift gears, I pray the very gears of our hearts click and lock into place.

The reality is, there's intense power in the truth and fire we're diving into.

I also know in the midst of great challenge can lie great danger.

Dave Zuleger once noted, "Christians often unintentionally heap harmful expectations on one another to 'have it all together' in suffering."

If you're anything like me, you can beat yourself up pretty badly. I revel in a mountaintop experience or revelation and then become discouraged when I sink to the bottom of the ocean again only a couple days later.

Don't you wish there was a button you could push to keep the bad days away? To never sin or stumble again? To keep your emotions and perspective continually aligned with God's?

Until heaven, we are faltering humans, wrapped in flesh. Fortunately, God knows our frame, keeps in mind that, *"we are but dust."*

So, if you feel fired up to choose a different spirit and allow God to fuel you with faith and perspective, prayer answered.

But if you feel pressure to "perform" or "have it all together" then let me remind you, no one gets it right the whole way.

No one walks through any season without mistakes. No one suffers perfectly.

I sure haven't.

Nor have any of our heroes in Scripture.

We talked a lot about Abraham's faith. Read again this verse I included about him earlier:

*Abraham **never wavered** in believing God's promise. In fact, his faith grew stronger, and in this he brought glory to God. He was fully convinced that God is able to do whatever he promises.* (emphasis mine)

The verse basically says Abraham suffered perfectly, that he *"never wavered."*

The only problem is, and I say this respectfully, *that's not true.*

Yes, he was a man of audacious, self-denying faith. He continually stepped out into the unknown. His whole life was a journey of trust. He raised a knife to sacrifice the dearest portion of his heart. He kept trusting against all disappointment in God's promises. He truly is the father of our faith.

Yet we also have recorded times when he doubted. We read of backpedaling and lying to foreign leaders out of fear.

We stumble uncomfortably across verses revealing moments of impatience where he took matters in his own hands. Case in point, the awkward story of Sarah convincing him to sleep with her maidservant to hurry up the process of an heir.

So then why does Scripture say he *"never wavered?"*

I believe one reason is because life is not defined by our *periodic stumbles,* but by the *overall posture* of our heart. Abraham's posture continually leaned forward in abandoned trust and confidence in God, *even in* his human moments of disappointment and disillusionment.

The other reason, the even more exciting reason, the reason that brings me to joyful tears, is I believe when God writes Abraham's story, or your story and my story, for that matter, He writes it in *grace.*

Steep your soul like tea into the following words:

> *He made known his ways to Moses,*
> *his deeds to the people of Israel:*
> *The Lord is compassionate and gracious,*
> *slow to anger, abounding in love.*
> *He will not always accuse,*

*nor will he harbor his anger forever;*
*he does not treat us as our sins deserve*
*or repay us according to our iniquities.*

*For as high as the heavens are above the earth,*
*so great is his love for those who fear him;*
*as far as the east is from the west,*
*so far has he removed our transgressions from us.*
*As a father has compassion on his children,*
*so the Lord has compassion on those who fear him;*
*or he knows how we are formed,*
*he remembers that we are dust. (Psalm 103:7-14)*

God's default nature is grace. It's who He is.

The same is true of his pen.

As he writes, the ink drips with mercy. It splashes with grace.

It tends to downgrade failures to footnotes, celebrate steps of obedience, and highlight the victories of trust and surrender.

In case you find that a bit optimistic, take time to re-read the faith almanac of Hebrews 11.

If you're familiar with the stories of Samson, Rahab and others, it's honestly shocking they even made it into the Bible. Much less into the hall of fame faith chapter. Much less in a positive light.

One would assume the gross moments of David's story would at least earn an asterisk by his name.

But no.

When God writes the story of our lives, He writes it in grace.

You can't look at Noah or Gideon or even Abraham (or you or me, for that matter), without realizing we serve a God that oozes compassion.

He demonstrates a preposterous amount of mercy with you and I. And His goodness fills the cracks of our shortcomings as we trust and follow Him.

There was only One who suffered perfectly. There is only One in whom we place our trust. There is only One upon whom we set our gaze.

Our majestic, wonderful Savior.

Jesus.

How I walk through the valley matters, yes. But my hope is not in how I walk through the valley. My hope and tust comes from knowing there's a great Shepherd with me *in* the valley.

The reason we can know our story has a good ending is because there's a Hero in it. And *thank God* that hero is not me.

No, *our story* is actually a secondary role in the *Hero's story*. And He wins.

I love Caleb. He was a warrior, through and through.

Yet I believe just like every character and story of Scripture, he is merely a signpost to Jesus.

*Caleb* was a foreshadowing of *Christ*.

And his *different spirit* was just a hint at what we could have in the *Holy Spirit*.

At the end of the day what I need more than anything is to experience a dynamic, overflowing relationship with the Holy Spirit.

At the end of the day, I need to stop trying so hard to be the hero in my story, and instead fix my eyes on the Hero who has already promised victory.

Jesus, the ultimate Wilderness Warrior.

The One our eyes are on. The One who is going to lead us through.

Our giants may be big, but Christ is bigger.

He comforted His disciples with these words: *"I have told you these things, so that **in me you may have peace**. In this world you will have trouble. But **take heart! I have overcome the world**."*(John 16:33, emphasis mine)

No matter what the past or present may hold, His shoulders are broad enough for our burdens and blame. His blood rich enough to wash all our transgressions downstream. His perfect work on our behalf forever settled in the universe.

I've set some pen and words to depict the wilderness warrior that is Caleb. But let's take in a glimpse of that eternal Lion out of Judah's tribe:

*Then I saw heaven opened, and a white horse was standing there. Its rider was named Faithful and True, for he judges fairly and wages a righteous war. His eyes were like flames of fire, and on his head were many crowns. A name was written on him that no one understood except himself. He wore a robe dipped in blood, and his title was the Word of God. The armies of heaven, dressed in the finest of pure white linen, followed him on white horses. From his mouth came a sharp sword to strike down the nations. He will rule them with an iron rod. He will release the fierce wrath of God, the Almighty, like juice flowing from a winepress. On his robe at his thigh was written this title: King of all kings and Lord of all lords.* (Revelation 19:11-16 NLT)

It's *this Warrior* who fights for us, loves us, defends us, strengthens us, and carries us.

Our strength. Our King. Our redemption. Our Leader.

The Warrior of all warriors.

We'll make it through because our hand is in His, and He never lets go.

While we're in the desert, tempted to look down, tempted to look to the side, even tempted to gaze too long within, we set our affections, hopes, and dreams back on the Person of Jesus.

Yes, while everything crumbles like sandcastles around us, we fix our eyes like flint towards the Rock of ages.

He and He alone *"is the author and perfector of our faith."*

○ ○ ○

And so here we are.

Full circle on this man named Caleb, and how his life can change our life.

As the waitress bussed the empty dishes that day at J. Christopher's, fire was beginning to crawl into the marrow of my spine.

Caleb's story. His spirit.

I felt the Lord showing me the connection of the whole heartedness that fueled him.

Other revelation and meat from the last few chapters came later on.

But one last arrow was about to shoot ripples of heat and hope through my soul.

Still processing Caleb's spirit and whole heart, I adjusted my empty coffee mug to the right corner of the table, and let my eyes settle in deeper to Joshua 14 where Caleb is giving his speech to Joshua forty years after that spy mission. The words in bold below leapt off the page and into my heart:

*"Now then, just as the Lord promised, he has kept me alive for forty-five years since the time he said this to Moses, while Israel moved about in the wilderness. So here I am today, eighty-five years old!* **I am still as**

*strong today as the day Moses sent me out; I'm just as vigorous to go out to battle now as I was then."* (Joshua 14:10-12, emphasis mine)

Forty-five years later. Four and a half more decades of hardening battle and difficulty and deserts.

But just as strong. Just as agile. Fire still in his eyes.

He came out the other side even better.

And isn't that what happened to our Master as well?

Do I really need to remind us even Jesus went through the wilderness?

I'll skip past elaboration of all the powerful parallels.

How, as discussed in Chapter 2, the Israelites entered the wilderness right after their Old Testament *"baptism"* of the Red Sea and Jesus entered the wilderness immediately after his *baptism* by John in the Jordan.

Or how the Jews spent *forty years* in the wilderness and Jesus spent *forty days*.

Or all the quotations and allusions made by Jesus from this Mosaic period while he was in the desert.

No, I want to hurry past all of that and exclamate the very first sentence we read after Jesus left the wilderness:

*Then Jesus returned to Galilee, **filled with the Holy Spirit's power**.* (Luke 4:14, emphasis mine)

I don't care your denominational background. That is where you shout.

And in that moment, I sensed the Holy Spirit speak as strongly to my heart as I have ever felt:

*"Russ, not only did Caleb not lose his life in the wilderness, he didn't lose an ounce of his strength. And neither will you. Not only are you not going to **die** in this season, you're going to live to **thrive** in the next one. On the other side of this wilderness is not less joy, but more joy. More joy, more wisdom, more strength, more integrity and more blessing. Trust me. Choose a right spirit. And just wait and see what's on the other side."*

And that's when my eyes went from glassy red to bleeding tears as I felt the fierce Presence of God's love and power sit down at the booth with me. Churning things within me. Healing me with octane courage and lifted perspective. Putting gale-force wind back in the dilapidated sails of my spirit.

I believe that's what He longs to do in *you*. If I could be so bold to speak straight to your heart:

You're not going to die in this valley. You will live to climb another mountain.

Waiting on the other side of this season is not a sea-sick, anemic you. No, it will be a stronger you. A wiser you. A more Christlike you.

Let me remind you what's beyond the desert if we don't faint—verdant pastures of the promised land.

Desert mirages may have washed away your vision. But the land is still there. And you will make it.

Even Jesus needed the wilderness. And He came out the other side even stronger.

So will you.

Don't wait until you're in Jordan to lift your head. Lift it now.

Wash your face. Square your shoulders. Focus your eyes.

Walk like a king, for the King is in you.

Remember, you can't choose your *season,* but you can always choose your *spirit.*

Oh, the power of a different spirit.

More than that—oh, the power of the Holy Spirit.

The Spirit of truth and strength and fire.

I encourage you to find a private space as you close this chapter.

Get alone with God. Cry out to Him.

Receive fresh strength and power from the Helper called to your side. He is waiting to strengthen, renew and refresh you from the inside out.

Lift up the horn of your life and ask God to fill it with fresh oil.

*"But because my servant Caleb has a different spirit and follows me wholeheartedly, I will bring him into the land."*

## WILDERNESS WRITINGS

(Notes from the Section—What stood out?)

_____

_____

_____

_____

_____

_____

_____

_____

_____

_____

_____

_____

_____

_____

_____

_____

_____

## DESERT DECISIONS

(Future Applications—What steps are you going to take?)

_____

_____

_____

_____

_____

_____

_____

_____

_____

_____

_____

_____

_____

_____

_____

*the*

# VEAL

*of*

# VISION

## Chapter Fifteen

### SOUP THAT STEALS:

*How Vision Creates Strength "God gives us a vision of
the future so we can endure the pain of the present."
–Rich Wilkerson Jr.*

*"The most pathetic person in the world is someone
who has sight but no vision."–Helen Keller*

*"Leave the broken, irreversible past in God's hands, and step
out into the invincible future with Him."–Oswald Chambers*

It is awkward to stare for hours at a detailed
statue of a naked man.

Yet over eight million people a year visit the Galleria
dell'Accademia in Florence to do just that. They stand, sit, even
kneel at the foot of Michelangelo's *David*. I never understood all
the fuss. Then I went to Italy.

After a few surreal days of boating through the dreamy
channels of Venice, we made our way to the arts-soaked world
of Florence. Cheese, wine and statues swirled around us like the
crows of the Coliseum. I had felt like James Bond in Venice, soon

to be a gladiator (with a taste for gelato) in Rome, but currently an artisan in Tuscany.

*Veni, vidi, vici.*

In all reality, I thought I'd seen enough statues and paintings to last a lifetime. Then I took an espresso and museum map into the Gallery. At the end of a hallway, time stopped. I stood there, dwarfed beneath the seventeen-foot masterpiece of stone that burned Michelangelo's name into the stars.

It was breathtaking. My dad went to work with his camera by instinct, tourists buzzed and gasped, and teenage girls took carefully crafted selfies in front of the colossal nude to edit later for Instagram. I sat down and took it in. The sheer size and precision to detail overwhelmed my senses.

*David* has an interesting history, though. The marble block was originally excavated in 1464 by another sculptor. Work began on the stone but was abandoned at least twice. Problems were found with the quality of the rock and the tediousness of the work.

Then Michelangelo came along and saw the potential. He saw the future, and then he created it.

Just like the Promised Land waited forty years for a people with vision to enter, the marble waited forty years for someone with vision to turn it into the masterpiece it was always destined to become.

Legend has it, before he began sculpting *David*, Michelangelo would sit for hours staring at the marble statue. When asked what he was doing, he would respond "working."

He was cultivating a vision before cutting into a stone.

After completing another masterpiece, he famously remarked, "I saw the angel in the marble and carved until I set him free."

As we continue our journey through the wilderness, let me ask you, what do you *see*? Is there an angel appearing in the marble?

What are you moving towards in your heart? What kind of future are you envisioning?

Is the pain of the desert so deep you can't help but keep looking at the difficulties?

If so, I pray by the end of this section your confession will become Paul's confession:

> *We don't look at the troubles we can see now; rather, we fix our gaze on things that cannot be seen. For the things we see now will soon be gone, but the things we cannot see will last forever."*[1]

I pray your eyes become a chisel, carving into the dry, stony confusion of this season.

Truth is, the wilderness is often the time when vision is lowest. Yet it's the time when vision needs to be highest. Vision in the desert isn't a luxury, it's a necessity.

o o o

Vision is an inspiring word.

It's also life-and-death material.

As usual, Solomon sets it plain: *"Where there is no vision, the people perish."* (Proverbs 29:18 KJV)

Lack of vision actually causes *death*. Death in *every area*.

Think about it. If you don't have strong vision for your marriage, it won't last. When feelings fluctuate, there must be more than butterflies. There must be a covenant tied to a preferred future for a lasting love and family.

The same principle drives finances, health, everything.

Why? The crux of it can be found in the ESV translation of the same verse: "Where there is no prophetic vision, the people *cast off restraint.*"

With no golden horizon to beckon me forward, I'm prone to just switch off the GPS. To wander, derail, eventually compromise.

But the more I value the future, the more value I'll place in my decisions in the present. The focused stock I put in *what's coming* determines how I invest and protect *what's now*.

Vision, therefore, is what produces strength.

Take your guilty-pleasure snack, for example. Let's say it's a Snickers bar riding shotgun all day, tempting you, taunting you.

However, you know tonight you'll be dining at your all-time favorite restaurant, lingering long over your dream dishes. Bacon-wrapped filet mignon, truffle butter dripping off the sides. Lobster risotto. Maybe a Cheesecake Factory bastion of chicken pasta and *Adam's Peanut Butter Cup Fudge Ripple Cheesecake.*

*Sing to me, Adam.*

Either way, chances are you'll have the grit to skip every second-rate snack as you walk the red carpet towards your evening culinary dreams.

Or....

That week includes lackluster take-out and grey cold cuts birthed in grocery chains. You're going to cave and indulge, aren't you? Why not, right?

"Why not?" is the spirit that flourishes when we lack strong vision. If there's not a "great meal" to look forward to, we "cast off restraint" and merely react to whatever's staring us in the face.

When dating, if we don't have strong vision for that magical wedding day and the feeling of entering marriage in a healthy, guilt-free, God-honoring way, we will "cast off restraint" when it comes to our purity and emotional health in the present.

If we haven't cultivated a compelling financial vision of a generous and debt-free landscape, then we will "cast off restraint" and "devour all we have," living budget-less and unintentional. We'll just eat up our money on the way to nowhere.

If we haven't captured a vision for our health, we'll ride a nutritional merry-go-round. We'll "cast off restraint" and opt for quasi-foods cheaply exchanged through window squares and *Reese's* wrappers will pile up into mountains of condemnation on the coffee table (just me?). Instead of prioritizing our energy and vitality to fulfill God's call, we'll "live to eat" instead of "eat to live." We'll simply lack the motivation necessary to bypass the cheap fats and sugars that call our names in the moments of convenience. Bring on the kale chips.

Marriage. Finances. Health.

Passions. Career. Parenting.

Across the board, the principle applies.

*"Where there is no [prophetic] vision, the people cast off restraint."*

So how would you assess your vision tank right now? Empty? Full? A quarter tank and beginning to leak?

Do you have *spiritual* vision?

Do you have a vision of the kind of man or woman you want to be? The kind of intimacy you desire to enjoy with God? The level of passion for His Word and Presence?

How much like Jesus do you want to become? What kind of eternal impact are you hungry to leave behind?

A strong vision for who you're becoming can funnel the choices you make and the life you live. A strong vision for where you're going will put steel in the spirit right where you are.

Truth is, one of my burning hopes in writing this book is to fill you with white-hot vision while you're in the wilderness.

I know if you can onboard some vision for what's beyond this season, that will cause hope to surge in your soul, giving you the strength you need to make it to the other side.

The Promised Land is ahead. Can you catch a glimpse?

○ ○ ○

It cannot be emphasized enough—vision is even more important in the wilderness.

It's when our souls are emptiest that we're most tempted to make life decisions not informed by vision. Choices fueled by temporary frustrations instead of future hopes.

God knows I have.

And so did a guy named Esau.

It's circa 1873 BC and Rachel and Isaac finally conceive.

You might recall the whole exodus story occurs right after Genesis ends. God made an oath to Abraham, promising to provide him an heir and change history through his family tree. People, land, worldwide blessing, *the whole shabang*. Isaac is Abraham's boy, ticket to said oath, the son of promise through which the nations and the true-blue *Son* of promise will eventually come.

Isaac is also your average Joe, faults and all. He and his wife's opposing favoritism towards their now-grown twin-boys is thinly veiled, if at all. Esau, red, hairy and made for hunting, brings back the wild game favorites that makes Pops proud. Jacob picks herbs and writes poems, more than happy to be doted on by mom.

Dysfunction abounds in the home. Tensions run high. And the birthright blessings heading Esau's way only serve daily helpings to the elephants in the corner. This ancient privilege will endow Esau with family leadership, a special paternal blessing (later to be hijacked by Jacob as well) and double the inheritance. Talk about hitting the lottery just for coming out first.

But alas, one fateful day changes it all.

Isaac is at his nightly post, rocking chair facing west, Rachel humming and knitting on the right. Jacob mans the kitchen, peppers sliced and seasonings measured, soup almost done.

Esau, in contrast, has been in the tree stand since before sunrise, bow drawn, quiver emptying. And missing his targets.... All. Day. Long.

Defeated, frustrated and starving, he returns. His weekend of bow-hunting has turned out emptier than his stomach. *Yeah, but I bet momma's boy has a full belly right now. Bet it's been a fried artichoke and carrot cake kind of night for those two. Tough, tough life....*

Frustration boils over to a familiar resentment by the time Esau makes it home. He slams the door behind him and throws his bow against the wall. It hits harder than he'd meant, sending arrows flying into the ottoman. He's stopped in his tracks, though, by what he smells from the kitchen. Aromatics of meat and spice crash over him in salty, Mediterranean waves.

He glances to the corner. A table is set for one in the family dining area, solitary wooden bowl by solitary wooden spoon. Steam wafts in from the kitchen and out walks a grinning Jacob, licking a single finger. *You have got to be kidding me....*

I'll let you read the rest for yourself:

*One day when Jacob was cooking some stew, Esau arrived home from the wilderness exhausted and hungry. Esau said to Jacob, "I'm starved! Give me some of that red stew!" (This is how Esau got his other name, Edom, which means "red.")*
*"All right," Jacob replied, "but trade me your rights as the firstborn son."*

*"Look, I'm dying of starvation!" said Esau. "What good is my birthright to me now?"*
*But Jacob said, "First you must swear that your birthright is mine." So Esau swore an oath, thereby selling all his rights as the firstborn to his brother, Jacob.*
*Then Jacob gave Esau some bread and lentil stew. Esau ate the meal, then got up and left. He showed contempt for his rights as the firstborn.* (Genesis 25:29-34 NLT)

Amazing. Just like that, Esau traded his *future*. For *soup*.

The family blessing, influence and wealth was ahead of him, and in a moment, he shrugged it off for beans and lentils.

Before we get judgy, let's be honest. We do, too.

We trade the health and appearance we crave for fiteen-minute meals.

We trade quality time with our Creator for a few more minutes of sleep.

We trade financial freedom and opportunity for deals we can't resist.

We trade the preciousness of purity for a moment of pleasure.

We trade what we want most for what we want right now.[2]

We all make bad trades, some worse than others. But never are bad trades made more than *in the wilderness*.

Hundreds of years after the journey of the children of Israel, King David looked back on their time and wrote:

*But they soon forgot what he had done and did not wait for his plan to unfold.* **In the desert they gave in to their craving**; *in the wilderness they put God to the test.* (Psalm 106:13-14, emphasis mine)

In the place between deliverance and destiny, the Israelites burned with craving, and it ended up burning them in return.

Be very, very careful when you're hungry in soul. Very, very careful when you feel empty. You'll make bad trades. You'll trade great things for okay things. Permanent things for passing fancies. Birthrights for Chef Boyardee. A calling for a crockpot. Destiny dreams for desert deals.

When you're hungry, in body or soul, everything looks *better*. That deal. That extra sleep. That vacation. *Someone else's spouse.*

I mean, come on. It's bad enough to trade in your future for food. But it was *soup*. Not honey-bacon mac-and-cheese. Not hot molten chocolate souffle. No porterhouse. Just soup.

Can we all agree? Even at its best, soup is just *okay*....

But again, it says he arrived home *"from the wilderness"* and he was *"exhausted and hungry."* In that condition, everything is amplified isn't it? Every emotion. Every temptation.

And the enemy knows it. That's why every desert season has its own *soup de jour*.

The children of Israel had it.

Esau had it.

Even Jesus had it. He prayed and fasted for forty days. It's there, *in the wilderness*, that the enemy whips up three different bowls of temptation. All a la carte. (Unlike Esau and the children of Israel, however, Jesus sent every dish back to the kitchen.)

Might as well write it down: The enemy will present a spicy bowl of soup for every bland season.

And the enemy knows you well enough to know just how to season it.

Consider Esau's particular bowl. Interesting that the text tells us the stew was red. We are told only verses earlier that Esau was red-haired. Then we find out Esau was later nicknamed "Edom," meaning, you guessed it, *red.*

Call it a stretch if you want. But I don't think those details are coincidence, and coincidence or not, they point to a fundamental truth. The enemy studies us, knows us and tempts us with our greatest personal cravings. His strategy in our dry times is that we will default. Then once we default, to *define* us by those moments, in order to ultimately *destroy* us by them. It's the plan every time.

Fortunately, *"we are not unaware of his schemes."*[3]

Reminders don't hurt, though.

So, remember—he knows your family's history and he knows your DNA. He knows your chemistry. He knows your biography. He knows the way you screwed up the last time and the thirty times before that. He knows the lies you're tempted to believe, the people you're tempted to listen to, the moments you're most susceptible, and the prime triggers of your flesh.

In my life, I've found the enemy seems to put the bowl in front of me and wait. Wait and wait. Until I give a little taste. And then the more I taste it the more I want it.

Notice as well that Esau's consequences didn't catch up with him that day. They rarely do.

I can only speak for me, but I know I've had certain bowls of soup I've dabbled with too long. Relationships in my past and harmless habits I knew I was to let go of, but I kept picking that bowl up and putting it back down. Picking it up and putting it down. And it cost me.

You have anything like that?

Every day we must choose to keep destiny in front of us.

I don't know what your "bowl of stew" is. Maybe it's too many glasses of wine at night. Maybe it's porn, romance novels or serial dating. Maybe it's numbing yourself in relationships, work, or social media. Perhaps it's settling where you shouldn't settle or shutting down emotionally.

See, Esau was a man of spiritual apathy but carnal ferocity. And in his deepest moment of loneliness and emptiness, he defaulted. He downed that bowl of red stew and I bet he even licked the bottom. After a few minutes of pleasure, though, regret was the only thing remaining for a long, long time.[4]

We need to remember the smell of soup can remain long after the taste is gone. We need to remember a mere sampling of the bowl in one season can become a lingering bondage in the next. We need to remember what the sweaty, yelling preacher said about sin is true: "it'll take you further than you ever wanted to go, cost you more than you ever thought it would cost, and stay longer than you ever thought it would stay."

The smells of the bowl might be calling your name even now. Maybe screaming in your face is more like it. But I'm writing this chapter because I want the veal of your vision to become bigger than the veal in your spoon.

If you don't, you just might block your future with a bowl.

o o o

Sometimes the fragrance of the bowl is made up of the flavors of the past.

We saw earlier how the children of Israel *"gave in to their craving."*

What exactly were they craving?

We read:

> *"If only the Lord had killed us back in* **Egypt,"** *they moaned.* **"There we sat around pots filled with meat and ate all the bread we wanted.** *But now you have brought us into this wilderness to starve us all to death."* (Exodus 16:3 NLT, emphasis mine)

They were craving Egypt. They were longing for the *past.*

This moment occurs six weeks after their deliverance from Pharoah.

Incredible. Less than two months ago they were *slaves*. Back-breaking work from sunup to sundown. No future or freedom. Only shackles. Whipped and beaten and dehumanized, with no end in sight.

Now they're free. God has performed show-stopping miracles. They have a new name and identity. The Promised Land is only a few mile markers out.

Yet they are so discouraged and hungry, the past actually begins to look better than the future.

Ever been there?

Sentimental for a season when you were a slave?

For an uber-nostalgic soul like mine, there's a single line from the prophet Ezekiel that haunts me. The prophet warns a sinful, stubborn people of their impending judgment, spiking the gavel with this statement:

*"You won't think back on Egypt with stars in your eyes."*
(Ezekiel 23:27 MSG)

Do you have any stars in your eyes for Egypt? Any tender, sympathetic glances towards sin? Any reminiscing over seasons God delivered you out of?

Here's the truth. Without strong vision, when your soul feels hollow your heart will stay stuck in the past, often with rose-tinted glasses. And that is a future-killer, for sure.

Your life simply can't move forward if your feet are facing backward.

But I believe God *can* give you vision, vision strong enough to unstick you from the past and decimate any delusions about your bowl in the present.

Vision will fill you with a great hunger for the greater things ahead, the future and goodness God has promised, just beyond the horizon.

Maybe you don't feel very confident about the future right now. Say this out loud anyway:

> *I remain confident of this:*
> *I will see the goodness of the Lord in the land of the living.*[5]

We read in Hebrews that Jesus, *"for the joy awaiting Him, endured...."*

Through vision, Jesus passed on the bowl. Now the grave has been opened and the universe rearranged.

As we learned, Caleb kept vision alive in the desert and, unlike his peers, took his rightful place across the Jordan. He passed on the bowl and inherited the land.

Sadly, Esau had an incredible destiny, too. He could have been the heir to usher in the Hero of the world and live out his days in the shade of God's smile and blessings, his name forever etched in the legacy to come. If he'd only slowed down long enough to cool his emotions and set vision back in front of his weary eyes, maybe he could've mustered the strength to pass on the bowl as well instead of passing on his future.

I don't know what the enemy's got simmering for you, but you can pass.

Let's commit. Steak over soup every time.

## Chapter Sixteen

# DEATH BY DISTRACTION:
### *How Vision Creates Focus*

*"March on, my soul; be strong!"–Judges 5:21*

*"Your life is controlled by what you focus on."–Tony Robbins*

*"The successful warrior is the average man,*
*with laser-like focus."–Bruce Lee*

D e s e r t   o r   n o t ,   v i s i o n   i s   a   n u c l e a r   f o r c e .

As discussed, vision gives strength. Without it we "cast off restraint" and choose "bowls" over blessings. Embracing it, however, produces restraint instead of regret.

Vision also provides focus. Focus for the season and focus for the day to day.

I'll tell you a secret.

I used to be obsessed with Martial Arts.

Not interested. Obsessed.

I bought every Bruce Lee film ever made, ate short grain brown rice every meal to enhance my *chi"*[1] levels, and practiced my strikes and forms for hours every day. Even though I was only a middle-schooler, I studied Eastern philosophy like a madman and bought beginner books on Korean and Chinese.

To this day Colt swears I had an Asian accent when he met me. To this day Colt exaggerates.

Humor me, though, as I relate one of my favorite Martial Arts career "highlights."

See, I was a proud member of a Tae Kwon Do traveling tournament team.

I know, right?

On this particular day, I capped off the demonstration by breaking three boards on fire. Yes, you read correctly. *On fire….*

Now, we won't discuss the actual ease of this particular feat, the embarrassing fragility of these planks (I'm almost certain I saw someone sneeze near one once and the board exploded, but I can't prove it), or how we placed pennies between the boards to help the physics.
The point is, you should be impressed.

Anyways, tournament day arrived. Adrenaline and Gatorade shot through my adolescent body as I waited my turn to shine.
I saw it all in my mind. I saw my hand slice through the wood and fire like a samurai of old, invoking the cheers of parents and the gasps of peers. I was already looking forward

to watching it back in slow motion the next morning over toast and jelly.

Only problem, the photographers—my *parents*—had not yet arrived.

I glanced impatiently towards the door over and over. Time was ticking and I was next. I adjusted and readjusted my purple belt, looked over in awe at the Korean student cutting flips on the mat, and then looked back over at—

Ah! Right there! My precious mom and dad, over in the top corner of the bleachers. I had somehow missed them. I smiled and waved, but they didn't smile or wave back. That's weird.

*Andddd*…they didn't have the camera out yet.

Subtly, I began to motion with small, polite nods of my head towards the direction of their camera case.

They didn't move.

My head twitches became bigger. I began to articulate with my face as well, head tilted, lips drawn in on themselves, eyebrows raised high in you-better-hurry contempt.
Still nothing. Only a slight look of confusion beginning to appear on their faces. And I was about to walk to the middle of the gym and change Martial Arts history, *undocumented*.
Subtlety was gone. I started making wild camera charades with my hands, eyes wide and pleading.

What were they *doing*?!

Now I had their attention. My dad stood to his feet and shoved his palms in the air in one great, big, violent shrug.

I gave a last disapproving glare and let it linger. Then I shook my head in frustration, walked forward and did my magic anyways.

Afterwards the inquisition began:

"Great job, son! You sure–"

"Thanks…. But mom! Dad! Why wouldn't you get your camera out to record?!"

"Son, we did…why were *you* screaming at that random couple in the corner?"

Yes, 7th grade. The year I discovered I needed glasses.

Funny as it might be, my blurry vision that day affected me. It caused me to focus my attention in the wrong direction, creating frustration for myself and others. It also got me nowhere.

Once glasses, then contacts, then LASIK (thank God) filled my eyes with clear vision again, I knew where to look and where not to.

Focus, we discover, is the equal and powerful handmaid of vision.

I believe it was Andy Stanley who lamented the tragedy of when "our rearview mirror becomes bigger than our windshield." When we believe our best days and moments are all behind us and we're longing for the past more than leaning towards the future. That's the day our soul begins to die.

So, as we ride through the Sahara, we're going to stretch out that curved, laminated glass in front of us and breathe and sleeve-wipe until we at least make out shrubs in the distance. There has to be some rays of vision rising in the horizon.

But if the windshield is vision, the steering wheel is *focus.*

Focus drives you to where you're going.

The vision of shimmering diamonds *tomorrow* captures the heart of the archeologist, fueling the focus to put hand to spade *today.*

Thus, if God's beginning to fill your heart with vision for a season beyond this pain, and I pray He is, what's your focus for this season?

Usually, the more external the vision, the more obvious the focus.

If it's paying off debt in six months, the daily budget and spending focus becomes pretty apparent. If it's a ripped six-pack in Tahiti this July, well, let's throw out the sugar and get to the crunches.

Other times the focus is more of an internal posture.

Late summer of 2015, when my hero and pastor moved to the other side of the country, I felt the weight of the church sink deep into my shoulder blades. By instinct, in that season I focused on keeping myself spiritually full, made my presence and leadership as available to staff as I could, and began driving our current values and culture as intentionally as ever before.
Not too profound, and things I should do all along, I suppose. But the laser focus served me well.

For a while.

Within a few months, seeds of deep frustration were making flowerbeds of poison ivy in my spirit. I was striving and pulling and pushing, with nothing to show but splinters and thorns. And then one call with a Yoda-figure in my life recalculated my perspective. I still remember the velvety assuredness of his words:

"Son, there's new leadership and vision now and things are changing. Until God shows you what's next, it's time to stop fighting for what you want and be faithful in what God's asked."

He might as well have jerked the steering wheel from my hands. That U-turn of focus salvaged my sanity and permitted me to lean into a new mindset for that season.

No more fighting and striving.

Simple, humble faithfulness. That became the focus.

I want you to know, God not only imparts vision for the future; He grants strategies and focus for the present.

He did it for kings in the Old Testament and His followers in the New Testament. He's done it for me and He'll do it for you.

In Scripture, we see a God who delights when people come to him for help. Likewise, we see Him displeased when kings and prophets don't "inquire of the Lord" to know His heart and plan on serious matters.

This is good news. We don't have to beg. God desires to help us even more than we desire to be helped.

If you feel like you're in the dark as to what your focus should be, let this promise enter your heart:

*If you need wisdom, ask our generous God, and he will give it to you. He will not rebuke you for asking.* (James 1:5 NLT)

I love the added assurance He won't rebuke or be frustrated with me for asking.

At times I worry I might be a nuisance to God. How insulting that must be to His Father's heart. Like any decent earthly dad, but to the nth degree, He loves me and aches to teach and guide me as His child. To give me a new course direction where I need it. A new anthem, even.

I want to say like David, *"My heart is stirred by a noble theme."*[2]

Late into every November, I begin to ask God for a theme for the next year. Sometimes it's just a word, a verse, or a thought.

How clarifying, how invigorating, when God stirs our heart with a new theme. With a fresh focus. With a lifting and energizing perspective.

So, ask! Our Father delights to help and guide His kids.

I remember asking God for very specific guidance one weekend. I was about to return from my time away after my desert crash of 2016. As eager as I was to re-engage, I was about to wade back into some rather wonky, complicated situations, both relationally and ministerially. The thought of it brought a great deal of anxiety to my heart. I needed a game plan. Friday morning, I asked God to give me one.

That night I stood in the kitchen of some dear friends, Amanda and Jose. Their kids are my god kids. Most of the family asleep, we talked long over the season, the comfort of long friendship mellowing out some of my inner tension. And then without warning, the tone of Amanda's voice changed. I took another sip of Lacroix and lifted my elbow off the island. I saw it in her eyes. Strength began to enter the room as she talked, and then it escalated. I felt it, that familiar divine shift as the words poured forth, as if from some invisible sink, direct and unbroken. I quickly sensed her words weren't so much *her* words.

"I really believe this is your approach for the next few months…."

My thirsty spirit received it like water.

The next day, a lifelong friend called from Dallas.

"I've been praying," he started. "I'm not trying to be weird or speak out of place, but I feel like God dealt with me about your next season and the strategy He wants to impart to you. I felt like He shared with me that you are to…."

It would be hard to describe the confidence instilled in me that weekend.

The two "words" locked together in perfect harmony, creating a new compass deep inside.

Paul reminds us, *"By the mouth of two or three witnesses every word shall be established."* (2 Corinthians 13:1 NKJV)

By the confirmation of these encouragements, God implanted a profound strength and focus onto my mind. Insecurity gave way to boldness.

Yes,*"…a word in season, how good it is!"* (Proverbs 15:23 ESV)

Words in season. They're both meat and map for the dark days.

I believe there's a word in season for you. A divinely given compass.

We find this through time with Him, in His Word and through His Spirit.

And many times God will speak or confirm what we sense through a God-filled believer. I don't know your background. I don't know if you're freaked out by the prophetic or even familiar with it.

*Pssst.* Some Christians are *weird.* I get that.

God knows I've seen the goofy and the garbage.

But while I'm exhorted to "test everything," I'm also commanded not to "despise prophecy." (1 Thessalonians 5:20-21) That is, when a human being allows the Spirit of God to use them to deliver a specific encouragement or guidance.

I'm fortunate to have a handful of normal, balanced friends who happen to flow in the genuine gifts of the prophetic. And I have to tell you, when the road is steep, I'll take that over rubies and diamonds.

If you need a word in season, knock until the door opens.

The Captain of heaven still gives battle plans to the soldiers who ask, and I for one am grateful.

o o o

While we seek and discern what a focus for this season might be, I can immediately help us understand what our focus is *not*.

Our focus should definitely *not* be on the things we can't control.

The extent to which we try to control people and circumstances is the extent to which we experience anxiety and stress. It's also fruitless.

It's even quite ironic, if you think about it, that the things we have *total* control over—our spirit, our devotional life, our disciplines, our attitude, our response, our decisions—are the things we often focus on the least. Meanwhile, the things we have *no* control over—other people's opinions, other people's actions, the economy, the diagnosis, what the future might bring—tend to be the things we focus on the most.

Let's change that, shall we?

I'll tell you a second secret.

I used to be a Manager at a clothing store called The Buckle.

It's a mid-to-higher end eclectic retail with nearly a hundred brands, free alteration, a lay-away program, custom-fit-jean experience, the whole nines. Ah, I can still see the hole punches in my Buckle primo card now....

The buzz was real. Oh, and if you were a pastor and didn't shop there, turn in your resignation now.

It was the place to be.

Unless someone greedy and inexperienced "helped" you, that is. In that case you might still have scars. Say it with me, even as the painful memories arise, *"No, thank you, I'm just looking...."*

I learned a great deal during my time with the company. A lot about leadership, organization, sales, conflict resolution, every John Maxwell quote you'll ever see on Facebook, you know, the good stuff.

One simple exercise stands out above the rest. I picked it up from a young hotshot who took over during my last year. He was red-blooded and cocky, and I liked him a good bit. He echoed the corporate disdain for excuses, bemoaning above all else the forbidden phrase, "the mall is dead today...."

"All a state of mind," he'd remind us. "And you set the tone by your language and energy for the day."

One day in particular, he was rather bothered by the chorus of complaints. He called a meeting, had each of us pull out a piece of paper and pen, and instructed us to draw a line through it. We labeled the right side "Controllables" and the left side "Uncontrollables."

We started on the left.

"Okayyyy." He took a robust gulp of his vitamin water and stared us down, tapping his beaded bracelet with a Bic pen. "What are some things we *can't* control?"

Answers flowed:

"How many people are at the mall."

"How much they buy."

"What product we have."

On and on. We transitioned to the right side. To the things we *could* control:

"Our smile and our attitude."

"Our energy and pace."

"How much product we show and how well we show it."

"How many guests we call."

"How many projects we finish and how clean we keep the store."

"How much merchandise education we invest in."

On and on.

A simple exercise. A profound one, too.

One I confess I have carried on into the rest of my life.

In fact, why not give it a shot right now?

Let's think of all that's irking us, the hard yards we've trekked, the ones still to trek, all the pain and all the grief. And then let's get to listing:

## THE UNCONTROLLABLES

_____

_____

_____

_____

_____

_____

_____

_____

_____

_____

_____

_____

_____

_____

_____

And then:

## THE CONTROLLABLES

_____

_____

_____

_____

_____

_____

_____

_____

_____

_____

_____

_____

_____

_____

Notice how I gave us more lines on the second one. I knew we'd need them.

The exercise, of course, is not to minimize the reality some of us are facing or to be trite.

But the longer we live, the more we come to grips with our humanity and realize how little control we have. And I'm convinced peace comes as we release and trust what we can't control to the Father's hands and by His grace lean into the things actually under our stewardship.

Let's keep our eyes on the right side of the page.

o o o

It never ceases to amaze me what a gracious gift the proper focus is and what a deadly distraction the wrong one can be. Distraction is a killer.

About a year before I moved to the Midwest, Georgia passed aggressive "distracted driving" laws. Understandably. Texting and driving destroys lives.

It doesn't matter how big your windshield is if your eyes are on a text message.

Yep, it's worth repeating: distraction's a killer.

If the enemy can't defile you with sin in the soup, he'll try to distract you with a clanging spoon to the floor.

He'll clang the spoon of other people's opinions.

He'll clang the spoon of "what if" and "if only" and "I'll never."

He'll clang the spoon of yesterday's mistakes, today's anxieties, and tomorrow's unknowns.

He'll clang the spoon of what other people might be doing, thinking, saying, planning.

But God longs to give us a refreshing and Spirit-sharpened focus for the exhausting distractions of the desert.

In fact, I'm going to give you a secret weapon, a practical broadsword that has helped me fight off some of my most stubborn mental enemies.

It's a redirecting phrase. And I'd like you to say it with me. *Out loud.*

Here it is, in all its glory:

"Yeah, but that's not my focus."

Feels good on the tongue, doesn't it?

Try it again.

*Thoughts about what he/she might be doing are beginning to ruin my morning. I even heard that—*

"Yeah, but that's not my focus. I have no control over him. I am setting my mind on the goodness of God. I can't control her. But I can control my spirit."

*I still can't believe I did _____. Who am I to think God could ever love me or use me now—*

"Yeah, but that's not my focus. Like Paul said, 'This one thing I do—forgetting what's behind and pressing forward....' I can't do a thing about yesterday. Yesterday is under the blood and today His mercies are new. Today I can live for God. Today I can trust He's using the good and the bad to...."

You get the point. Grab the hilt of this sword and try it out this week, deflecting the enemy's tactics, continually setting your mind on fruitful things, choosing peace instead of worry and joy instead of angst.

Whatever frustrating or discouraging thought comes knocking, "Yeah, but that's not my focus...."

I'll stay informed. I'll know the facts. But the lion's share of my attention? I've already been told where to put it:

> *"Summing it all up, friends, I'd say you'll do best by filling your minds and meditating on things true, noble, reputable, authentic, compelling, gracious—the best, not the worst; the beautiful, not the ugly; things to praise, not things to curse."* (Philippians 4:8 MSG)

That's my focus.

o o o

I'll end the rabbit trails on focus, save one last observation. This is one to put in a to-go box for later:

We won't just be *affected* by our focus; we will be *formed* by it.

The ideas we savor most, the frequent place of our mental leaning, the proclivity of our thoughts and desires, theses will shape who we are. "As goes our attention so goes our lives."

We find this golden truth in the casing of 1st John 3:2-3 (TPT):

*Beloved, we are God's children right now; however, it is not yet apparent what we will become. But we do know that when it is finally made visible, **we will be just like him, for we will see him as he truly is. And all who focus their hope on him will always be purifying themselves**, just as Jesus is pure.* (emphasis mine)

It melts the mind to think of us being like Jesus. It's a promise nearly too wondrous to imagine. Yet that is our future. But did you catch the connection? The writer says, "we will become like Him" for "we will see Him."

In other words, we become what we behold.

This can be observed in the dramatic and the mundane. We see Lot's wife turning to salt and oblivion as she looks disobediently to the past. We see Israel's sons and daughters healed simply by looking at the serpent on the pole of Moses. We see, even more glorious, in John 3:14 that the serpent was a foreshadowing, a teaser if you will, to Christ, so that as He is raised up all who look to Him for life and salvation will find it.

We see the become/behold principle in the practical. If you struggle with alcoholism, don't look at alcohol. *"Do not gaze at wine when it is red, when it sparkles in the cup,"*[3] Solomon warns. Sexual immorality, no different. Job said, *"I made a covenant with my eyes not to look with lust at a young woman."*[4] What we look at on our screens, whether the screens of our devices or the screens of our minds, will eventually make its way into the movie of our lives.

We *become* what we *behold*.

Our energy literally flows to the direction of our eyes. This is why Jesus said, *"The eye is the lamp of the body. If your eyes are good, your whole body will be full of light. But **if your vision is poor, your whole body will be full of darkness. If then the light within you is darkness, how great is that darkness!"**[5] (emphasis mine)

If you try to walk in the opposite direction in which you're looking, you won't get far. But the more shocking truth is we don't just *walk* in the direction of our focus; we begin to *become* the object of our focus.

Not, obviously, in a hyper-literal sense, but even deeper actually, in the long arc of our life and in our very essence, the tissues of our being conforming to the power of our gaze.

Need a new strategy to change how you live? Change where you look.

*And we all, with unveiled face, **beholding** the glory of the Lord, **are being transformed** into the same image from one degree of glory to another. For this comes*

*from the Lord who is the Spirit.* (2nd Corinthians 3:18
ESV emphasis mine)

The becoming accompanies the beholding.

To bring it home for someone like me, this means I can't
keep obsessing over my failures and rubbernecking my mistakes.
That doesn't help me change; it only fuels shame, and shame will
drive me right back to the very things Jesus is trying to free me
from.

We must face what we need to face and deal with
ourselves honestly. But as Robert Murray McCheyne, the great
Scottish writer and Pastor of the 1800's, advised, "For every look
at yourself, take ten looks at Christ."

Yes, even in all our talk about the spirit we choose
and the ways we walk in the wilderness, the eyes of our heart
should place their deepest gaze not on our performance or our
disciplines but on the marvelous person of Jesus. Only then will
we experience a confident and free life, living *from* victory and
not *for* it.

What we behold—in other words what we contemplate,
chew on, listen to, read, circle back to in our thoughts, feed into
with our desires—*this is who we're becoming.*

So even when we inevitably complicate things, we have
the writer of Hebrews to fan away the fog, reminding us the clear,
central key to the Christian life:

"**Let us fix our eyes on Jesus**, *the author and perfecter of
our faith.*" (emphasis mine)

May we lift our eyes to the hills, where our help comes from[6], our focus steady on the Lord.

May the Spirit *"open our eyes to see treasure."* To see Christ.

May we become fixated on God again. Obsessed with peering into His glory and goodness.

Some of us think we've seen it all, our eyes bored with religion.

We need a moment like Job, nose to carpet, saying *"My ears had heard of you* but now my eyes have seen you."[7] (emphasis mine)

We need to quit talking about the burning bush or merely acknowledging it from the corner of our eyes but become like Moses and "turn aside to see it" for ourselves, drawing nearer and nearer, until the flames dance in our eyes.

Some of us are the prophet Isaiah, having been around this thing for a long time. But we need an Isaiah 6 *moment*, where we realize we haven't seen anything. A moment of vision, where God's glory comes billowing over the mountains and into the smallness of our rooms, shaking the foundation of our comfort and dusty shrunken theology, the pillars trembling and the angels thundering. A moment in which pride and apathy are disintegrated and we're small again, both terrified and mesmerized by a glimpse into glory. A moment where we realize just how "other" God is and it begins to humble us and change us and fill us. A moment of rapturous wonder that turns us back into kids, dreaming of how wildly beautiful God really is.

We need to fall in love again.

You know, I've said it once, but I can still taste the golden, halcyon days of first walking with Jesus. How I would turn Him like a diamond over and over in my thoughts, often for hours. I remember the lazy joy that would fill my heart during my walks between class, singing to myself the first worship song I ever learned, based on Isaiah 40:

*Do you not know? Have you not heard? The Lord is the everlasting God, the Creator of the ends of the earth. He will not grow tired or weary, and his understanding no one can fathom. He gives strength to the weary and increases the power of the weak.*

Twenty-two years later and I can still recall the melody as easily as my own name. I can still remember not understanding how any Christian could ever be bored again. I can remember the eternal youth and excitement filling and bursting the banks of my heart as I would sing of and contemplate this great God. And I can remember wanting to grab my classmates and scream the song. Did they not know?!

Without realizing it in those days, I had curated a garden in my imagination for me and the Lord. The truth is, we spent a lot of time in that garden. And truth is, that garden changed me.

To be honest, I think I need to get back to that garden. I sometimes wonder if the greatest gift I could give myself and others would be to perch myself by the windows of God again and drink in His colors. To sit still long enough to peer into the kaleidoscopic splendor of the Everlasting One.

Who knows?

The cure for our ailing, divided souls could be a long, indulgent view of Jesus.

And the more the eyes of our heart become captivated with Him, the more we're going to be made more and more like Him without even noticing.

## Chapter Seventeen

## WEAK IN THE WAIT:
### *How Vision Creates Hope*

*"When we are tempted, Satan distracts us from Christ's beauty. When we sin, he distracts us from Christ's mercy."*
*—Emma Scrivener*

*"You've gone into my future to prepare the way, and in kindness You follow behind me to spare me from the harm of my past."—Psalm 139:5 TPT*

*"It's kind of fun to do the impossible."—Walt Disney*

Without vision things perish.

Bank accounts. Marriages. Businesses. Muscles. Spiritual lives.

You name it.

At the top of this perishables list is *hope*. And hope is something we can't go on without.

You may be familiar with the *Survivor's Rule of Three*. It states a person cannot survive:

- 3 Months without companionship or love
- 3 Weeks without food
- 3 Days without water
- 3 Hours without shelter in extreme conditions
- 3 Minutes without air
- *3 Seconds without hope*

Circle that last one. We'll last a while without necessities, but only seconds without hope.

It's written into our skin and soul.

To be honest, I've noticed in my own life I can often trace a lot of my grated nerves, low-boil sadness, and even irritability to a simple lack of hope.

It's just so easy to get there, isn't it? Enough disappointments, enough letdowns, enough time passing between your prayers and the answers, between your dreams and the fulfillment, hope just begins to leak and eventually fade. You pin your best moments as all behind you and lose the energy to look ahead with any sense of expectation.

And this blueness of soul, this unblushing sickness stretches to every organ of life.

For starters, it's an infection to courage.

Fear is often thought to be the opposite of courage, but that's not true. The opposite of courage is not fear. The opposite of courage is discouragement.

When we "encourage" someone we literally "put courage in" them. We release confidence into their spirit.

Discouragement, on the other hand, causes us to draw back and live small lives. Hope's the antidote.

A lack of hope causes a root of anger as well. Take a sweeping look at the most troubled neighborhoods. They're usually the most hopeless. Hopelessness breeds a kind of violence in the soul, whether it ever manifests externally or not.

Notice the trend in your own life. With shallow waters of hope come deep waves of frustration. Always. And unaware of the source, we tend to aim all our malice and angst somewhere else, usually at *someone*. As Mark Twain once said, though, "anger is an acid that can do more harm to the vessel in which it is stored than to anything on which it is poured." We're wounded and worried, and we just keep aiming our angry arrows at our objects of wrath even though time and again they only boomerang back on ourselves.

But like knobs of butter that sizzle away in the pan, a spirit of fret and complaint will melt away against the heat of fresh hope.

Relatedly, a lack of hope travels through soil to merge with the root of unforgiveness. The less vision I have for tomorrow, the more I'll sit in the wounds of yesterday, nursing them with salt and reinforcing narratives. Ever ran into someone still rehearsing the same story of hurt from three years prior?

A new finish line on the horizon, though? Well, that'll get me on my feet, help me dust myself off, and give me energy to let go as I move forward.

At some point, as mentioned earlier, like the prophet Samuel I have to hear God's loving voice ask me, *"How long will you grieve over [Saul].... Fill your horn with oil and go."*

The moment we stop living as a victim is the moment we can begin living with vision.

Without vision, hope takes wings and leaves the scene. And as we can see, a lack of hope makes us sick in every way.

○ ○ ○

I remember running down the hill to Crater Lake in Oregon in the summer of 2016, trying to outrun my thoughts. Some of the loss I've touched on crescendoed the night before in an argument over the phone that left me devastated. I felt so disappointed, and even more, I felt numb.

My family and I were about to enjoy one of the most scenic boat rides in the states, and all I could do was run, run and run, hoping I could outrun whatever it was I couldn't feel yet in my anesthetized state. Then in my mind, seemingly from somewhere beyond the pine trees, came the voice of my old Pastor, whispering to me the words of Solomon:

> *Hope deferred makes the heart sick,*
> *but a longing fulfilled is a tree of life.*[1]

"Right now, you're just heartsick, son," I felt him say.

He was right. The emotional awareness began to wash over me like warm water, loosening my defenses, swimming in my thoughts. The tears came then. And as my family ambled slowly down the mountain behind me, I kept running down towards that lake, tears blurring the branches, secretly wishing I could just keep running for days.

I was heartsick.

The Passion Translation of Proverbs 13:12 puts it even plainer:

*When hope's dream seems to drag on and on,*
*the delay can be depressing.*
*But when at last your dream comes true,*
*life's sweetness will satisfy your soul.*

Are you heartsick today?

Do you have some deferred hopes? Things you thought would take place by now? Some issues you thought you'd be past? Some dreams you're close to giving up on?

Are your hands still empty as you've waited and waited, looking for any sign God is going to move in the dreams and aches of your heart?

Maybe you can relate to the words of the Psalmist, *"I'm homesick—longing for your salvation; I'm waiting for your word of hope. My eyes grow heavy watching for some sign of your promise...."* (Psalm 119:81-82 MSG)

The delay can be depressing.

The delay between desire and birth. Pain and healing. Egypt and Jordan.

I love David's plea in Psalm 119 (MSG), *"Take my side as you promised; I'll live then for sure. Don't disappoint all my grand hopes."*

"Come on, God" he pleads. "You gotta come through in the end. Please don't disappoint me."

The question is, what do we do when our grand hopes *are* disappointed? When God hasn't come through? When He hasn't done things the way we wish He would've? Or by *when* we wish He would've?

I'm so glad our heroes in Scripture experienced this.

I'm so glad David and Joseph experienced decades of delay between God's promises and the fulfillment. I'm glad Isaiah and Jeremiah penned their words of sorrow and despair. I'm glad the pages of the Bible are still wet with the tears of their writers.

We get to warm ourselves by the fire of their emotional honesty.

We also get lift off, to hot-air-balloon altitude and perspective, to lean over and survey the longer and *better* kind of stories God tends to write. That's a life-giving thing to take in as we're down here on our small patch of earth scratching our heads, stuck in scenes we're convinced are the end of the whole story.

We also see, cliche as it may sound, that God often doesn't meet our expectations because He is planning to *exceed* them.

When disappointment hits, we get to the bedrock of our trust in God and on where we're actually placing our hope. Then we get the opportunity, if that hope is misaligned, to place it squarely back on God Himself, a hope that will never disappoint.

It might be time to let hope back in. To make the Lord our hope, trusting He'll make every other dream He has for us come true in its proper time.

○ ○ ○

Sometimes hope seems like a cruel and impossible request.

I'm sure that's how Job from Scripture felt. A nice vocabulary of disaster had descended on his life like a Tarantino film and health had sapped clean out of his body.

In that state of mind, Job didn't see any use in retaining expectation that life could get better. So, he necked the vinegar of self-pity and asked, *"What strength do I have that I should still hope? What prospects, that I should be patient?"²*

I'm glad *someone* else has felt that way before.

Everyone has if they're honest. And yet the choice to hope remains flat and open on the table even when sadness and hurt fester beneath the wood.

In Psalm 39, for example, David's angry. He's frustrated at God, others, and life in general. We read, *"...but my anguish increased. My heart grew hot within me."*

Then in verse seven, he turns a corner. He asks the question we all need to ask, coming to the conclusion we all need to come to:

*"But, now, Lord, what do I look for?*
*My hope is in You."*

He's saying, *God, I feel so let down. I've run out of places to look to even feel better. So now, I'm putting my hope back in*

*You, and as I do, I feel strength forming under my heart again. For You said, "Those who hope in Me will not be disappointed." (Isaiah 49:23 ISV)*

There is a fountain that never disappoints and drinking from this fountain, keeping hope alive and fresh in our hearts, is vital to stepping into all God has in front of us. Here's a promise for the desert to highlight in your Bible:

> *Do not fret—it leads only to evil.*
> *For those who are evil will be destroyed.*
> **But those who hope in the Lord will inherit the land.**
> (Psalm 37:8-9, emphasis mine)

Again, at the end of the chapter:

> *"**Hope in the Lord** and keep his way. **He will exalt you to inherit the land.**" (Psalm37:34 emphasis mine)*

Hope, tethered to God and His promises, is an invisible rope that pulls us into the future God has planned.

And hope is a choice we can make.

In fact, let's skip a few pages over to Psalm 42. Here David again searches for words to describe the pain he's experiencing:

> *My tears have been my food*
> *day and night,*
> *while people say to me all day long,*
> *"Where is your God?"*

*These things I remember*
*as I pour out my soul:*
*how I used to go to the house of God*
*under the protection of the Mighty One*
*with shouts of joy and praise*
*among the festive throng.*

He's on a diet of tears, and memories of better days are kosher salt to open wounds. But then he pivots and starts talking to himself, giving marching orders to his own soul:

*Why, my soul, are you downcast?*
*Why so disturbed within me?*
**Put your hope in God,**
*for I will yet praise him,*
*my Savior and my God.*

He presses palms to eyes and dries them, then takes a breath and looks in the mirror. A surge of holy iron stands him up straight. Chin lifted, he puts his heart in check and preaches to himself, begins to "bake his own cake," as the old-timers would say.

*Hope in God, David. You're going to make it. God's got this. He's with you. He's for you. Come on, now. He hasn't brought you this far to fail you now. Eyes back on the Lord. Hope, hope, hope in Him again!*

The pattern repeats three times in the same chapter.

David acknowledges the pain and releases it, raw and unfiltered, in the safety of God's love, and then makes the decision to *hope in God*.

He speaks to his own heart and strengthens Himself in the Lord.

It may sound easier said than done, but hope is a choice we can make.

As Pastor Jason Laird says, *"hope is not discovered; it is decided."*

It's a decision to say, "what I had in mind has not come to pass and I feel such loss and emptiness. But I am choosing to shift and put my emotional energy in *You*, God. I believe You're big, I believe You're good, and I believe the story will not end without You having the last word."

It's reminding ourselves how faithful God has been in the past and how faithful He will be in the future.

It's transferring our peace from how much we can control to a trust in how good He is and how great His plans are for our destiny.

We decide to hope.

Sometimes the situation is so bleak we even have to *dare* to hope. Here's the full context of that verse from earlier in the book:

> *I will never forget this awful time,*
> *as I grieve over my loss.*
> **Yet I still dare to hope**
> *when I remember this:*

*The faithful love of the Lord never ends!*
*His mercies never cease.*
*Great is his faithfulness;*
*his mercies begin afresh each morning.*
*I say to myself, "The Lord is my inheritance;*
*therefore, I will hope in him!"*
*The Lord is good to those who depend on him,*
*to those who search for him.*
*So, it is good to wait quietly*
*For salvation from the Lord.* (Lamentations 3:20-26 NLT, emphasis mine)

Hope. The greatest dare we'll ever take.

For me, one of the greatest hope daredevils of all time is Abraham. His power to choose hope no matter what. His ability to wait on God with expectation even when all seems lost.

He'd been promised a child and a future beyond imagination. Though he was far from perfect, he had tried his best to walk in obedience to God, enduring incredible pain and disappointment along the way.

And now, he's old. Apparently, the promises are duds, the dreams are shreds and for every motivational speech about "how good God is," he can hold up decades of "real life" evidence that apparently it just isn't in the cards for Grandpa Abe.

And yet we read:

*"**Even when there was no reason for hope, Abraham kept hoping**—believing that he would become the father of many nations."* (Romans 4:16 NLT, emphasis mine)

Have you ever been to a place where hope doesn't even seem logical anymore?

Yet even when it didn't make sense, Abraham chose it anyway. The NIV phrases it this way:

*"Against all hope, Abraham in hope believed...."*

I like that.

Let's keep reading.

**For God had said** to him, *"That's how many descendants you will have!" And Abraham's faith did not weaken, even though, at about 100 years of age, he figured his body was as good as dead—and so was Sarah's womb. Abraham never wavered in believing God's promise. In fact, his faith grew stronger, and in this he brought glory to God. He was fully convinced that God is able to do whatever he promises.* (Romans 4:18-21 NLT, emphasis mine)

God had spoken. So, Abraham believed.

Don't be discouraged if you can't relate to the "never waver" part. As mentioned earlier, a fine-combing of Abraham's biography will reveal just how gracious God is when He recaps our story.

The point is, Abraham kept going, kept believing, kept trusting, even when the promise was now literally and physically impossible. He'd logged in enough miles with the Almighty to know "impossible" is usually God's starting line. And as he held on in hope, even with bloody fingers, his spiritual muscles grew. Paul says his "faith grew stronger" and He "brought glory to God."

When He was knocked down, He got back up. When the Lord spoke, he moved. He was just audacious enough to take God at His word, to hope against all hope there is a God in heaven *who is able* and *will fulfill His plans and purposes for me*, no matter what.

In fact, if we back up earlier in the chapter, we see that Abraham *"received the promise by faith"* just like we do today, and we catch a line I'd love to see stenciled over every closed door in my life:

> *"This happened because Abraham believed in the God who brings the dead back to life and who creates new things out of nothing."* (Romans 4:17 NLT)

That line alone is enough to make wet branches catch fire.

We serve a God who can revive the dead and disposed and materialize new futures out of vacuous voids.

What a reminder for my own heart. And the truth is, Abraham's story not only has the potential to breed fresh hope; it gives us a taste of what can happen in the waiting.

The Bible tells us Abraham's faith actually *grew.*

This seems counterintuitive. Let's be honest. Many times the wait itself is *precisely* what crushes our spirit.

*"The delay can be depressing...."*

This is why Abraham's miracle was so staggering when it finally came to pass. We'll all have tests of our hope and our faith. And often our faith is tested not by the size of the miracle but by the size of the delay before it comes.

Yet despite what we may think, we don't have to come out the other side of this season shriveled and reduced. We can actually be expanded. If we let vision take its proper hold, then much like a woman pregnant with child, our anticipation will only swell in the wait. The pain may increase with time, but so will the desire and expectation.

Look at Paul's words:

**That is why waiting does not diminish us, any more than waiting diminishes a pregnant mother. We are enlarged in the waiting.** *We, of course, don't see what is enlarging us. But the* **longer we wait, the larger we become, and the more joyful our expectancy.** *Meanwhile, the moment we get tired in the waiting, God's Spirit is right alongside helping us along.* (emphasis mine)

We can let the size of the delay crush our spirit, or we can pour gasoline on the vision and let the size of the delay enlarge our desire. Then, when the *longing* is *fulfilled*, oh how sweet the fruit from that *tree of life*.

God is with us in the waiting. He's with us in the disappointment. He resonates with our pain.

But in this liminal place of life, between Egypt and Canaan, we must allow the breeze of fresh vision to blow through us again, bringing the fragrance of hope along with it.

Instead of the wait reducing us, may hope swell inside us.

In fact, I pray for you what Paul prayed for the Romans:

*May the **God of hope** fill you with all joy and peace as you trust in him, so that you may **overflow with hope** by the power of the Holy Spirit.* (Romans 15:13, emphasis mine)

o o o

On the subject of hope, I'd like to administer a little to anyone who feels like Esau. To anyone whose mind is still on the "bowl of soup" you've already eaten.

If you're anything like me, I cringe when I remember. Mistakes that still haunt my mind. Follies that chip away at my confidence for a brighter tomorrow. Whispers of shame from under the pillow.

Yes, I have bowls I would give nearly anything to take back if I could just reverse time. God knows I do. I have a feeling it might be the same for you.

The truth is, our choices do help form our future. And there are things we cannot take back.

But while we own this, while the fire of regret and sin still burn our skin at times, while we must come to terms with what Dr. Tozer referred to as "the irreversible law of consequences," while we curse our own damned stupidity, we are also to remember we kneel daily before the fresh, rising mountain of God's mercy.

It is in front of this mountain, with humility and hope, that we must let our tears fall.

A mountain where the faithfulness of God stretches past the blue and into the dark.

A soaring summit of grace that extends higher than any star.

An avalanche of compassion.

It's a high place where we learn God specializes in redemption and delights in restoration. A place, in fact, for us to be happily mystified by a God who can somehow restore even the years the locusts have eaten.

A place to be reminded we're not defined by our darkest moments and God isn't caught off guard by our worst mistakes. A place to consider the ugliest stains of our Bible heroes' humanity and remain mesmerized God can still use *anyone*.

It is a mountain I have spent much time before. Begging God to create clean heart valves inside of my sinful soul and—whatever you do, Lord—please, please don't remove the sweet, healing Presence of your Holy Spirit from my life.

At this mountain are the holds of God's promises. We place our feet there. We're reminded when we're faithless, He's still faithful. We're reminded He'll complete the work He began in us.

It's at a mountain, in fact, God first makes a full declaration of His name and personality. At Mt. Sinai, *in the wilderness*, after Moses pleads for God to reveal Himself and show His glory, the introduction of all time:

*Then the Lord came down in the cloud and stood there with him and proclaimed his name, the Lord. And he passed in front of Moses, proclaiming, "The Lord, the Lord, the compassionate and gracious God, slow to anger, abounding in love and faithfulness, maintaining love to thousands, and forgiving wickedness, rebellion and sin. Yet he does not leave the guilty unpunished; he punishes the children and their children for the sin of the parents to the third and fourth generation." (Exodus 34:4-7)*

Oh, how that mountain must have smoked and shook as God flipped on the loudspeakers of heaven, His words rolling like thunder over the hills.

"Alright, Moses, here is what I am like:"

Compassionate.

Gracious.

Slow to anger.

Abounding in love and faithfulness.

Maintaining love.

Forgiving.

And just.

That's who God is. Read back over the words and phrases. Feel the lightning heat of that eternal Heart towards *you*.

Speaking of Moses, his life illustrates how brilliantly God can redeem the irreversible.

In case you didn't know, I have to break it to you. Our original wilderness guide never made it to the Promised Land.

It's true. Sadly, as recorded in Deuteronomy 32, God tells Moses he will see it with his eyes but never enter it with his feet.

The Lord references a moment of bizarre but deep violation back in Numbers 20. An incident at the waters of Meribah Kadesh. In a display of deep casualness, Moses disobeyed direct instructions, operated out of frustration towards the people, failed to uphold the holiness of the Lord, and then took credit for God's glory in a manner so public God had to draw a line in the sand for the sake of His name and the sake of the people.

To his credit, Moses brought up the issue a few times in prayer, yet never complained. He just faithfully continued to lead the people and serve God. Sure enough, Moses died on Mount Nebo, gazing across at Canaan, the precious vision dimming as his eyes closed on this life. His friendship to the Lord was so precious, though, we are told the Lord Himself buried him there on the mountain.

Bittersweet and a little depressing, to be sure.

And yet.

Let's fast forward a few thousand years.

Jesus is walking the earth.

The end of his life is nearing. He takes his three closest friends with him on a pretty arduous hike, most likely up to the top of Mount Hermon. Peter brought the charcuterie, James the Chardonnay and John the notepad.

Chardonnay glasses drop and shatter, though, as they look up to see Jesus engulfed in light. And just like that, he's not alone. Two other figures emerge from the curtain of eternity. They talk with Jesus, awe and familiarity mingling like the light and the words.

One of these figures is Elijah.

And the other?

Moses.

Standing on a mountain. *On the other side of the wilderness.*

*In* the Promised Land.

Yes, he's been in heaven. But still.

It's nearly cinematic, no? Stunning, visceral, glorious and full circle.

Somehow Moses *did* still get to his purpose.

That's just like God, isn't it?

o o o

Where there's no vision, we perish. In every area.

The inverse is also true. Where there *is* vision, we flourish. In every area.

Relationships. Finance. Spirituality.

A quick, fun story. Lee, youth pastor, you remember him. He moved to Greenville, South Carolina from Kentucky when I was in the seventh grade. Immediately things began to take off in the youth group. But as the ministry grew so did his waistline (*his words*). I suppose I didn't really notice at the time, though as I think back, we did stop by Wendy's *a lot* as the years progressed.

One day, Lee took his family on a cruise. At one of the islands, his youngest daughter McKenzie asked if they could take a special boat ride excursion. To Lee's embarrassment, however, the ticket-box regretted to inform him he was too heavy for the small, wooden vessel.

Line-in-the-sand moment for Lee that day. He knew things had to change.

When he got back to town, he joined a gym, subscribed to *Men's Health*, and—here's the vision part—placed a blown-up photo of Brad Pitt in his gym bag to keep him in check should the Twinkies come calling. Yes, I made fun of him.

Lee lost over a hundred pounds that year, though, and packed on solid strands of muscle in place of the missing flesh.

*The 700 Club* flew him out to be interviewed on TV. Then, *USA Today* came to town and did a story on him and my best friend and I got to be with him in the photos (just thought you should know). A few Hollywood agents even contacted Lee about the movie industry. No kidding.

Maybe I should place a picture of Brad Pitt in *my* gym bag come to think of it.

I still think I won't.

But Lee had a picture he was moving towards.

It reminds me of my favorite definition of vision:

"Vision is a mental picture of a preferred future."

It's a picture Lee needed.

It's a picture even Abraham needed.

We read earlier about Abraham's great faith, how he took every paragraph from God to the bank. However, even the father of our faith needed a picture.

God spoke to him in Genesis 12, inviting him on a journey, bundling his carry-on with nothing but promises that seemed too good to be true. By Genesis 15, years had passed. Life put Abraham through the ringer and the years have far out-paced Sarah's capacity to bear a child. The promise of descendants and blessing have faded like morning from the light of their eyes.

And then we read in Genesis 15, *"the word of the Lord came to Abram in a vision...."*

God brought vision. In this vision God reminds Abraham the Lord Himself is His shield and reward.

Abraham brushes that away with complaints of dead dreams.

God's gracious, though, and—how beautiful is this—"**He took him outside** *and said, 'look up at the sky and count the stars— if indeed you can count them.' Then he said to him, 'So shall your offspring be.'"*

God took Abraham outside. Outside of his disappointment. Outside of the disillusionment about how things were supposed to go. Outside to some fresh air to let God's perspective back in.

Abraham had been in the tent too long. He needed to see a picture of the future again.

That's what real vision is. It's what this chapter is about. God taking us by the hand, out of the tent, saying, "Come on. We've had some rough miles. Let's look at the stars again. Let me renew you with a fresh glimpse of my promise and what I have in store. Go ahead. Try to count the stars, Abraham. My plans are beyond anything you can wrap your mind around."

He showed Abraham a mental picture of a preferred future.

God has that for you, too. It's not a picture of you languishing in sorrow, washed up on the shores of yesterday's crumbs. It's a burgeoning horizon of His Spirit doing beautiful things in and through your life.

Seek Him for it. Imagine. Pray. Ask Him to give you a picture of the season and plans He is drawing you into.

Get away if you have to. I hear Mark Batterson in my mind saying, "A change of *pace* plus a change of *place* equals a change of *perspective*."

Rent a cabin. Taste some salty air by a beach. Or just walk *outside*.

Either way.

Let's leave the tent of fear and doubt.

Let's go out to the stars and *dream*.

o o o

I once heard Erwin McManus say, "'Desert' is codeword for 'future.'"

I think it's true. I think we ought to turn our mirages into mood boards.

Maybe a "hope list" just to get started. You know, a sort of melange of goals, bucket list and vision.

I made one a few years ago and keep it on my phone. It ranges from spiritual aspirations and character formation, to my desire to publish a book (here we are), to the dream of my parents holding my son on a Carolina coast with my future family, to having a bite at the pub in London that was frequented by C.S. Lewis and J.R.R. Tolkien, all the way to the ridiculous and whimsical, such as "Lost Week" in Hawaii, closing my eyes there by the tree line to hear the way Claire says Charlie's name, the Smoke Monster lurking nearby.

I keep the list close and I go back to it every few months.

Try it.

The thing is, everything goes awry in us when our hope tank is low. That's why I need to remind you the God who created the stars knows you by name and hasn't forgotten your plight. It's why I remind you He can still make the sun stand still, donkeys converse, water leap out of stone, and fling down fire from heaven to kiss offerings of faith. And He can still fulfill His purpose for you.

And it's why we place our fingers around the gas handle and squeeze, filling our hope buckets with the fuel of vision.

Vision and hope really are synonymous in that way. Two sides of the same coin. So, whatever it takes to top off the tank right now, let's get at it.

Let's go outside and look at the stars again. Let's let our spirits begin to taste the things God is preparing. Let's push the bowls away and feast on the veal of vision. Let's stare at the marble until angels come out.

As we've seen in these last three chapters, we're vulnerable in the desert without vision. Vulnerable to either be taken out by *temptation*, knocked off course by *distraction* or destroyed by *discouragement*. But high-watt vision will dispel all three like sunlight to darkness.

So, let's turn up the wattage.

And then let's dip our ideas into ink.

You know, some people don't love New Years. But I'm all about it. It's one of my favorite times. My nostalgia combined with my ambitious, dreaming spirit can barely take the combustion as the final days of December tick away. I'm both reminiscent and scheming, "Long December" by Counting Crows looping in the car, the rustic voice wondering if this year might be better than the last.

Anyways.

As I mentioned earlier, I usually have a theme in tow by November I'm praying over. I'm also making a "Top Moments" highlight list for the closing year along with goals for the following. Early in High School this was 947 some odd random things that had no chance of happening. I've evolved. Somewhat. I now have manageable goals and plans. But you better believe they're God-sized goals, large and magnetic, to pull me with enthusiasm into the next year.

Several thousand years ago, the Lord spoke to a prophet named Habakkuk. As He was concluding, God gave both an immediate instruction and a timeless principle concerning the vision. He told the prophet to *write it down: "Write the vision, and make it plain on tablets, that he who reads it may run."* (Habakkuk 2:2 MEV)

I'd like us to close out the chapter by doing just that.

Let's set our heart and eyes and pen on fire.

Let's spread our hands out over the table, take a deep breath and pour copious amounts of caffeine.

Let's pray.

Let's write.

What if the desert is where we decide to dream again?

I can hear Relient K even now, singing about paper and expensive pens and how nothing in the past can keep us from the future.

What will you write?

I don't know.

Maybe you'll sketch a simple cartoon mouse that will turn into miles of magic and wonder and rollercoasters that scream into the sky.

Perhaps you'll type up a personal code for the kind of person you'll become in faith and the iceberg of integrity you want undergirding your life, letting that begin to push into the rest of your decisions.

Maybe you'll journal some relational vision.

True story, that girl I was planning to build my family and life and ministry with? In the same season of its collapse, *three* different people from *three* different states called me within *three* weeks with the same message, "Russ, God has heard your prayers. But he wants you to write the list of what you're looking for in Mrs. Moore. Not a genie in the bottle of every preference. But vision. You have not because you ask not."

Just in case they weren't all crazy, I got to writing. What could it hurt? Funny enough, sadness slowly changed its clothes into excitement, not to mention clarity. Sometimes when I'm weary in the waiting, I'll spread those papers before the Lord like Hezekiah. They're gold leaflets in my hand and I'm asking God to look down at what's been written, a thousand tears and sleepless nights and prayers laced in every word.

Now. In all transparency I'm still single as of this writing. So, if you know someone....

Again, who knows? Maybe it's vision for your family or your finances or your health or to eradicate poverty or disease.

Perhaps simply for the season beyond this season.

A few months ago, I was preparing a message on this principle and I holed up downtown to prepare. There's a little family-owned vegan restaurant in the cozy city where I work. Granola families bring their kids there to play on wooden slides in the back while they eat hummus and kale.

I was fortressed in my normal corner. A simple table of worn wood saddled with over-sized leather chairs stained by the sun. The platform it's on is elevated and feels invincible and large windows bring the light in from behind you. I had brought along my journals of the last few years, all goat skin and tear-spotted, ready to go back in time.

It's odd reading your own words, drinking in your own heart. Remembering the tears and the emotions. I really did feel like that past season would never end. I had felt so alone. So abandoned. So washed up.

Yet I had written down vision. Vision for my next season in ministry. I'd even been bold enough to get specific in what I was believing for next. A kind of grit had mixed in with my grief, and my refusal to settle caused tension in some relationships. However, even when the presented opportunities seemed like the only potential options, I somehow believed. By God's grace I somehow waited for God's best.

I also knew my waiting required participation. Late one night, I read *The Last Arrow* by Erwin McManus and a deep knowing came over me. A bold but peaceful kind of resolution. I knew that I knew that I knew. I had to draw a line in the sand and move forward. I went to the bank the next day and opened a new savings account, informing the teller I wanted it nicknamed *Next Arrow*. If I hadn't heard from God by a certain time, I would step out in faith, into the unknown, scared but trusting.

God moved and opened the next door in his fashionably late fashion, and I didn't have to touch any of the savings. The point is, the *written vision* had moved me to *working action*, and had kept the waters of my hope from growing stagnant.

So even as my food arrived, I stayed huddled down over the journals, my eyes moving with tears from heartbreak, to hope, to promise, to vision, and then back again, over and over, like the merry-go-round life can be.

My food was growing cold, so I took in a nice plume of herb-spiced egg and jabbed some avocado with my fork. But I began to swell inside even more from the Spirit so heavy on these pages of God's faithfulness, swell inside at how good God had been to me on my journey. I never thought I'd live in the Midwest. I now see cornfields and eat *pierogies* and love the city of Columbus and I have no idea what the future holds. But oh, what God has done. What He's done for me. Through me. *In* me!

The tears came fuller and swifter and my hands folded back into my lap. Someone else can eat this food. And don't tell me God-given vision won't see you through.

So, what will you write?

Maybe someone reading this will let destiny flow prophetically from their pen to paper for the church.

A few years ago, we wanted to honor our Lead Pastor in a special way. We had come out of a season of pain and pruning but joined to the hip with supernatural expectancy and favor. Like Jacob to Israel, we changed our name, sharpening our values and breathing new air and meaning into the culture.

Yet we knew the heart of our Pastor and his mission had never changed. We found the original scrap of paper he had scribbled vision on over 15 years ago. His heart and vision now and then were identical. We looked at the incredible thing God had built. We got emotional over the campuses now alive and thriving, the families forever changed, the legacies eternally impacted. We surprised him with a black marble plaque, something a little more modern and inspiring, but etched with the same words he had written before, just like Habakkuk thousands of years prior, *"that they may run with it."*

Tears were shed.

This is also the story of Hillsong, the first ever global church. Brian Houston of Australia had written down "The Church I See" back in the 80's. He envisioned a Spirit-filled church of grace, faith-filled in confession, youthful in spirit and anthems of worship scratching the corners of the earth. And now here we are. The rest of the story's in the amber, as they say. The impact of what Pastor Brian "saw" and then wrote down is now changing culture, damaging hell and creating beauty for the Kingdom on every continent besides Antarctica. The spirit of Hillsong and its glorious message of the Gospel is penetrating and flourishing in cities like Paris, London, LA, New York, and dozens more.

Maybe you need to write down "The Children I See" or "The Business I See" or "The Life I See."

What do you see beyond this divorce? This depression? This transition? This loss?

And do I really need to remind you by now that nothing can hinder? That it doesn't matter your age?

Too young? Do we need to visit all the teenagers and young men in Scripture that became kings and prophets? Or peruse the canals of history to speak with the Mozarts and the Blaise Pascals?

Too old? Should we speak with Moses, our wilderness guide himself, who was eighty years old before he saw the burning bush and stepped into his call? Or we could just brush the biographies of the Julia Childs and the Smith Wigglesworths and even Colonel Sanders.

*"You are never too old to set another goal, or to dream a new dream,"* C.S. Lewis said.

And we certainly can't be tempted to think our past is too dark for God's grace. We know God's story in Scripture is riddled with killers, liars and prostitutes. The Apostle Paul himself, who wrote a third of the New Testament, murdered Christians for a living before his conversion. Something tells me he has you beat.

So, let's get our pens ready.

As we write, let's write with fresh lens. Let's throw away the outdated lens of failure, shame and hurt. Let's replace them with a new lens. Ephesians 3:20 is a great one to get us started:

*"Now to Him who is able to do exceedingly, abundantly above anything you could ever ask, think or imagine…."*

Let's make it grittier, down into the skin, with the Message translation:

*"God can do anything, you know—far more than you could ever imagine or guess or request in your wildest dreams!"*

Now.

Start writing.

## VISION

*"What I see"*

_____

_____

_____

_____

_____

_____

_____

_____

_____

_____

_____

_____

_____

_____

_____

## WILDERNESS WRITINGS

(Notes from the Section—What stood out?)

_____

_____

_____

_____

_____

_____

_____

_____

_____

_____

_____

_____

_____

_____

_____

## DESERT DECISIONS

(Future Applications—What steps are you going to take?)

_____

_____

_____

_____

_____

_____

_____

_____

_____

_____

_____

_____

_____

_____

_____

*the*

# ARRIVAL

*of the*

# PROMISE

# 1 250 BC.

*It's early morning. Dark and quiet, just a few sand cats, their claws against shrubs.*

*I can only imagine what Joshua is thinking.*

*He's been sitting under an acacia tree for hours, nibbling at a few wild berries, not even trying to resist all the thoughts. He's indulging them, matter of fact. They've been swimming over him since evening, leaking into the dreams of fitful sleep through the night, now brewing strong like coffee in early dawn.*
*He looks out over the hill and sees a whisker of gold beginning to rise. Picking at his beard, he sighs deeply.*

*It's been forty years.*

*Forty years since the pain of Egypt. Looking down he can still make out scars on his wrists. The iron of the shackles left deep grooves in the flesh above each palm. He can picture himself stacking bricks, day after day, night after night. He remembers the fireside talks. He remembers looking up at the stars toward a God who apparently had forgotten about them and covered His ears to their cries.*
*He remembers Moses. Oh, how that mysterious man came out of nowhere. He and Aaron. No one believed them. Even after their little magic tricks.*

*Could anyone really believe Pharaoh would ever let them go? Could any Hebrew still dream they'd ever be free?*

Like a tide sweeps away the shore, so time had done with their hope, sweeping it clean from the heart of men and women.

Yet, something in that peculiar people had hoped, hadn't it? They'd kept crying out. Some had kept daring to believe that one day, just maybe, deliverance would finally come.

Then, suddenly, God burst onto the scene like fireworks.

Joshua leans his head back against the trunk and closes his eyes, letting the movie replay. All those plagues, so terrifying and majestic. The signs, the wonders, the words, the miracles. That first Passover Meal, the smokiness of the roasted lamb, the terror of the blood-streaked doorposts.

The hair stands to attention on Joshua's arms as the Red Sea waters stand to attention in the eyes of his mind. The memory rolls all around him, faint but somehow near.

What a party that was on the other side. Oh, how they danced.

A single tear escapes without struggle and falls on his left scarred wrist as he smiles deep from inside.

But then the desert years.

It's so odd, funny almost, the nature we have as humans. How electric the power of those first miracles, how throbbing the joy of their hearts. And then thirst, hunger, and discomfort quickly clawing it all away like rats on refuse.

His mind went like a film over those early wilderness days, the growing complaints, the manna, the quail, the water from rocks. The energizing defeat of the Amalekites and the organizing insight of Jethro. The eleven days stretching to weeks, then months, then years.

He both soared and hurt at the memory of Mt. Sinai, the thunder and lightning and glory. God giving them covenants and plans as a society. They were becoming a people and they were being promised a land and future. New laws were stretching their minds and humanizing their hearts. Protocol to protect. Offerings to atone. Priests to minister. And sabbath—a delighted command to rest!

Yet he could also still see the people restless at the foot of the mountain while God spoke to Moses at the summit. If you try you can nearly taste their idolatry. Picture it, will you? That dull calf of melted gold, hard as their hearts, resting lazily in Aaron's complicit hands.

Joshua's thoughts turned darker still as he remembered all the jealousy and immorality that began to color the camp, all amid the bitter impatience and escalating disbelief of what God had promised. If he was honest with himself, Joshua had had nights where he too wondered, will I ever see this land I've heard so much of?

And then he saw it, took it in for the first time on that infamous first scouting trip. His eyes had grown wide, dreamy and eager, the first time they rested on the land. It's all been worth it, he remembered thinking. The thick and plush valleys, pregnant with crop. Waterfalls gathered from the mouth of rivers, sliding down mountain walls, sweetening the soil of the hills. In the flatlands, field after field shone with evergreen potential. He'd easily been able to envision the fill of livestock among the plains, even taste the flesh between his teeth.

And the fruit! Grander than anything he could dream up. One single cluster of grapes so large it had to be carried on a pole, a man on each side (he could've sworn someone spotted him behind the bushes that day).

Unfortunately, the giants of the land were also large.

Beast-like humans towered by small trees and blocked out the sun. They looked angry at life itself.

*And there you had it. Scouting report complete. The future homes, memories and God-given promise swelled in the eyes of two. The terror of giants swelled in the eyes of ten.*

*Caleb was not silent. Oh, how the fire blazed in his eyes. The anger at their disbelief and cowardice. A dispute had broken out a mile out of sight and then a long, silent trek back to camp.*

*God was not happy, either, and things got really sticky for Moses.*

*Speaking of Moses.*

*It would be a long time before Joshua didn't wince at the memory of his name.*

*How easily Moses had swum his way into the young man's heart, mingled into the posture of friend, father figure and hero, all at once.*

*He'd treasured their chats at tonight, remembered mustering up the courage to ask, "Moses, what's He like? When you see Him face to face. Those forty days on the mountain, under the cloud, let's go over it again, Moses. Please, tell me more."*

*Of course, Joshua had developed his own walk with God. When everyone else stood at their tent from a distance and watched their leader go in to meet with God, Joshua was the young aid who would stay there with Moses. He lingered there. He'd been taken up the mountain, too. And what he saw and heard...oh, there are things he would never repeat in this life. Words don't exist for them anyway.*

*Still, to sit in that premier front bleacher seat of the intimacy God and Moses shared... How about the time Moses came down the mountain with his face glowing, soft sun sputtering out of his* countenance? It was like God had bottled up a few ounces of glory and shook the splendor out over Moses in the fashion of a spring rain.

And yet Moses was so down-to-earth average, wasn't he? Limped along with his own insecurities like the rest of us.

The glory only seemed to make him more acutely aware of his humanity. Humility seeped from his bones. Like other mortals, he made mistakes. Oh, how he made mistakes.

In fact, it's why he wasn't here now.

*Oh, God, could you not have just let him go with me to the other side? Just for a while?*

What Joshua wouldn't give for one more night by the fire, watching wisdom form and roll off Moses' tongue. Dreaming out loud about the future. Even just to hear his laugh again, that dry, simple humor of Moses, usually self-deprecating, his jokes always betrayed ahead of time by a certain shine in his eyes and twitch of his mouth.

By now a spoonful of sun was tipping over the horizon, its gold beginning to spill on to the hills. Most of the men were up. Behind the trees to his left, Joshua heard water splash and hiss against the final embers of last night's campfire.

"Today is the day," he whispered to himself.

He flicked a small lizard off his knee, brushed and then slapped his thighs before standing up with a grunt.

His thoughts had filled him with wonder and pain and sadness.

They'd also filled him with hope.

*In fact, as the sun was beginning to rise, he felt strength rising with it.*

*He brought forth like fine china the words of the Lord to the table of his mind.*

*God had spoken clearly. He would be with Joshua as He was with Moses.*

*He would never leave or forsake Joshua.*

*Joshua, therefore, was to be strong and courageous. "No one will be able to stand against you all the days of your life," the Lord had promised.*

*God had committed to give Joshua every place he set his foot.*

*His part was to walk with God, careful to obey, and follow him wholeheartedly.*

*That had been an overwhelming night soaking in those promises from the mouth of God. He'd relayed God's words to the people, and they'd volleyed back their support. "As we followed Moses, so we will follow you." Spies had been sent out, they'd consecrated themselves for the miraculous days ahead, and now, here they were.*

*Finally.*

*After forty years, forty years of wandering, sin, pain, disappointment, hopes raised and then hopes dashed, failure, death, loss, and everything in between, God's people were about to enter the Promised Land.*

*"Joshua. It's time."*

*He didn't turn his head. He'd recognize that gruff voice anywhere.*

*After a long silence, he turned and looked into burning eyes. Even under that stoic expression, he thought he detected a slight grin of determined mischief.*

*"I'm ready, Caleb,"* he responded. *"Let's go."*

## Chapter Eighteen

CROSSING JORDAN

*"Hope is the feeling we have that the feeling
we have is not permanent."–Mignon McLaughlin*

*"Everyone on earth has a treasure that awaits him."
–The Alchemist (Paul Coehlo)*

*"The Promised Land always lies on the other side
of the wilderness."–Havelock Ellis*

I hope this book has strengthened you deeply, encouraging you to hold on to God, clinging to His arm as He walks you through whatever desert season you're in. I pray you're able to look back on this difficult time one day and hear God say:

*"I remember your youthful loyalty,
our love as newlyweds.
You stayed with me through the wilderness years,
stuck with me through all the hard places."*
(Jeremiah 2:1-2 MSG)

Let's stick with God. Better chapters lie ahead.

But after this painful season, then what? What exactly *is* "Canaan" for us here in the twenty-first century? What does that represent? What does *the other side of the Jordan* look like on *this side of heaven*?

In the first chapter we defined *the Wilderness*. In the last few chapters, let's define *the Promised Land*.

First, let's be clear, there *are* finish lines to cross in this life. Thank God.

There *are* Jordan moments.

Highlights. Mountaintops. Crossing overs.

There *are* climactic scenes where we finally stand in front of the person we've waited for our whole life, see our future in their eyes, and whisper our vows through tears.

There *are* moments where our trembling fingers click "submit payment" on our last debt, we realize we're finally free, slice scissors through that final credit, and call up Dave Ramsey to give that blood-curdling "debt free scream."

There *are* special episodes where we step on the scale and we'll never tell anyone we almost cried, confidence and energy surging through our body as we resist the urge to hop in the car, drive to the beach, and revel in our new reality.

These moments are real. Let's not minimize them. They're *mental pictures of a preferred future*.

After heartsick years, they are longings fulfilled, blooming like a "tree of life."

I've encouraged you to write out vision, in fact, for some of these moments and seasons. And I'll be the first to wave you on, right here at the end of this book, and say "go for it!"

I pray waves of these moments sweep over you in the months and years to come. I'm believing for double blessings to chase you down all your days.

However.

If we're honest, you and I also know there's no complete resolution in this life. It's true. It's beautiful, bittersweet, and kind of sad, but true.

People get married yet still wake up lonely some days. They reach their goal weight but still find imperfections or get sidelined by a surprise diagnosis. They win their sixth basketball championship in Chicago but still need to try something new.

Some people even experience everything this earthly life could offer, marrying supermodels and winning Super bowls but still saying like quarterback Tom Brady, "there has got to be more than this." All over Hollywood and ESPN are modern-day examples of Solomon crying "vanity!"

In fact, sometimes new victories give way to new battles. I won't go all *"new levels, new devils"* on you like the old preachers do. But I will say, let's cheer for Joshua crossing the Jordan, but let's also remember he had to quickly replace *Nikes* with army boots and war over the land he was to possess.

Even in the promised land there are giants to fight, and the first thing Joshua saw after he crossed the Jordan was a thirty-foot wall.

Yes, God gave them an astonishing victory over Jericho and the walls buckled like Jenga, but future battles still remained.

Yes, they consecrated themselves for three days before stepping behind the Ark of the Presence into the Jordan, but sin was still found in Achan's tent and brought destruction to the camp.

You get the point.

If we put our ultimate hope in this life, all our eggs in this planet's basket, we will be let down. *Every single time.*

"There's no finality this side of heaven," Leonard Ravenhill once said.

Conflicts still exist, and climaxes still lack the kind of resolve only eternity can bring.

We ache for resolution in this life, though, don't we? An everlasting itch of the soul, if you will, that earth never can seem to scratch. In fact, it'd be very easy for me to go all poet-in-the-woods on you here and dive deep into the nostalgia of our humanity's homesickness. I'll resist, and we're going to explore this a little more in the last chapter, but here's the truth—*we're all trying to get back to Eden.*

Adam may be your great-great-great-great-great-to-the-nth-degree-grandfather, but a keen scent of his memory lingers inside you. Something in you knows you were made for Eden, made to be clothed in glory, made for satisfaction. Therefore, something in you also knows something is incredibly missing. And we live our lives trying to find what that is, continually hoping beyond all hope *if I can just get there*, life will be complete.

The bad news is Eden is not coming back. At least not yet. A restoration of all things is in the works, but if you look for Eden in the Promised Land, the milk will taste sour. Only eternity contains the foam of that creme.

On the other hand, however, the New Testament "promised land" for the believer is *not* just heaven. I do not believe that is what Canaan represents for the Christ follower. I believe there is a *promised land* available to walk in now before we ever transition to eternity.

So, what is it?

I believe the *promised land life* is *the life you were created and destined to live.*

It is the "mountainous air" of higher living most Christ-followers sadly never step into. It is the *"pressing forward to the high call of God in Christ Jesus,"* as Paul said.

It's a life where the promises and truths we read in Scripture become actualized in day-to-day, gritty, glorious living.

It's a life of untold blessing, victory and peace.

I trust I don't have to over-preface this is no waving of the flag for some prosperity gospel, where we all become healthy and wealthy in this life.

It is, however, stepping into the reality of Ephesians 1:11 (MSG, emphasis mine):

> *It's in Christ that we find out who we are and what we are living for. Long before we first heard of Christ and got our hopes up,* **he had his eye on us, had designs on us for glorious living,** *part of the overall purpose he is working out in everything and everyone.*

Designs for *glorious living*.

Perhaps you've never considered God has those for you. But He does. They must be entered into with intention and perseverance, but they *are* available, nonetheless.

Yes, there is an ultimate promised land called heaven. However, I emphatically believe there is a symbolic promised land here on earth awaiting each believer, the kind of life that brings some heaven to *here and now*.

Not a utopian, every-wish-fulfilled peak, some kind of euphoric climax where every dream comes true and all the tension is resolved. If we wait for that, we'll keep waiting.

But there is a life God longs for us to enter before we leave earth to go to heaven, and that is, namely, beginning to live more from heaven *towards earth*. A place where we're living into rich grooves of purpose. A realm where we're tasting the higher plains of higher living, deeper freedom, life-giving intimacy with God. A dimension where we're kissing the sunrise of fruitful days, the kind of destiny days God had in mind when He breathed us into existence.

It's a John 10:10 kind of life, the kind where Jesus came to *"give us life and life to the full."*

A full life.

An overflowing life.

A surrendered life, detached from the weightiness of sin and distraction.

A powerful life, energized by a soul-filling friendship with the Spirit, His wind in my sails and at my back.

A joyful life, with laughter, unspeakable peace and hope.

A heated life, untouched by the tepid waters of lukewarmness, but ablaze with the life and warmth of God, His fire in my eyes.

A contagious and expanding life, "rivers of living water" spilling out of me and onto others, making the world thirsty for what I've got.

It's a life not full of comfort, but full of purpose. A life not full of safety, but full of risk.

A life driven by the adventure and destiny only God could dream over the pages of my life.

This is the life where I'm living by passion, not obligation; by expectation, not dread.

A life where I'm living with eternity in mind, in step with the Spirit, trusting God when the road is steep, knowing in the dark hours reward and paradise and golden streets are just around the corner.

This is a life where I rise above insecurity, the fear of man, traps of materialism, and false promises of the world. Yes, it's life at a higher hill, a higher way of thinking, a higher way of living. It's becoming the highest expression of my potential as a human made in God's image, the highest expression of love, compassion, kindness, and joy. It's walking in supernatural contentment from a place of loving acceptance in the Father's pleasure, free to love those around me.

This is also a life we must *choose* to step into.

As Pastor and Bible Commentator Warren Wiersbe points out, "Too many Christians are 'in between' in their spiritual lives—between Egypt and Canaan. They have been delivered from the bondage of sin, but they have not by faith entered into the inheritance of rest and victory."[1]

See, promised land living is a future that will never be entered by default or accident, only by faith and intention.

It is a kind of reality that is free, yet costly.

It's receiving mercy and eternal life as the jeweled gifts they are, but continuing on, stepping into the sacrifice and commitment necessary to walk fully in the rich calling of God.

This can all sound a bit lofty but promised land living can be as grandiose as yielding to an ever-nagging call to ministry, public service, or leadership, or it can be as simple and human as beginning to smile at the person behind each counter. As deep as a ground-opening underworld in the Spirit in which you begin to plumb the depths, or as daily as waking up in the morning with expectation and prayer instead of dread and phone addiction. It can be freedom and blessing in finance and career, but also being present, engaged and intentional with your family and friends.

It may be the same life but a different life. It might mean quitting your job. It might also mean bringing passion and purpose and an eternal lens to your current job. It could mean fording the rivers of your view of and love for people different than you politically, your perception beginning to shift as God broadens your mind and melts your heart with empathy and compassion.

It might be your money, time, and energy changing color and shape under the beams of a new sun, the same scenery outside but a different geography inside, paradigms flipping mindsets and emotional patterns awkwardly on their head.

Promised land living.

It is a high level of living in the grace and purposes of God.

It's a land Jesus died to give us, but just like the children of Israel, that doesn't mean we don't have a part to play or giants to fight.

It's a life upstream for salmon and uphill for men and women. John Maxwell once said, *"most of us have uphill hopes; we just don't have uphill habits."* The ways of God and the leading of the Spirit can bring us to this land, though, this "glorious living" Jesus had in mind for us all along.

It's a life where we search out our inheritance and learn how to walk in it.

See, the children of Israel had an inheritance waiting them. Land and abundance and blessing.

And so do we.

Here's just some of what Paul said to his friends in Ephesus in the first chapter of his letter, trying to describe the inheritance they had coming:

> *Praise be to the God and Father of our Lord Jesus Christ, who has blessed us in the heavenly realms with every spiritual blessing in Christ…. He chose us in Him before the foundation of the world…in love He predestined us for adoption to sonship through Jesus Christ…to the praise of his glorious grace…in him we were also chosen…that we might be for the praise of His glory… when you believed, you were marked with a seal, the promised Holy Spirit, who is a deposit guaranteeing our inheritance until the redemption of those who are God's*

*possession—to the praise of HIs glory.... I pray that the eyes of your heart may be enlightened in order that you may know the hope to which he has called you, the riches of his glorious inheritance....*

As a believer I'm rich. Filthy rich.

I just gotta live like it.

Well-known author and pastor, Dr. A.W. Tozer, once remarked, "I believe most of us will barely get our feet wet in eternity before bowing our heads in shame and humiliation and saying, 'my God! The riches there were in Christ and I've come to the judgment seat nearly a pauper....'"

Promised land living means beginning to cash the checks *now*. Activating the promises of God and walking in His fulness on *this* side.

Until we get to heaven, it will never be a *perfect* life in Jesus, but it can be a *progressing* life in Jesus. Pressing on to walk in the kingdom ways of "love, peace and joy in the Holy Spirit."

I don't think we have to wait until we die. The kingdom is near. Heaven can begin to invade *now*.

Jesus paid the price for us to walk in the "more" He purchased for us with his blood. We're coheirs with Christ. More than conquerors.

So, let's spend our days in the river of God's fullness.

I love the picture painted in Psalm 84. I want it to tell my tale until the day I see God face to face:

*And how blessed all those in whom you live,*
*whose lives become roads you travel;*
*They wind through lonesome valleys, come upon brooks,*
*discover cool springs and pools brimming with rain!*
*God-traveled, these roads curve up the mountain, and*
*at the last turn—Zion! God in full view!*
(Psalm 84:5-7 MSG)

I'm raising a toast. Here's to *grace days* ahead.

o o o

I'd love to tell you once you get past a certain mountain there will be no more giants to fight. I wish I could report a pain-free promised land on this side of eternity's curtain.

It's funny. I'm in my own promised land right now, the one I wept and prayed and fasted for. The pain of a few years ago has nearly dissolved on the tongue, but there's an aftertaste, and I still remember the longings, all the desperate prayers hurled at those yellow walls of my kitchen in Atlanta.

But here I am. I'm in a new city with incredible friends at a thriving church I'm thrilled about, right in the middle of God's will. Prayers answered. Jordan crossed.

And yet, as I type these words it is July 9th, 2020. The year feels like a page out of Revelation. One hundred and twenty days ago on March 11th, our leadership team called an emergency meeting to discuss COVID-19. The writing was on the wall and we sprang into action, moving services online and sending out communication.

That night I was hammering out e-mails sitting beside the other Location Pastor when reports spilling from TV braked our typing to a halt. Cases were skyrocketing, travel restrictions were being rolled out, Tom Hanks had the virus, and the NBA postponed their season. You could see fear spread like thin spiders across the faces of news correspondents. I called a loved one on the way home that night and said, "mark this evening–the world is about to change."

It's now been a hundred and twenty days of quarantine. Over half a million people have lost their lives worldwide. Societies have shut down and economies have collapsed.

One hundred and twenty days. One hundred and twenty days of no physical worship services, good weeks and bad weeks, social distancing and no hugs, working nonstop hours to still do church, racial injustice and riots and division, murder hornets, *Tiger King*, anger and suspicion and conspiracy theories, political hostility and polarization, Saharan winds, being alone way more than is healthy for a human, worrying about my older parents across the country, normal life tensions amplified by everything, thinking I've had the virus twice only to finally go to the hospital with bags packed and test negative, and the way things are going, probably aliens invading Toronto later this evening.

And this is my Promised Land.

This is the dream, Joseph.

Currently, we had plans to safely reopen physical gatherings at our church this weekend. We'd had an inspiring, life-giving vision night with volunteers to prepare. *Finally*.

Then the country spiked again, and a quarter of our staff were exposed to someone who just tested positive. So, we had to send out communication to cancel our first back-in-person service before it even began, while some of us–that included me–waited to see if that meant we had the virus too.

In the meantime, I became internally out of breath from a relational kick in the gut I just received that I won't dare to bore you with the details of. I'll just say that even apart from all outside apocalyptic occurrences, my heart was gutted.

A few minutes ago, I parked under a tree. I wanted to find a safe but not-at-home place to be alone, work, and sit today. I began to get out of the car, but then gripped the steering wheel with my left hand and leaned back with a sigh as the tears came. I almost don't want to tell you I cried, because I feel like I've said that twenty times in this book already and you're going to think that's all I do, but honestly, it's fine. I cried. The tears leaked down my face. Eventually, I yielded to the inward flood rushing over me and leaned forward and buried my head into the rubber of the steering wheel and shook, my body racking with sobs for all the grief, and all the loss, and for all the things I don't even know how to name right now that are happening in my heart.

Welcome to life on earth.

Welcome to the Promised Land, Joshua.

As the tears slowed to a trickle, a song playing from my car caught my attention. The lyrics to Pat Barrett's song "Land of the Living" began to materialize and resonate in my mind for the first time. A song about healing again, feeling again, and seeing God's goodness in my life.

Maybe this is my new song in the night.

I already know. I will feel again, and I will heal again.

All I know is He's seen me through a lot, and He'll see me through this.

All I know is I will see His goodness in the land of the living.

I will continue to cross Jordan Rivers into new promised lands.

That doesn't mean I'll never see a desert again. It doesn't mean I'll never have to kill another giant or take another mountain.

It just means I'll be ready the next time I do.

It means I'll never be alone while going through it.

It means a *promised land life* can still be lived out, even during a wilderness season.

It means the best really is yet to come.

*What a God we have! And how fortunate we are to have him, this Father of our Master Jesus! Because Jesus was raised from the dead, we've been given a brand-new life and have everything to live for, including a future in heaven—and the future starts now! God is keeping careful watch over us and the future. (1 Peter 1:3-5 MSG)*

## Chapter Nineteen

PROMISED LAND

*"So, the Lord gave to Israel all the land he had sworn to give their ancestors, and they took possession of it and settled there."–Joshua 21:43 NLT*

*"After long training (forty years!) the people are addressed by Moses as if they are capable of doing what they have been created and saved to do: live as the people of God in the Promised Land of God. Live holy lives. Live the creation-salvation revolution. It has taken them a long time to grow up."–Eugene Peterson*

*"If you believe in this story...finish it."*
*–Mrs. Wheeler (Stranger Things)*

The moment their feet touched water's edge, the great Jordan River gathered itself up and piled away at a distance. Similar to the Red Sea miracle but different, God's methods remaining ever fresh, ever new.

Upon crossing, they elected leaders for the twelve tribes and set up corresponding stones at a place called Gilgal.
Then the men circumcised themselves. Then Jericho fell.

Then, If you were to cram in some movie candy and hit *fast forward*, you'd glitch through Achan's sin, Ai's destruction, covenants renewed, Joshua telling the sun to stand still, the Gibeonite deception and then *finally*—hit *play*—time has come for this bountiful, divinely gifted land to be divvied up like a pizza from Greenville Avenue.[1]

I can only imagine the moment, what it must have felt like for these people.

Hearts electric with realization, hands rubbing together with anticipation, joy unbearable in hearts seeing the dream come to pass in front of their eyes.

The time had come.

Land was distributed to the twelve tribes to inhabit, build, cultivate, and make babies in.

Most of them settled west of the Jordan. Reuben, Gad, and the half-tribe of Manasseh settled east.

One group, however—the *priests,* to be specific—was given no distinguishable land.

We read, *"But Moses gave no allotment of land to the tribe of Levi [Levites were the priests], for the Lord, the God of Israel, had promised that he himself would be their allotment."*[2]

Another translation says the priests were to be given no land allotment because the Lord Himself would be their "inheritance."

Seriously?

Sure, cities and pastureland were parceled out to them, and their inheritance included daily food and continual vocation. But still, no major land allotment.

How unfair is *that*?

Yet our initial reaction may reveal something of how we think and what we value.

See, the children of Israel got some land.

The priests got *God*.

God in all His fullness. God, His favor and essence, their continual portion. *The Lord* was their inheritance.

Unfair?

It'd be like agonizing over the dirty street corner given to Bill instead of me, because I only get *the Universe*.

These priests, these men who walked the tabernacle floors when the clouds got thick and throbbed with divinity, God's glory coming down, unbearable in splendor—I can assure you there was no complaint about their end of the deal. They knew what we need to know, that the promises never compare to *the Promiser*.

As discussed, there is a promised land *life* available in this earthly life.

But let's press deeper still, to the promised land *itself*.

God.

This isn't semantics here. No, this must sink deep down into our core. God Himself is the promised land our hearts were made for and have been dreaming of all along.

As St. Augustine of Hippo famously said, "You have made us for yourself, O Lord, and our hearts are restless until they rest in You."

The Priests knew this.

They knew their greatest joy would not be their property, but God's *Presence*.

They knew the first thing God did once He delivered the people was bring them to a mountain to experience and worship Him (I hope you're still dancing).

They knew God was their inheritance and that He was bigger than their wildest dreams.

They knew God was the best Promise of all.

Our wilderness guide, Moses, knew it too.

Entire books could be written on the destiny-dividing difference between Moses and the people he led, but this one's by far the most important: the children of Israel were beside-themselves-obsessed to get to their treasures; *Moses had already discovered his.*

This is why he laid on the mountain talking with God while the people tinkered restlessly below with their sad idolatries.

This is why the Israelites were forever complaining, discontent, and constantly longing for comforts of the flesh. Moses, meanwhile, imperfect though he was, walked steady under the umbrella of God's smile, surrounded in the comfort of God's Presence, invigorated by the divine friendship, always craving a deeper encounter with the God he loved and treasured.

Not long after Moses came down from the mountain, gripping the God-etched tablets, after the gold-calf-revival service down below, we read this beautiful, passionate request straight from Moses' heart to God's:

*"Now—show me Your glory."* (Exodus 32:18)

Moses wasn't content to know God as an acquaintance. He wanted to experience all of Him. So, he marshaled the nerve to ask.

God was pleased.

He told Moses no human eye could take in His unveiled form and make it out of the moment alive. So, he tenderly hid Moses in the cleft of a rock. There, ensconced by stone and God's protective Hand, Moses' eyes shut against God's palm, and God's searing goodness passed by, allowing Moses to linger upon the blazing trailing comet of His glory from behind.

Oh, the gravitas of this moment.

Oh, how little I settle for.

But back to the difference of Moses and the people:

"Show me the *goods*!" was the cry of the children of Israel.

"Show me Your *glory*!" was the cry of Moses.

The people were consumed with the benefits of God's hand. Moses was passionate about the pursuit of God's *face*.

The people craved deliverance. Moses craved the *Deliverer*.

The people wanted God's blessings. Moses wanted God *Himself*.

This is even more on display in Exodus 33 just verses before Moses asked to see God's glory, right after he'd come down from the mountain to find the idol in the people's hands.

God got angry. He shared his anger with Moses and told him to take the people and leave.

> Then the Lord said to Moses, "Leave this place, you and the people you brought up out of Egypt, and go up to the land I promised on oath to Abraham, Isaac and Jacob, saying, 'I will give it to your descendants.' I will send an angel before you and drive out the Canaanites, Amorites, Hittites, Perizzites, Hivites and Jebusites. Go up to the land flowing with milk and honey. **But I will not go with you**, because you are a stiff-necked people and I might destroy you on the way.'" (Exodus 33:1-3, emphasis mine)

To a selfish child, it almost sounded too good to be true. They had rebelled against God, and yet, because of the promise God had made for this group of people, He was about to finally get them out of this godforsaken wilderness and send them on ahead to their own Canaan Calabasas, overflowing with lobster and *Perrier*. He still promised to defeat all their enemies. He even promised to send one of His very own angels along to accompany them even though He Himself would no longer be going.

This was about to be the best day of their lives. The promise had finally come true. The deliverance was finally here. The destiny had finally arrived.

But look at Moses' response:

> Then Moses said to him, "**If your Presence does not go with us, do not send us up from here.**" (Exodus 33:15 emphasis mine)

No matter how many times I read this I'm still floored.

To Moses it didn't matter how great the future dreams, nor how painful the current circumstances. If God Himself wasn't the central part of the package, he wasn't interested.

Moses had tasted life, real life, actual *glory*, and it had ruined him. Moses had spoken face to face with the Maker, felt the current of His power run through His bones. He'd never again be content with a form of religion or mere blessings as replacement for the substance of God's tangible Presence and friendship. Foot-of-the-mountain living would never again hold appeal.

The Message Translation paraphrases Moses' response like this: *"If your presence doesn't take the lead here, call this trip off right now."*

If Your Presence isn't in it, call it off, God. Leave me right here.

And remember, when Moses said *"do not send us up from here,"* "here" was the *desert*. "Here" meant hunger, thirst, discomfort, sorrow and loss.

And yet Moses would've rather had problems and pain *with* God's Presence than the promised land *without* it.

I can't help but hope that's the posture of my heart.

I think it's pretty safe to say this was *not* the general posture for most of the Israelites. Can you imagine if the same proposition had been given to them as was given to Moses? They'd have booked a one-way flight that afternoon!

Sure, they mourned when they heard God's words of displeasure. But you and I both know that conviction would've been short-lived. If these grumblers constantly craved the memories of *Egypt* without God's Presence, they definitely would have taken the *Promised Land* without it!

Remember as well, unlike the people he was leading, Moses had been raised in a palace. He'd grown up in Egyptian luxury and ease.

He'd already tasted the limit to which worldly pleasure can bring anything lasting and fulfilling. The metallic emptiness of the earth's way no longer whet his appetite. He craved eternal things now.

*He [Moses] regarded disgrace for the sake of Christ as of greater value than the treasures of Egypt....*[3]

No deception of materialism or fleshly allure remained inside Moses. Unlike the children of Israel, he'd been there, done that. He knew there was no pillow soft enough to heal a mind and no house big enough to fill a heart. He knew we're all made and shaped for no less than God Himself.

o o o

My sophomore summer of high school, I went to the Dominican Republic on a mission trip.

It was exotic and romantic in all the ways I'd imagined, minus I didn't see anyone raised from the dead.

It transformed my heart, though. Long-lasting friendships formed and I showered in streets, slept on the floor, ate actual green eggs every morning, met God in beautiful new ways, dreamed about girls back home and laughed my guts out under burning orange skies.

I also had one of the most terrifying flights of my life.

We were there for a couple weeks and halfway through we'd had to charter a small toothpaste tube of an airplane to hop over to a nearby island. I've never loved flying as is, even though I travel quite a bit, but watching them duct-tape part of the engine back on and give a thumbs up in front of a toothless grin (at least that's how I remember it) before we taxied out placed a flaming iron of panic square in my chest.

By God's saving grace, I swallowed a most wonderful morsel of news early in the flight that numbed my nerves and kept my mind distracted—the pilot was Mandy Moore's dad.

Mandy Moore, if you don't know, was the pop-star crush of nearly every boy growing up in the 90's. She captured my heart in the movie *A Walk to Remember*. Now she *crushes* my heart on TV in *This is Us*.

To this day, I can't remember how I heard the news about her pilot dad. I just remember immediately ripping out a piece of paper and pen to declare my love.

This was my chance. She was beautiful. I heard she was a Christian. I was in love with her. And now her dad was the pilot of my flight. That's called *fate*, my friend.

I went to great lengths to tell her the good news that I was single, also a Christian, and would love to take her on a date were she ever to venture near Greenville, South Carolina. I sprayed some travel cologne on that baby, sealed her up, and handed it to the pilot on the way out.

"Can you give this to your daughter?"

He grinned and told me to have a good day.

The weeks after the Dominican trip passed slowly. One week after I got back and two weeks after giving her father the letter, I had still received nothing.

I *did* receive a love letter, but it was from one of the girls on the trip I'd met (just thought I would insert that).

Then one day a large manilla envelope arrived in the mail.

It was from her.

Mandy Moore.

*See, she wouldn't have even had to change her last name....*

She had sent me a high-gloss photograph signed with the words, "Dear Russ, best of luck," and then she'd added a heart and her autograph.

Underwhelming response to my proposal, sure. But love unrequited aside, I melted. I couldn't believe it. I think I slept with it by my bedside for a solid year.

(Cue some Dashboard Confessional song about waking in the night with her picture clearly in sight....)

Here's the thing, though. At the risk of minimizing what Mandy and I had, we didn't really know or desire each other. I knew of her, but I didn't *know* her.

I *admired* her, but I couldn't say I *desired* her.

And I think that's the difference that makes the difference. Just like many people in church today, I would say the children of Israel *admired* God, but I'm not so sure they *desired* God.

They liked the idea of being good people, good Israelites, today what we would say good "Christians." I'm sure they thought God was a great ideal and they for sure wanted the blessings He could provide so they could live a happy life. Unlike Moses, though, God was not the central treasure and passion of their heart.

That is a destiny-dividing distinction.

I've shared often over the years that the only reason I think someone as jacked up as me has made it this long following Jesus, besides grace upon grace upon grace, is the fact that when God crashed into my world, I didn't fall in love with the perks, I became rapturously consumed with the excitement of *Him*. Downright ravished by the thought of knowing and experiencing Him. It's why my favorite parable Jesus ever used to describe what it's like when someone "gets it" is the example of someone finding a straight up *Blackbeard's Treasure* in their backyard one day.

See, obligation or even good intention is not the steering wheel of our lives. Desire is. When all is said and done, our lives will always go the direction of what we want most.

So, as we close out the final lap of this book, these are questions worth writing down to wrestle within our hearts:

*Do we desire God Himself? Is there a hunger in us for His Presence? Are we in love with what He can do or are we in love with who He is? Is God our ultimate Promised Land?*

If we're mere admirers of God and not desirers of God, we'll make an idol of the Promised Land.

Even worse, if God isn't our ultimate treasure and motivation, we might even bail out on faith when things don't go our way. We'll be the spouse that marries for money, but now the money's gone, and suddenly Florida and that new shiny co-worker are calling our name.

If God isn't our ultimate treasure and motivation, then when we do get blessings, they'll turn into bondage.

Interesting enough, the gold they used to make the golden calf when Moses took too long was ironically the same plunder God blessed them with when they left Egypt. But it wasn't enough to fill their hearts when their souls remained distant from a life-giving relationship with God.

Just practically, if God Himself isn't our ultimate destination, we will miss many precious moments of life waiting for "when." We'll make an idol of future promised land seasons, while always missing the beauty and purpose of the present season.

We'll fantasize about when I graduate middle school, then high school, then college, then marriage, then kids, then career, then...and we'll let the felt absence of future blessings rob us from the actual joy of present blessings, not to mention the ultimate Blessing that life was created to revolve around in the first place.

The balance of living a vision-filled but present life, as I once heard Pastor Judah Smith put it, is "to live *in* the moment but *for* the future."

See, the continuous deception of "when I get there" is a thief of moments. But a passionate pursuit of the Presence of God is oxygen that will breathe *into* our moments.

I'm still working on this, trust me, but I've found life gets rich and I get freed up to enjoy the journey when I come to the place in my heart where God truly is the Promised Land. God, *You* are the summit of all my hopes and dreams. You are my big, great obsession.

I'm praying like crazy for some "land." Trust me.

But like the priests, *God, You're my portion. You're my daily bread and water. You're the lily of the valley and the great morning star. Everything that the deepest parts of my soul have ever longed for all find their home and fulfillment in You.*

It's okay if we're not there yet.

Again, the good news is the longer we walk with Jesus, the easier it is to fall in love with Him. The easier it gets to enjoy the journey with Him in the car, no matter how much we want the road trip from hell to finally come to an end.

The longer we're with Him, the more we begin to notice His smile tucked inside of His ways. We discover His kindness and faithfulness.

The more we walk through lonely valleys with Him, the more we experience how extravagant His love and care is for us, and in return it deepens our affection and love for Him.

Like spoiled children the Israelites were obsessed with God's *gifts*. But like Moses I want to be obsessed with His *Presence*.

Sure, Moses deeply anticipated the coming Promised Land. He dreamed of it. No doubt he was looking forward to no longer laying his head on rocks and fighting off thirst and coyotes.

Yet he discovered a freeing, invigorating secret along the way. The blessings aren't the Promised Land. God is.

In every season, the treasure chest of delights that is God is more than enough.

In every season, during the cold nights, we must continue to feed the fire of our passion for Him.


○ ○ ○


I spent the summer after Argentina seeing some unbelievable things. I saw God answer the kind of prayers and perform the kind of healings and miracles that if I were to put them here in print, you most likely would not believe me.

And yet I was frustrated.

I would read of Moses' encounters with God, envision the events on the pages of Scripture, and I'd get a little green with envy.

I wanted what Moses had. No, I don't live for sensational moments or mountaintop highs, I get that. But Moses asked to see His glory. I wanted to as well.

In the middle of that summer, I was with a church group doing ministry at a summer camp in Chicago, rolling this frustration around in my head like bitter licorice.

Before service one night I flipped open my Bible and read the following:

*The old way, with laws etched in stone, led to death, though it began with such glory that the people of Israel could not bear to look at Moses' face. For his face shone with the glory of God, even though the brightness was already fading away. Shouldn't we expect far greater glory under the new way, now that the Holy Spirit is giving life? If the old way, which brings condemnation, was glorious, how much more glorious is the new way, which makes us right with God! In fact, that first glory was not glorious at all compared with the overwhelming glory of the new way. So, if the old way, which has been replaced, was glorious, how much more glorious is the new, which remains forever!* (2nd Corinthians 3:7-11)

In other words, Moses had nothing compared to us.

I can't promise you what kind of spectacular, highlight-reel moments you might experience. That's not the point.

But I can tell you this. You and I live in the days where Jesus has come to earth and sent His Spirit to live in us. He's paid for all our crimes and given us grave-destroying power and life-producing promises. He destroyed the veil between us and God's Presence so that we can enter anytime, anywhere.

Plus, I can tell you, no matter how long you've followed Jesus, there are more Mt. Sinais to climb. Let's keep pressing into the cloud.

# Chapter Twenty

## CANAAN & EDEN

*"I'll see you in another life, brotha."*
*—Desmond Hume (LOST)*

*"My days have passed, my plans are shattered. Yet the desires of my heart turn night into day; in the face of darkness light is near."—Job 17:11-12*

*"Your calling is not to stay alive but to stay in love."*
*—John Piper*

I believe and pray you're nearer to your next promised land season than you ever imagined.

But even after that, there's more.

In *The Chronicles of Narnia*, C.S. Lewis puts image and soul to what for many of us remains flat and mental—the life beyond this life. The extraordinary beyond the mundane. The Eden that can and *will* return.

Even in our best promised lands on this side, in our most honest and alone moments, we acknowledge that an ache remains. Something is still missing. The yearning to return to Eden still lingers and echoes through the corridors of every human.

This is where our sights and imaginations must remain tethered to the life beyond this life. We have to remember there's more. We have to remember God is on a mission to restore *everything*.

Narnia remains just on the other side of this mysterious wardrobe we're in.

We must keep this in view when we begin to set unrealistic expectations on an earthly life. I say this as an audacious dreamer who is ludicrously optimistic about the future and what can be experienced in this world.

Yet the older I get, the more I'm learning there are no final resolutions of the soul on this side, at least as far as I'm concerned.

I'm learning to live boldly for the dreams I still have and the people that still need hope. But I'm also learning not to put all of hope's eggs in the basket of a blink-of-an-eye, millisecond life that's "just a vapor" in light of eternity. Instead I'm learning, ever so slowly, to push my investments and hopes into a homeland that will last forever.

Once the Israelites crossed the Jordan, there were still giants to fight, loved ones who died, wounds that never quite healed, and mysteries of life that never completely wrapped up. And I can tell you, no matter how large and ripe the grapes tasted in Canaan, it never quite tasted like Eden again.

That isn't pessimism. It's realism. And embracing a hope-filled reality in a fallen world is a healthy dichotomy that can liberate us to dream, to believe, and to be filled with unspeakable joy and adventure while simultaneously steeling us against the poison-tipped rhetoric of any televangelist—or politician, for that matter—who would like to sell us on a way to get back to Eden on this side.

I hope you don't find what I'm about to say disappointing and I think you know this anyways, but let's settle the matter. No matter how beautiful your life and my life become, the ache will remain.

In my view, no one speaks more pointedly and beautifully on this than C.S. Lewis. The following quote from *Weight of Glory* is rather lengthy, but worth the absorption:

In speaking of this desire for our own far off country, which we find in ourselves even now, I feel a certain shyness. I am almost committing an indecency. I am trying to rip open the inconsolable secret in each one of you—the secret which hurts so much that you take your revenge on it by calling it names like Nostalgia and Romanticism and Adolescence; the secret also which pierces with such sweetness that when, in very intimate conversation, the mention of it becomes imminent, we grow awkward and affect to laugh at ourselves; the secret we cannot hide and cannot tell, though we desire to do both. We cannot tell it because it is a desire for something that has never actually appeared in our experience. We cannot hide it because our experience is constantly suggesting it, and we betray ourselves like lovers at the mention of a name. Our commonest expedient is to call it beauty and behave as if that had settled the matter. Wordsworth's expedient was to identify it with certain moments in his own past. But all this is a cheat. If Wordsworth had gone back to those moments in the past, he would not have found the thing itself, but only the reminder of it; what he remembered would turn out to be itself a remembering. The books or the music in which we thought the beauty was located will betray us if we trust to them; it was not in them, it only came through them, and what came through them was longing. These things—the beauty, the memory of our own past—are good images of what we really desire; but if they are mistaken for the thing itself they turn into dumb idols, breaking the hearts of their worshipers. For they are not the thing itself; they are only the scent of a flower we have not found, the echo of a tune we have not heard, news from a country we have never yet visited.

As I type this, I'm outside in Bexley, one of those trendy little blocks sandwiched between wealthy neighborhoods and rougher patches of town. Today is rare, especially for Ohio. It's 75°F in November and I'm watching the dimmers of the sky slowly turn clockwise, dusk marrying the gold, burnt orange, and oaken colors of autumn, fading sunlight cascading through the leaves.

It's such a beautiful evening, I nearly can't enjoy it.

Call me a tortured soul, accuse my enneagram four wing of soaring, but nights like this tug out an ache in me that has only grown with age. The beauty, the nostalgia, the memories beyond my memories, the urges I can't name, the restless yearning. All that unnamed yearning. It all hurts.

It's as if there's some kind of whispered conversation occurring in the subterranean places in me, but I can't quite decipher the language.

And I just have to hope, I have to know beyond all knowing, the mystery inside me points back to the Eden inside me. I have to know one day the second Adam will take me by the hand and lead me back to the land the first Adam messed up. Only this one will be restored, and the golden healing and magic of those days will last forever.

I feel that all of this, and what Lewis wrote, is not only quite moving, but quite freeing. When we can take the pressure off this life to satisfy every eternal craving, we can be liberated to enjoy it and serve this world while we're here.

The bad news is utopia isn't arriving.

The good news is the kingdom has already come.

The kingdom of God—the culture and rule of heaven— is something we can step into, experience and be wholly transformed by.

We can even walk in its spirit and produce its fruit. But one day, oh, one day, we'll also walk its streets and take hold its leaves. We'll breathe in final healing and step into a divine, reclaimed humanity we were always meant for. We will see *God.*

The dance for now is simply to live in, pray down, and transfer the oxygen of that eternal reality into the current here and now. That is where contentment and satisfaction begins. That also, by the way, is where we generate the most profound and lasting impact here below.

In fact, while I'm already over-sharing Lewis quotes (who doesn't?), here's his take on the matter:

*"If you read history, you will find that the Christians who did the most for the present world were precisely those who thought most of the next."*

I want to step into my *promised land life* as I press on to know my *promised land God*, keeping in mind my true eternal *promised land home* and hopes all still lie ahead of me in eternity.

*"The Lord will surely comfort Zion and will look on all her ruins; He will make her deserts like Eden, her wastelands like the garden of the Lord."* (Isaiah 51:3)

o o o

I'm one of those weird guys who's thought about my wedding a lot.

I can't wait to meet the girl God has for me. I can't wait to see her walk down the aisle. I want to have around fifty groomsmen, and I want the wedding to be modern, minimal and yet edgy enough to never forget, while upheld with some timeless elements and feel, a trestle of tradition if you will. I want a sunset and I want a Scottish guy to play bagpipes, haunting and tantalizing, like the ones from *Braveheart*. I want there to be a lot of people there, everyone happy, everyone in love. I want a memorable reception, full of macaroni and cheese casserole, pour over coffee stations, food far too bougie to pronounce, and every type of meat, cheese and *hors d'ouevre* imaginable. Everyone will be dancing, close-up magicians will be executing some micro magic by the dessert table, old friend groups will be laughing too loudly by the wine bar, heck, artists might be painting near the beach for all I know, a surprise musician might make the rounds, and there will be enough merriment to keep people smiling for a year.

I'm getting older in life, so I guess I better start saving for that one.

It'll also just be nice to not be at someone *else's* wedding for once.

I don't know about you, but I've been to a lot.

I've attended too many to count, I'm a serial groomsman, and tomorrow I'm officiating a small ceremony somewhere out in the middle of nowhere for a couple that attends my church.

I've also been to all *kinds* of weddings. Some are just odd, some are fine but fade into the winter of my memory like snow, while others stand out like an Indian summer in the north, piercing and beautiful.

I attended one of the latter a few years ago in Cincinnati. I'd driven in from Atlanta, found a last second "plus one" from Lexington and snuck in just in time. Close to a thousand packed out a rustic, startling cathedral. The grandiosity of it all took my breath. Blessings and prayers poured forth from the family like oil, carrying in a scent of heaven, and you could almost smell the thick myrrh of blessing that drenched the moment, the couple, and the generational prayers they represented.

After the ceremony we were all escorted outside under starch white tents to mingle and refresh while we awaited our seating back inside for a wedding course from something off one of Chef Ramsey's cooking shows. I still don't know which diamond company his dad owns, but I want to find out.

Much earlier in life, I was taken aback by the wedding of my best friend's older sister. Danielle was Miss South Carolina and became like a surrogate older sister to me as well, especially during my awkward adolescent years. And let me tell you, the regality and beauty of her wedding did not disappoint. A horse-drawn carriage pulled her like a southern princess over hills painted by a setting sun and her radiance cast a kind of Bardic spell on everyone present. I think angels even began to sing. Bagpipes led the procession (sound familiar?) as her dad floated her across the field to an open-air, high-roofed barn. Time shrunk, audible gasps punctuated the night, and the Spirit kissed that ceremony so tangibly everyone could feel it on the skin of their arms.

My favorite wedding memory of all time, however, was a vow renewal ceremony with Marc and Colleen.

Marc was one of my best friends through high school and early college. Though much older than me, he possessed a youthfulness of spirit that magnetized my company. He also owned a mansion— literally, a designated historical landmark—a mile from my house. So yeah, that had its perks.

He and his wife Colleen own the largest bridal festival company in the southeast and my friends and I would help them pipe-and-drape arenas all over that part of the country to earn our first few grown-up paychecks. He also coached our church basketball league, though, don't tell him I said this, I'm not sure he'd ever seen a game in his life prior to that season. I think he just wanted to be one of the guys.

All that to say, I knew when he asked me to be part of his vow renewal, this would be epic.

Fast forward to that summer.

They paid for twenty of their closest friends, plus photographers, to go on an
all-expense paid week-long cruise together. Hundred-dollar-a-piece leis were imported from Hawaii and on the ceremony day we donned them along with our off-white linen attire as a Jamaican church of God minister led Marc and Colleen

in a tropical vow renewal. Congos began to play on the outside as drippy New Found Glory riffs began to play in my mind. Colt led an acoustic love song to seal the deal, and then we were walked over to shore-side tables weighed down with lobster, hot dessert and chilled champagne, the warm waves lapping at our toes while we dined in the sunset.

I mean, come on.

Of course, all this is nothing to some of you who have perhaps attended an actual celebrity wedding.

Out of curiosity I looked up the top five most expensive of all time. Chelsea Clinton's trailed in last at a mere five million dollars. Perhaps not surprisingly, Princess Diana's marriage to Prince Charles took the proverbial wedding cake at *one hundred and ten million dollars.*

Let's be honest. It's mindless but delicious entertainment to read of the unbridled luxury of Jennifer Anniston or Kanye's ceremonies and after parties.

But….

Here's why I semi-brag and even bring any of this up. If we're going to train the feelers of our mind to begin to explore heaven again, here's an icebreaker…what will *heaven's* wedding be like?

All things love, after all, including marriages *and* weddings, are but shadows of the real thing waiting on the other side of Narnia's wardrobe.

*And the angel said to me, "Write this: Blessed are those who are invited to the wedding feast of the Lamb."* (Revelation 19:9 NLT)

Paul had a vision of paradise, much of which he was forbidden to even try to express here on earth and of which he could only shake his head in staggering awe and write *"no eye has seen, no ear has heard, no mind can conceive what God has in store."* I can't help but wonder if part of that had to do with the upcoming wedding.

Can you imagine the colors? The sights and sounds? The people, animals, and creatures? The food, drink, and tastes? The sounds, the music, and the centuries upon centuries of dancing to follow?

What will God say? What will God *do*? What will *we* do? Can you imagine the maddening joy?

Sorry, *Vanity Fair,* anything on earth is a kid coloring crayons by the trash compared to what's to come.

I'm just trying to get your mind to feast for a minute on the upcoming permanent promised land. The initial celebrations if nothing else. To allow these thoughts to become the apricity to your cold desert nights.

I can't wait for the wedding in heaven. I can't wait to dine with Jesus. Ask all my questions. Put a ring on my finger. Be made whole by His smile.

Are you imagining it now?

Chris Rice, a Christian artist from the 90's, wrote a song called "Deep enough to Dream" in which he keeps dozing off, dreaming of heaven. It's a beautiful song, sickly-sweet and innocent, like most of his others. But I love the bridge and the childlike depiction of heaven he indulges about breaking bread with our heroes, and the peace and holiness of the air, and all the colors and creatures. You should listen to it after this chapter if you get the chance.

I cannot wait for that day. See, whenever I read the verse that says we will not marry in heaven, it kind of makes me sad to be honest. No marriage? No romance? No sex? This has almost depressed me at times—especially if I don't marry before I die. No *sex*??

But I think this is because I forget about the *Sacred Romance*[1]. I forget it came first, that it is a hundred times greater and purer and more satisfying. I forget that the most exhilarating love and life I could ever hope to experience on this broken planet will pale miserably in comparison to the moment I reach out and touch His face.

o o o

I don't know what you think about all those people who write books claiming to have been to heaven and back.

Right or wrong, I tend to be skeptical.

I once went to dinner with a family whose son had clinically died and come back to life. He had seen and reported back some impressive things to be sure, even near-death views and earthly details surrounding the hospital and the events of his experience he would have had no way of knowing. His story has inspired and comforted families all over the world.

They even wrote a book based off the events called *Heaven Is for Real*. To date it's sold a million and a half copies. The follow-up movie grossed over a hundred million dollars at the box office.

I remember being at BD's Mongolian Grill in Lexington, Kentucky, sitting across from this five or six-year-old boy fresh out of paradise. I had already scarfed down my salty bowl of Asian confusion and between sips of my soda, I kept trying to pry some kind of secret out of his eyes.

*Did you really see Paul? Did you really see heaven? What's it like? What should I know?*

But he just kept playing with his toy truck in between bites of chicken nuggets.

I've read dozens and dozens of books on heaven to be honest, especially early on in my faith. To me the most convincing is *90 Minutes in Heaven* by Don Piper (not to be confused with John). There's a realism, a weightiness, a grittiness to the book that is stripped of sentimentality and false happy endings and it rang a true note inside me when I read it.

My favorite book on heaven, though, isn't any kind of biography or near-death experience. It's a book simply called *Heaven* by Randy Alcorn. It's intriguing, balanced and refreshing. Do yourself a favor and at least buy the devotional.

In the book he picks up on a theme so woven throughout Scripture I think we miss it in our angels-on-clouds, Sunday school idealizations of heaven.

Heaven, for all it will include and not include, will primarily be a *restoration* of everything God originally had in mind, only better.

Heaven will not be *out there* somewhere. It will be *on earth*. A renewed earth. Eden restored.

*Then I saw a new heaven and a new earth, for the old heaven and the old earth had disappeared. And the sea was also gone. And I saw the holy city, the new Jerusalem, coming down from God out of heaven like a bride beautifully dressed for her husband.*

*I heard a loud shout from the throne, saying, "Look, God's home is now among his people! He will live with them, and they will be his people. God himself will be with them. He will wipe every tear from their eyes, and there will be no more death or sorrow or crying or pain. All these things are gone forever." (Revelation 21:1-4 NLT)*

Beautiful, isn't it?

That's the first paragraph in the second to last chapter in Scripture. The chapter title in my Bible for the next chapter, the very last chapter in the whole book, Revelation 22, is literally "Eden Restored."

*Then the angel showed me a river with the water of life, clear as crystal, flowing from the throne of God and of the Lamb. It flowed down the center of the main street. On each side of the river grew a tree of life, bearing twelve crops of fruit, with a fresh crop each month. The leaves were used for medicine to heal the nations.*
*No longer will there be a curse upon anything. For the throne of God and of the Lamb will be there, and his servants will worship him. And they will see his face, and his name will be written on their foreheads. And there will be no night there—no need for lamps or sun—for the Lord God will shine on them. And they will reign forever and ever.*

Genesis to Revelation.

What began in a garden ends in a garden.

What was broken from the *fruit of a tree* was restored through what Jesus *did on a tree* and then ends with the *leaves of a tree* that bring the longed-for healing of all nations and all people.

What began in Eden ends in Eden.

A new, glorious creation to steward.

Whatever we know of that eternal promised land, three diamonds emerge from this earth-side of eternity, three truths about what will make heaven so painfully beautiful, our minds can't come near the shores of its oceans to even conceive it.

Three P's: Presence, Paradise, and Purpose.

*Presence.* Specifically, the Presence of God.

This one swallows up the other two and even if the other two realities ceased to exist, this alone would make heaven *heaven*.

God is there.

Words would fail if I spent a thousand years trying to articulate and hypothesize what it will be like in my renewed, glorified body to see God. To see Jesus. To be exposed to His splendor, His nearness, and the light of His glory. The thought of beholding my Maker, of seeing the source of life I've always talked about *in person*. Losing myself in the oasis of who He is.

Heaven isn't heaven because of gold streets or no pain. Heaven is heaven because of God.

And yet, it will also be *paradise*. Jesus straight up told the broken thief on the cross next to him that he was about to join Him in paradise that evening.

No pain, suffering, injustice, sickness, illness, loneliness, death, fear, insecurity, loss, anxiety, sin, disappointment or temptation. Can you imagine?

On the contrary, there will be *"pleasures at his right hand forevermore"*[2]. Joy unspeakable, peace incomprehensible, love supernatural, reunions with loved ones, sights and sounds to behold, a God to encounter, a universe to explore, colors and delights and experiences we could never even imagine with our finite minds as we kick our feet along this clod of clay. Our senses will be exploding from day one.

But it's the third "P" of heaven we tend to think about least.

There will be *purpose* in heaven.

Some people secretly, shamefully nurse a terror they will be bored in heaven.

This is because we don't understand the first two "P's" to any measurable degree.

But it's also because we forget the third.

Heaven will not consist of lying around on clouds playing harps like the horrible, milquetoast Hallmark cards we've seen.

In Eden restored, just as life was in Eden uncorrupted, there will be *things to do*.

Even before Eden was tainted by the fall, God had entrusted Adam and Eve with purpose. Work was given *before* the fall. That first couple was blessed with the opportunity and obligation to produce, to multiply themselves, and to steward the wonderful creation God had provided.

In the new Eden, the joy and satisfaction of worthwhile labor will not only continue; it will be redeemed and intensified.

As Randy Alcorn points out, "The New Earth isn't a blissful realm that we'll merely visit, as vacationers go to a theme park. Rather, it's a realm we'll joyfully rule with Jesus, exercising dominion as God's image-bearers."

We see this truth all through Scripture. Our inheritance as God's children in eternity will not just be in what we *have* or what we *experience*, but in what we *do*.

Consider this familiar passage for one example: *"Well done, my good servant!' his master replied. 'Because you have been trustworthy in a very small matter, take charge of ten cities.'"*[3]

In heaven, there will be—without the painful, anxious curse of the fall—a continually self-renewing, joyful, replenishing and eternal work we will have the joy to be a part of. Perhaps for you, if you're faithful with a little on this side, it might even be to rule a city. Or ten.

What will all this look like?

We have the rest of our lives to dream and consider that.

And we should.

"Our liveliness in all duties, our enduring of tribulation, our honoring of God, the vigor of our love, thankfulness, and all our graces, yea, the very being of our religion and Christianity, depend on the believing, serious thoughts of our rest [heaven]."–Richard Baxter

o o o

So, what do we until then?

Surely, we don't fall into the fatalistic, lazy "rest, relax and be raptured" of past generations.

Nor do we hunker down with the equally unhealthy "everything's-going-to-hell-in-a-handbasket" spirit of fear and self-preservation that cause people to withdraw from engaging with society and the mission of God's love for people.

No, until we cross the threshold of death into our everlasting Eden, we cultivate and enter into the penultimate promised land of "abundant life" on this side.

By God's grace and with the help of His Spirit, we allow ourselves to become everything God had in mind and we knock down every giant in our way that would keep us from the fullness of His abundance and His promises.

And in all that, we live with *purpose*.

In fact, I emphasized the third "P" of heaven not only to whet your appetite for your eternal promised land. I also say it to leave you with one last note as you enter your "earthly" promised lands. We must always remember in every season, no matter how great, we have been entrusted with both the privilege and blessing of *purpose*.

On the morning of May 20th, 2000, a wispy-haired, earnest preacher named John Piper took the platform at the third ever *Passion Conference* to speak to college-aged students looking for a deeper sense of meaning and spirituality. Gusts of wind blew away his notes and hair as he navigated the distracting elements to deliver his message.

Dr. Piper had asked God before he spoke for "a prophetic word that would have a ripple effect to the ends of the earth and to eternity."

I think God did.

Piper's ministry changed dramatically from that point. The book *Don't Waste Your Life* emerged from the sermon's theme and is still lapping the shores of time and hearts. It changed my life when I went off to Argentina for college.

Twenty years later, they passed out a free copy to all 65,000 students that attended this year's *Passion Conference*, and I had the personal privilege to hand them down like special reserve mints to some of the college students in our church.

Back to that original message, though.

"You don't have to know a lot of things for your life to make a lasting difference in the world," he started. "You don't have to be smart, or good-looking, or from a good family. You just have to know a few, basic, glorious, majestic, obvious, unchanging, eternal things, and be gripped by them, and be willing to lay down your life for them."

Several minutes in he laid out the comparison that helped form a generation. He told the true story of a couple at his church in their 80's who dedicated their lives as missionaries to the poor. Recently they had died in a tragic accident. From there, he asked the young crowd if this older couple, having given their earthly all for God's glory and sacrificed so passionately for people, now standing in the Presence of God, should consider their lives a tragedy.

The crowd answered with a resounding *no*.

From there he juxtaposed a familiar tale from the pages of a recent *Reader's Digest* of a couple in their late 50's who retired and moved to Florida, spending all their time trawling on their boat, perfecting their golf swing, and collecting shells.

Here's where the tension builds. Here's where the bomb lands.

"*That* is a tragedy," he concluded, asking what the conversation was going to be when they entered heaven. "Look, Lord, here are my shells."

This may sound very harsh to our comfort-obsessed, Americanized ears, but I don't believe he was railing against retirement or enjoying life. I think he was railing against *wasting* our life. *Eternity* is what should burn in our hearts the older we get, not *epicureanism* or *ease*.

Holocaust survivor and psychologist Viktor Frankl once said, "When a person can't find a deep sense of meaning, they distract themselves with pleasure."

Even in the promised land on earth we should live for *purpose*, not *pleasure*. And ironically, in return, this kind of life will fill us with more *joy*.

In fact, let's circle back to hang out with Caleb one last time.

Over forty-five years have passed. He's eighty-five years old. He's been faithful. Only he and Joshua survived the previous generation, and it's time to inherit the land. So, Caleb asks for what's his and Joshua affirmed him and blessed him.

Wait, blessed him with what?

Watch this.

Joshua *blessed* him with the opportunity to fight another battle.

So Caleb, in case you forgot, decides to charge up the most challenging hill, against the most fortified city, take on the biggest battle himself instead of letting the younger soldiers do it for him, fight the biggest giants still alive, and then take his most desired land.

Caleb knew even then the promised land doesn't represent a problem free life; it represents a power-filled life where we fight hell and bear fruit. Where we cry tears and praise God. Where we suffer loss and experience glory.

Then, after Caleb conquered his land, something interesting happened.

He had been blessed with a giant to fight.

So, he turned around and returned the blessing.

Hidden in a somewhat obscure passage in Judges 1, we read:

*Then Caleb said, "Whoever attacks Kirjath Sepher and takes it, to him I will give my daughter Achsah as wife."*

*And Othniel the son of Kenaz, Caleb's younger brother,*
*took it; so he gave him his daughter Achsah as wife.*

I love it (though I'm glad marriage looks different now).
I love that the last thing we discover about Caleb is he gave his
nephew a purpose. He gave him a challenge.

He didn't hate his nephew. He loved his nephew. He must
have known one of the greatest gifts you can give someone in life
is a God-sized challenge and vision to run after. Another mountain
to take. A purpose to propel you forward.

The call to *choose your land*, and then go after it.

Othniel, his nephew who embraced the challenge, ended
up becoming Israel's first judge, by the way.

Caleb knew sometimes people can't recognize just how
big God is *inside* them until they experience a really big Goliath
fall *in front of* them.

So where does that leave us?

Now that you've been through this wilderness, one of
the greatest purposes you get to step into is helping other
people discover *their* purpose. Helping lead them through *their*
wilderness.

Have you battled sickness? You are positioned unlike
anyone else to help people battling *their* sickness.

Have you been through a wilderness of addiction? If so,
you can turn your hand back to lift someone else up, pointing out
the slippery rocks to watch out for.

Has your story been divorce? Depression? Failure? Doubts and deconstruction of your faith? Specific internal struggles? Loss and grief? Breakthrough from challenging environments?

Whatever your story, consider yourself ordained with a challenge and a purpose to be a guide in someone else's story.

I want to remind you the greatest blessing isn't comfort. It's meaning.

o o o

To return to the beginning of this chapter, let's set the record straight. Utopia is not arriving, not globally and not personally. In fact, something better has happened and is going to happen.

Eden, with everything God originally had in mind, will be restored.

And the kingdom of heaven has come.

Our posture on earth is not to wait blissfully for utopia.

Nor is it to curse the darkness, engage in culture wars, and make other people the enemy.

Our posture is to serve, love, pray, and shine bright, relentlessly bring the kingdom here and now.

I am praying while you do that you experience God's blessing richly envelop your life. I'm praying for His face to shine on you like the sun.

God is able to bless you abundantly.

I want to remind and speak over you again the promise of Isaiah 43:18-19:

*"Forget the former things;*
*do not dwell on the past.*
*See, I am doing a new thing!*
*Now it springs up; do you not perceive it?*
*I am making a way in the wilderness*
*and streams in the wasteland."*

I'm believing that for you.

There is nothing you have been through God cannot heal, cannot mend, cannot redeem and cannot leverage to propel you into a beautiful future.

You are not defined by your worst moments or what anyone has done to you. Your past does *not* have to hold you back. God is creating new things, even now, out of the soil of your life.

Allow faith and courage to move you.

May you be continually refreshed by His love for you.

May his favor rest upon you.

May His mercies undergird you.

I'm believing if it hasn't happened yet, that soon, very soon, your tears turn to wine.

I'm praying you're in or nearing the promised land.

And either way, if breath is still in your lungs, you still have mountains to take, a God to experience, giants to slay, people to love, victories to secure, and a world to impact.

Welcome to Canaan. Go choose your land.

*PS*—See you at the wedding.

"Who told you that night would never end in day?
Don't you know that day follows night, that flood comes
after ebb, that spring and summer succeed winter?
Be full of hope! Hope forever!
For God does not fail you."

– Charles Spurgeon

## WILDERNESS WRITINGS

(Notes from the Section—What stood out?)

_____

_____

_____

_____

_____

_____

_____

_____

_____

_____

_____

_____

_____

_____

## DESERT DECISIONS
(Future Applications—What steps are you going to take?)

_____

_____

_____

_____

_____

_____

_____

_____

_____

_____

_____

_____

_____

_____

# ACKNOWLEDGEMENTS

The richness of my life is relationships. To them I owe all.

At the top of that list is Jesus and the scandalous mercy and love He has drenched me with. His grace and friendship in my life are both meat and oxygen to my soul.

My parents. You have embodied the unconditional love of God in real time. Any good traits I have come from you. Mom, you are the kindest soul ever to walk earth. Dad, you're brilliant and a hero, and I love traveling the world with you.

To every pastor and/or mentor I've been fortunate to have in life, from early age to now: Jim Stephenson, Jerry Madden, Lee Claypoole, Clint Claypoole, Allan Malloy, Tim Moore. I honor you all. Pastors Tim, Lee, and Clint, in particular, you three have pastored and led me and shaped me through the most formative of my years. You'll never know what your influence has meant. Pastor Allan, thank you for extending to me the ropes of grace instead of the noose. Allison Rhodes and George Davis, thank you for serving as mentors in early years.

To Zach, Tim, Logan, and my sister Rebecca, thank you for so tirelessly reading, editing, and giving feedback. Also, to everyone at *Gatekeeper Press*, you have helped turn a lifelong dream into a reality, for which I am forever indebted. Jennifer, thank you for your patience, and Julie, for your thoroughness.

To the unofficial *HFTW* creative team of Kevin, Trae, Tucker, Christi, and Logan. Your eyes, minds and creative gifts have brought texture, beauty and visibility to what used to only exist in my mind. Thank you.

Finally, to my wilderness ropes—the companions that have seen me through the toughest times. To Colt, Amanda, Joel, Allen and Logan—your friendship has not just been survival to me; it's been life and color.

# ABOUT THE AUTHOR

Russ currently resides in Columbus, Ohio, and serves as an Executive Pastor at *X Church*. There he teaches, preaches, leads, creates content, and helps co-host a weekly podcast.

He loves traveling, reading, working out, getting lost, cooking, making Apple Playlists, live music, coffee-shop-hopping, talking theology and philosophy and politics, and eating food too hard to pronounce.

He'd love to know how to celebrate, listen or pray for you on your wilderness journey. Shoot him an email at contact.russmoore@gmail.com or connect with him on Instagram at @mooreruss. To be encouraged with more content from Russ or book him to speak, visit his website at www.hopeforthewilderness.com.

# NOTES

*Scriptures are all in NIV except when marked otherwise*

## Introduction

1. Wilderness Hospitality concept drawn from Dallas Willard's "Divine Conspiracy" pg. 102

## Chapter 1—No Wasted Tickets

N/A

## Chapter 2—Welcome to the Wilderness

1. https://www.earthdate.org/exploring-earths-driest-deserts

2. Ancient but mainstream personality typing system recently re-popularized by Ian Chron in his book *The Road Back to You.*

3. John Eldredge concept

## Chapter 3—The Wheel of Purpose

1. Psalm 22:1-5

2. Matthew 27:46

3. Donald Miller uses this phrase in his best-selling memoir Blue Like Jazz

4. Matthew 5:45

5. Romans 8:29

6. 2 Corinthians 4:7

7. 2 Timothy 2:21

8. Mark 2:22

**Chapter 4**–*The Unwanted Gift*

1. 1 Samuel 16:1

2. Genesis 50:20

3. Psalm 42:3,4

**Chapter 5**–*Dancing in the Desert*

1. This was a paraphrase. Here's the full quote. "He never concealed His tears; He showed them plainly on his open face at any given sight; such as the far sight of His native city. Yet He concealed something... He never restrained His anger. He flung furniture down the front steps of the Temple... I say it with reverence; there was in that shattering personality a thread that must be called shyness. There was something that He hid from all men when He went up a mountain to pray... There was some one thing that was too great for God to show us when He walked upon our earth; and I have sometimes fancied that it was His **mirth**." (Orthodoxy, emphasis mine)

2. Another Chesterton nod/phrase

3. John Piper, a well-known author and former pastor, famously contends that "God is most glorified in us when we are most satisfied in Him."

   One day, in a Q & A, he was asked the following question:

   "Given the emphasis of worship as the experience of being satisfied in God, how can someone worship God joyfully in the corporate service, if he or she is struggling with depression?"

   He spoke carefully, tenderly and passionately. And I hope his answer stirs and soothes your heart as much as it did mine.

   John Piper: "Being satisfied in God is not a description of any particular outward emotional state. You can be satisfied in God and be weeping your eyes out at the death of your mother. You can be satisfied in God while praying and aching for your lost child. And the form that satisfaction in God expresses itself with will vary according to all kinds of locations in life, experience in life... But what I would say to the depressed person is...

   There will be, if they're born again, a seed of contentment in Christ. A seed. And the form it might take is—'right now, I feel nothing. I am totally numb emotionally. But, I have a memory, that there was once a sweetness of affection, a sweetness of trust. A sweetness. And I by faith believe it's still down there. Because theologically the Bible says He'll be faithful to me.

   'And that I right now, in this room, while everyone's singing and I don't have any feelings to sing at all, am saying to Him, 'please—restore to me the joy of my salvation.'

   That sentence, coming out of your mouth, with the raw faith that is down there, is worship."

4. He asked the Lord for a song. God gave him one. From that evening on, when two am came, he had something. He describes that as the smallest breaking of the cloud that would eventually lead him back to the light of day. The song God gave him, by the way, is now being sung by heavy but hopeful hearts all over the world

## Chapter 6–Grace

N / A

*Chapter 7—Life in Death Valley*

N / A

*Chapter 8—Giants to Kill*

1.  2nd Chronicles 11:15—"... for the goat and *calf* idols he had made..."

2.  Name for the first five books of the Bible, believed to have all been written by Moses.

3.  Isaiah 29:13, Matthew 15:8

4.  John Bevere I believe coins and then expounds on this analogy brilliantly in his book, *Killing Kyryptonite.*

5.  Romans 3:23

6.  Ephesians 5:18

*Chapter 9—Rhythms*

1.  Exodus 16:31

2.  Numbers 11:7-8

3.  Exodus 31:17

4.  John Mark Comer has been re-popularizing this basic thought of Christianity in recent years. This idea that it's not enough to say and believe the things of Jesus and even just to do the things of Jesus, but that we must learn to live the *way* of Jesus (lifestyle, practices, rhythms).

5.  In *Sabbath*, Abram Heschel discusses the ancient Jewish belief that God literally is able to stretch out the fruitfulness and capacity of our work and time over the week when we take a day to Sabbath (much like the belief God is able to take out ninety percent and stretch it further when we honor Him with the tithe)

### Chapter 10–*Ropes*

1.  1 Corinthians 15:33

2.  Proverbs 27:17

### Chapter 11–*Revelation*

1.  2nd Timothy 3:16

2.  2nd Peter 1:19

3.  Pastor Chad Veach on communication

4.  Pastor Steven Furtick said this once in a sermon dealing with racism

### Chapter 12–*The Most Important Thing About You*

1.  "Only two survive"–Here is reference to Joshua and Caleb. To be more specific, these are the only two surviving adults of *that* generation. The children would go on to possess the promised land.

### Chapter 13–*A Different Spirit*

1.  First got turned on to this story in Mark Batterson's book "Play the Man"

2.  Mark 9:24

3.  Romans 10:17

### Chapter 14–*Whole-Hearted*

N / A

**Chapter 15**–*Soup that Steals*

1.  2nd Corinthians 4:18 NLT

2.  Many leaders/authors/pastors have spoken and written on this point/phrase. But I'd like to credit Pastor Levi Lusko for most likely hitting this point the hardest and most originally in the area of purity in his book *Swipe Right* and financial guru Dave Ramsey in all his best-selling books and material on how to have financial peace.

3.  2 Corinthians 2:11

4.  Hebrews 12:16-17

5.  David, Psalm 27:13

**Chapter 16**–*Death by Distraction*

1.  *Chi* or *Ki*–depending on which country and language–is an internal energy and force vastly recognized in the Orient and is used in medicine, Martial Arts and various fields

2.  Psalm 45:1

3.  Proverbs 23:31

4.  Job 31:1

5.  Matthew 6:22-23 Berean

6.  Psalm 121

7.  Job 42:5

**Chapter 17**–*Weak in the Wait*

1.  Proverbs 13:12

2.  Job 6

## Chapter 18  *Crossing Jordan*

1. I think the full Warren Wiersbe quote on the believer's "Canaan" is worth it to see—

   "It has been pointed out before that Canaan is a type of the Christian's inheritance in Christ. Canaan is not a picture of heaven, because the believer does not have to battle to gain his heavenly home. Canaan represents God's inheritance, given to the believer and claimed by faith. The victorious Christian life is a life of battles and blessings, but it is also a life of rest. In Hebrews 4:5 we see that the entering of the nation into Canaan is a picture of the believer entering into a life of rest and victory through faith in Christ. Too many Christians are 'in between' in their spiritual lives—between Egypt and Canaan. They have been delivered from the bondage of sin, but they have not by faith entered into the inheritance of rest and victory. How to enter and claim this inheritance is the theme of Joshua."

## Chapter 19—*Promised Land*

1. Greenville Avenue Pizza company in Dallas, Texas—best pizza in the world, hands down.

2. Joshua 13:33

3. Hebrews 11

## Chapter 20—*Canaan & Eden*

1. Luke 19:17

2. John Eldredge phrase

3. Psalm 16:11

Made in the USA
Columbia, SC
26 October 2021